FOUR
VIEWS
ON **THE CHURCH'S MISSION**

Books in the Counterpoints Series

Church Life

Evaluating the Church Growth Movement
Exploring the Worship Spectrum
Remarriage after Divorce in Today's Church
Understanding Four Views on Baptism
Understanding Four Views on the Lord's Supper
Who Runs the Church?

Bible and Theology

Are Miraculous Gifts for Today?
Five Views on Apologetics
Five Views on Biblical Inerrancy
Five Views on Law and Gospel
Five Views on Sanctification
Five Views on the Church and Politics
Four Views on Christian Spirituality
Four Views on Christianity and Philosophy
Four Views on Divine Providence
Four Views on Eternal Security
Four Views on Hell
Four Views on Moving Beyond the Bible to Theology
Four Views on Salvation in a Pluralistic World
Four Views on the Apostle Paul
Four Views on the Book of Revelation
Four Views on the Historical Adam
Four Views on the Role of Works at the Final Judgment
Four Views on the Spectrum of Evangelicalism
Genesis: History, Fiction, or Neither?
How Jewish Is Christianity?
Show Them No Mercy
Three Views on Creation and Evolution
Three Views on Eastern Orthodoxy and Evangelicalism
Three Views on the Millennium and Beyond
Three Views on the New Testament Use of the Old Testament
Three Views on the Rapture
Two Views on Homosexuality, the Bible, and the Church
Two Views on the Doctrine of the Trinity
Two Views on Women in Ministry

FOUR VIEWS ON THE CHURCH'S MISSION

Jonathan Leeman

Christopher J. H. Wright

John R. Franke

Peter J. Leithart

Jason S. Sexton, general editor
Stanley N. Gundry, series editor

ZONDERVAN

Four Views on the Church's Mission
Copyright © 2017 by Jason Sexton, Jonathan Leeman, Christopher J. H. Wright, John
Franke, Peter Leithart

This title is also available as a Zondervan ebook.

Requests for information should be addressed to:
Zondervan, *3900 Sparks Dr. SE, Grand Rapids, Michigan 49546*

ISBN 978-0-310-52273-7

Cover design: Tammy Johnson
Cover photo: Shutterstock.com, iStock.com

Printed in the United States of America

HB 09.11.2023

CONTENTS

Introduction: Recalibrating the Church's Mission
    by Jason S. Sexton 7

1. **SOTERIOLOGICAL MISSION: FOCUSING IN ON THE MISSION OF REDEMPTION** 17
JONATHAN LEEMAN

                     Responses
    CHRISTOPHER J. H. WRIGHT 46
    JOHN R. FRANKE 53
    PETER J. LEITHART 58

2. **PARTICIPATORY MISSION: THE MISSION OF GOD'S PEOPLE REVEALED IN THE WHOLE BIBLE STORY** 63
CHRISTOPHER J. H. WRIGHT

                     Responses
    JONATHAN LEEMAN 92
    JOHN R. FRANKE 98
    PETER J. LEITHART 103

3. **CONTEXTUAL MISSION: BEARING WITNESS TO THE ENDS OF THE EARTH** 107
JOHN R. FRANKE

                     Responses
    JONATHAN LEEMAN 134
    CHRISTOPHER J. H. WRIGHT 140
    PETER J. LEITHART 146

4. **SACRAMENTAL MISSION: ECUMENICAL AND POLITICAL MISSIOLOGY** 152

PETER J. LEITHART

Responses

JONATHAN LEEMAN 177

CHRISTOPHER J. H. WRIGHT 183

JOHN R. FRANKE 189

Conclusion: Recalibrating a Church for Mission
 by Jason S. Sexton 193

Subject/Author Index 199

Scripture Index 206

RECALIBRATING THE CHURCH'S MISSION

JASON S. SEXTON

You keep using that word. I do not think it means what you think
it means.

Inigo Montoya, *The Princess Bride*

So it goes with the church and its mission. Evangelicals especially use
the word "church" with great frequency, yet exhibit very little critical
reflection on what this word means. For quite some time it has been said
that evangelicalism has had no ecclesiology (doctrine of the church),
with Stanley Grenz concluding over a decade ago that "evangelicals
have never developed or worked from a thoroughgoing ecclesiology."[1]
This lack of developed ecclesiology largely springs from evangelicals'
participation in a wider movement—of the Holy Spirit, of people, of
denominations, organizations, and churches, etc.—where in fact *many*
ecclesiologies have been represented. None were industrial strength,
developed as robustly as they might have been, and yet this may have
been because any stronger representative ecclesiologies might have actually threatened the unity and momentum of the evangelical movement
and its wider ministries.

---

1. Stanley J. Grenz, "An Evangelical Response to Ferguson, Holloway and Lowery:
Restoring a Trinitarian Understanding of the Church in Practice," in *Evangelicalism and the
Stone-Campbell Movement*, ed. William R. Baker (Downers Grove, IL: InterVarsity Press,
2002), 228.

This leads to the second word, "mission." Amid efforts to sustain the momentum of the evangelical movement, whether as a whole or in its various parts, somewhere along the way mission became fuzzy. Local organizations emerged together with national and global ones displaying ecclesial hybridity whilst focusing on carrying out the mission of the church in its various forms and varieties. This included strong activities such as evangelism, preaching, pastoral care, justice ministry, and others. Somewhere amid this vibrant activity—funded in large part by the postwar moment of American affluence and evangelical expansion—churches began to farm out their work to other groups and gurus, making way for all sorts of innovative churches and Christian activity.

Corporatized and Colonialized Missions

Evangelicalism's expansion and the centralization of its activity often outside of local churches contributed to a corporatization of Christian activity within the evangelical movement. Despite a rich and lengthy Christian tradition of reflection on the subjects of the church and mission, mission in many ways was often reduced to a trope of orientation. In practical use it became not much different than what corporations use to focus their organizational strategies. *Mission* displayed particular and catchy approaches to the church's primary work, expressed in a mission *statement* that took primacy of place for articulating goals and a clear sense of purpose for Christian organizations or "ministries." One young church planter within a mainstream evangelical organization spoke of his experience preparing materials to display readiness for the church planting task, which would in turn help secure denominational support for the effort. Within the process of preparation, the organization's director of church planting emphasized that it was not the *theology* of the church (or a theology of mission for that matter) that needed to be emphasized; instead the entrepreneurial church planter's *mission* (and corresponding *vision*) were to be the focus. This was partly about branding, but also about keeping the vibrant goal in view, although it's not much different than business strategies from companies like Starbucks or Apple, often touted by church leaders as successful efforts to accomplish any organizational mission, including the church's.

The term "mission," then, is complicated. Yet the complexities inherent to its appropriation by a church eager to get on with its primary task are not lost merely on ways that mission mimics corporate capitalism. Growing concerns have emerged together with postcolonial sensibilities, leading many to reject and disaffiliate with older forms of hierarchical, hegemonic, and even violent notions of mission associated with colonialism.[2] While Lesslie Newbigin credits the ecumenical movement for the demise of the earlier colonial model of missions,[3] it's impossible to ignore today the growing history-consciousness that troubles evangelicals with details of a difficult (at times horrible) past, which in the worst cases brought various forms of harm to indigenous people groups, at times even approaching cultural erasure.[4] The colonialist missionary spirit is rightly blamed for things just now being discovered about the nineteenth-century Manifest Destiny consequences resulting in tragedies like the Trail of Tears, which devastated tribes during government-sanctioned Indian Removal, or the subsequent attempted genocide of Indians during the California Gold Rush.[5]

In America's Far West, this built upon an earlier Franciscan era of exploitation, imprisonment, enslavement, and removal of Native Indians from the land, through whatever means necessary. This colonial period provides an example of a kind of mission that Christians today want to largely disaffiliate with, especially with the utilitarian nature of those earlier missions, which were needed only until the natives were secularized, at which point the mission system would phase out. None of this can be easily disconnected from how those in the Far West think of missions today, or should, especially with the number of successful missionary organizations birthed in California during the latter half of the twentieth century. With a widely popular ministry launched

2. One example of this, although predating the colonial period of western civilization with its name association, Campus Crusade for Christ in 2011 changed its name to Cru, worried about negative associations with the medieval military crusades against Muslims. See Sarah Pulliam Bailey, "Campus Crusade Changes Name to Cru," *Christianity Today*, 19 July 2011, http://www.christianitytoday.com/ct/2011/julyweb-only/campus-crusade-name-change.html/.

3. See Lesslie Newbigin, "Mission to Six Continents," in *The Ecumenical Advance: A History of the Ecumenical Movement*, Vol. 2, *1948–1968*, 2nd ed., ed. Harold E. Fey (Philadelphia: Westminster, 1986), 173–97.

4. In the case of erstwhile support of slavery, see the Southern Baptist repentance over slavery, Gustav Niebuhr, "Baptist Group Votes to Repent Stand on Slaves," *New York Times*, 21 June 1995, http://www.nytimes.com/1995/06/21/us/baptist-group-votes-to-repent-stand-on-slaves.html.

5. Benjamin Madley, *An American Genocide: The United States and the California Indian Catastrophe, 1846–1873* (Newhaven, CT: Yale University Press, 2016), which charts over 300 massacres and mass killings.

through his 1949 Los Angeles crusade, much of postwar evangelicalism centered around Billy Graham. For much of his ministry, Graham was a member of First Baptist Church in Dallas, Texas, yet it was common knowledge that Graham was hardly ever there. What then did his membership in "the church" mean? And what did it mean in light of the challenge of local churches to display a kind of unity of mission amidst the juggernaut of evangelicalism that advanced in some ways on the backs of the churches, giving way to the emergence and strengthening of evangelicalism's great twentieth-century institutions?

Not dissimilar to Graham, Calvary Chapel in some ways represented a new kind of colonialism, and was said to have embodied the reverse of Manifest Destiny, where the Holy Spirit proceeds from West to East, from Orange County to the ends of the earth.[6] The situation has been exacerbated by evangelicalism's pragmatism, which prioritizes mission above nearly everything else, including ecclesiology. Calvary Chapel famously has no process for church membership, similar to many megachurches, which often makes membership and belonging largely arbitrary. In some cases, leaders of megachurches have found themselves speculating about whether the megachurches they help lead are even churches *at all*.[7] In recent history, approaches to mission have disclosed both various forms of racism and empire-building, manifest within groups ranging from the religious right[8] to more subtle displays. The latter has been found arguably in large ministries like Prison Fellowship, the strong existence of which (however inadvertently) enabled racist policies that contributed to mass incarceration, which disproportionately impacts African Americans and Latinos in the United States.

The Church's Ongoing Mission

The suburban megachurch of which I am currently a member, gives the largest individual portion (25 percent) of its budget to "missions," was

6. Philip Clayton, "Four Prophets: What the Free Speech Movement, Jesus Freaks, Esalen, and Goddess worship have in common," *Boom: A Journal of California* 5 (2015): 74.

7. See the AHRC-funded project led by Sarah Dunlop, "Megachurches and Social Engagement in London," where leaders of megachurches, which do much social good in London, were asked if they believe the megachurches that they oversee are in fact actual churches (http://www.birmingham.ac.uk/schools/ptr/departments/theologyandreligion/research/projects/megachurches/index.aspx).

8. Randall Balmer, "The Real Origins of the Religious Right," *Politico*, 27 March 2014, http://www.politico.com/magazine/story/2014/05/religious-right-real-origins-107133.

built on postwar white flight from urban Los Angeles. This particular church's overall mission statement, designated as its "vision," declares that it "*exists to develop, empower and release kingdom people and kingdom communities into missional engagement in their spheres of influence.*" While the church's *real* communal life is largely about joining small fellowship groups to meet with one another and be part of what it *really means* to be part of the church, missions is something almost ancillary, often presented as being done elsewhere and away from our suburban setting: for those people *over there*. It's done by donating money or volunteering time with the one-stop shop local nonprofit justice ministry that some leaders in our church founded with others to serve the homeless, the poor, and other people through various services in our city and region. This work displays something of our commitment to local missions, representing over close to 4 percent of the church's overall budget. Yet "global" missions funding comes out to about 21 percent of the church's overall budget. It's still not entirely clear how the church's stated mission (or "vision") drives what they do with "missions." According to the mission (vision) statement, church members ("kingdom people") are to view themselves as missionaries in their spheres of influence. Finding out precisely how the church does this kingdom-people vision in detail is very difficult, though, especially with megachurches whose budgets aren't always entirely transparent or visible to the public or members of the congregation. This provides room for flexibility of ministry in some cases; in the very worst cases, it opens the door for corruption and abuse.

Here is where a gap becomes obvious. With decades living in often white homogeneous (and affluent) suburban contexts, a disjunction sets in between church and mission, yielding forms of cognitive dissonance that are especially prevalent among younger evangelicals who struggle to remain in the church: the "nones." In this situation the church is something basic, situated *there* and somehow alive in its concrete presence. Missions, on the other hand, whether local or foreign, is something the church *does*, largely outside of the church. The book you are reading now, *Four Views on the Church's Mission*, wants to challenge this given notion. It proposes that mission is tied to the church's very being and constitution as the people who by the Spirit have dynamically become the body of Christ, the church. Unfortunately, evangelicals haven't quite figured this out yet, nor have we grasped with agreement exactly how it works. This book accordingly attempts to sort some of this out with regard to how we understand the church's mission.

This endeavor cannot be separated from doctrines of the church at play and what it means to be *church*. Yet rather than focusing on ecclesial features that may press into the conversation, which will display further differences in the contributors' views, yielding additional layers of complexity especially if other ecclesiologies (Catholic, Orthodox, etc.) were considered, the conversation in this book proceeds as an intramural Protestant evangelical one.[9] As such, the views represented in this volume showcase an intra-*evangelical* conversation seeking to bring mission and church more closely together, as it belongs.

The conversation is somewhat occasioned, if incidentally, by a moment of the church's attempt to recover a fresh vision of its mission amidst new and ongoing ecclesial alliances and coalitions. This has been developed in a number of movements: the so-called "missional conversation" prompted by Darrell Guder's 1998 book, *Missional Church*;[10] a recovery of the theological notion of *missio Dei* and its indebtedness to Barth and the ecumenical conversation;[11] ongoing reflections about the role of foreign and domestic missions amid increased globalization and transnational forces of culture transfer and migration, along with new ways of bringing traditional theological categories together to reframe how mission is done today.[12]

Being part of an evangelical conversation, the wider interest in mission cannot be separated from the exceptional work done by the Old Testament scholar and director of Langham Partnership and a major figure with the Lausanne Movement, Christopher J. H. Wright, whose own view is represented in this volume. Wright has spent much of his career both mining the Scriptures and then in turn finding a rubric with which to freshly view the Scriptures and the entire missional basis of the

---

9. For a wider approach adding additional ecclesial complexities to the conversation, see Craig Ott, ed., *The Mission of the Church: Five Views in Conversation* (Grand Rapids: Baker, 2016).

10. Darrell L. Guder. *Missional Church: A Vision for the Sending of the Church in North America* (Grand Rapids: Eerdmans, 1998).

11. See John G. Flett, *The Witness of God: The Trinity, Missio Dei, Karl Barth, and the Nature of Christian Community* (Grand Rapids: Baker, 2010), which traces a taxonomy of *missio Dei*.

12. For one attempt at this see Jason S. Sexton and Paul Weston, eds., *The End of Theology: Shaping Theology for the Sake of Mission* (Minneapolis: Fortress Press, 2016).

Bible for these things.[13] Chris's work has inspired a generation of evangelical engagement in thinking freshly about mission and has opened up a way—indeed, a *biblical* way—to do mission better today, which missiologists of all sorts began to pick up for their various expansive, creative, and even more rigorous missionary efforts in a fast-changing world.

The efforts, however, led recently to a trenchant reaction from a conservative wing of the evangelical movement, represented in the book by Kevin DeYoung and Greg Gilbert, *What Is the Mission of the Church?*[14] When I first saw and read this book, serving as the "mission and culture" book reviews editor of *Themelios*, a long-standing British evangelical publication that had recently been obtained and is now published by The Gospel Coalition, I wanted to see the book receive a critical in-house evangelical response, and I asked the leading Southern Baptist missiologist/church planter Ed Stetzer to review it. He heartily agreed, and the review went viral, causing a bit of a dust-up within the evangelical world.[15] At a basic level, the issue of disagreement was over whether mission is an expansive thing or a reduced thing. To put it crassly: expansionism versus reductionism; or, to reverse the connotations: convolution versus clarity and purity. This signaled a discussion that had been bubbling below the surface and had finally become fully manifest within the evangelical world. Like many things, the conversation developed even further into what might be understood and expressed in the four views presented in this book.

The Views on the Mission of the Church

Soteriological Mission. Represented by Jonathan Leeman from 9Marks, and closest to the view of DeYoung and Gilbert, Leeman brings layers of nuance to what he calls (although disputed) the fundamentalist perspective. Focusing largely on the mission of individual, personal

---

13. See Christopher J. H. Wright, *The Mission of God: Unlocking the Bible's Grand Narrative* (Downers Grove, IL: InterVarsity Press, 2006), 22, where he details the shift in emphasis from considering the biblical basis of mission to the missional basis of the Bible. His argument is distilled somewhat in Christopher J. H. Wright, *The Mission of God's People: A Biblical Theology of the Church's Mission* (Grand Rapids: Zondervan, 2010).

14. Kevin DeYoung and Greg Gilbert, *What Is the Mission of the Church?: Making Sense of Social Justice, Shalom, and the Great Commission* (Wheaton, IL: Crossway, 2011).

15. See a recap with Ed Stetzer, "DeYoung and Gilbert's *What is the Mission of the Church?*— My Review from *Themelios*," *The Exchange*, 14 November 2011, http://www.christianitytoday.com/edstetzer/2011/november/deyoung-and-gilberts-iwhat-is-mission-of-churchi—my.html.

conversion and redemption, he frames the discussion by highlighting what he deems a "broad mission" *to be* disciples or citizens of Christ's inaugurated kingdom, which is then distinct from the "narrow mission" *to make* disciples or citizens of that same inaugurated kingdom. This all relates to church authority, including how and where the church's mission of verbally proclaiming the gospel is carried out, and focuses its concerns on spiritual salvation and disciple-making as being of utmost importance and thus the church's primary task in the world today.

Participatory Mission. This second view is presented by Christopher J. H. Wright. This rather comprehensive view presents the church's mission as rooted in God's mission, unfolding in the pages of Scripture, in the history of Israel, and in the life of the church. The church's missional activities today, then, are participatory acts within God's great work for his own great purpose. This view renders specific acts of verbal gospel proclamation as ultimate insofar as they are participatory, but this also includes things like creation care and love for people and God's world, all of which amounts to participating in God's mission to heal and reconcile his whole creation.

Contextual Mission. The next view is represented by the lead coordinator of the Gospel and Our Culture Network, John R. Franke, who places an enormous amount of focus upon the particular contextual character of Christian witness. Grounded also in the dynamic Trinitarian life, this ecumenical vision of interdependence and contextual awareness means that particular forms of faithful witness and mission will look different in different places. Diverse contexts require this contextual approach wherein God's Spirit enables the church with power and discernment to adapt its mission to address local needs and concerns of the people where it ministers; the church in turn is shaped by these concerns. Centered upon the person and work of Christ, culturally diverse witnessing communities serve as signs, firstfruits, and instruments of God's reign now breaking into the world and bringing healing in very specific ways.

Sacramental Mission. The last view is given by Peter Leithart of the Theopolis Institute. This view of an ecumenical-political mission is shaped by the Christian act of baptism and the Lord's Supper, entailing a baptized believer's sacramental life that flows into world activities as an important feature of the church's cultural mission. The world needed fixing from its problem with the fall, which brought a strong division between garden and world, occasioning the split between communion with God and dominion on this earth as the original human mission. This sacramental life experienced by the believer and the church—this sacramental missiology—denotes an ongoing, visible, public, and political presence of the church as part of Jesus's social agenda of restoring the broken harmony of both liturgy and life together.

The views under consideration in this book cannot be separated from the particular ecclesiologies held by each of the contributors. This should be apparent, but it is not the primary focus of the chapters or the book. The matter is complexified within the wider world of Protestant evangelical theological discourse by the confusing character of what it means to be evangelical, exacerbated further by the current political situation in the US. Additionally, as all theology is expressed to some degree through biography, it follows that each of these positions is also personality-based, reflected by the people and institutions these thinkers have been shaped by, as well as by their experiences of church, and thus again is in no wise detached from their ecclesiologies. If there is one thing that evangelicals know about mission it's that it has everything to do with action and reality, despite how we might theorize about it.

We also acknowledge that all contributors in this volume are white males who have lived and worked primarily in the northern transatlantic setting, and therefore are reflective of far less than half of the Protestant evangelical experience, and a shrinking one. Aside from the emerging role women are increasingly playing in the future of what the church's mission is to look like, also missing are the significant roles that Black, Latino, and Asian evangelicals are making here, not to mention in other growing communities around the world where evangelicals of all kinds carry out vibrant apostolic ministries with a kind of power and outward expression of love that describes mission through and through, no matter what ecclesial structures may be extant. We are only learning about these movements of the Spirit to create the church in ways similar to the first-century situation, which Lesslie Newbigin says "began as the radioactive fallout from an explosion of joy," where mission's deepest secret is that it is acted out in doxology for the purpose that God may be glorified.[16]

---

16. Lesslie Newbigin, *The Gospel in a Pluralist Society* (London: SPCK, 1989), 127.

While more of these things will be revisited in this book's conclusion, what might finally be reiterated here is that the following chapters and relevant responses provide a deeply meaningful conversation that goes a good distance in excavating some of the big ideas present within evangelicalism that depict the range of views about not only what the church is, but also what it is to be and do in the world—its mission. We hope this book will be useful to the church, and especially to students and interested laypeople, as well as to mature pastors and scholars eager to get beyond the cognitive dissonance and back onto the task Jesus called his people to—to be his witnesses and to make disciples until he comes.

SOTERIOLOGICAL MISSION: FOCUSING IN ON THE MISSION OF REDEMPTION

JONATHAN LEEMAN

My next-door neighbor gently padded the dirt around his freshly planted sapling, looked up at me, and said with unfeigned sincerity, "Hey, I'm doing church work!" I didn't say anything but smiled politely. We were in his backyard and had been talking about his church, a congregation that belongs to one of the older mainline denominations, while he planted the tree.

The phrase "church work" struck me as awkward. Isn't church work what a pastor does? Or something that shows up in a church budget? Or on the list of ministry opportunities? Yet here my neighbor was claiming that planting trees belongs under the same banner.

Does it?

I pose the question because it is there in my neighbor's backyard, the pastor's job description, the church budget, or all of our lives, whether in work, rest, or play, where a book about the church's mission applies. To speak of the church's mission is to speak of the work that Christ sent the church to do. So what work does God give specifically to First Lutheran, to Second Presbyterian, to Grace Harbor, and to Capitol Hill Baptist (my own church)? To focus ministry or "church work" efforts on planting trees?

On the whole, the voices carrying on conversation about the church's mission tend to characterize that mission in either broad or narrow terms. Broad definitions will pack into the church's mission everything that Scripture enjoins of Christians—like stewarding the earth, paying taxes, or loving one's spouse. Narrow definitions insist on some kind of distinction between the individual Christian and the church, and then argue that not everything enjoined of individual Christians is enjoined of the church. The church's mission depends upon a subset of the biblical commands. Its corporate mandate is narrower.

Narrow definitions focus on *making disciples* of Christ. Broad definitions include making disciples, but also the broader enterprise of *being disciples*. Narrow definitions emphasize word ministry, like preaching and evangelism. Broad definitions insist more strenuously on words and deeds, "like the two blades of a pair of scissors or the two wings of a bird."[1] The analogy is not exact, but the comparison between narrow and broad is a bit like the comparison between the mission of a law or medical school and the mission of an actual lawyer or doctor (or both school and practitioner). One focuses on teaching; the other focuses on being or doing.

John Stott and Christopher Wright provide a good example of the broad approach: "'The word *mission* . . . is a properly comprehensive word, embracing everything that God sends his people into the world to do.' And that 'everything' is indeed broad and inclusive, if we take account of what the whole Bible shows us concerning what God requires of his whole people in their engagement with the world around them."[2]

Missiologist David J. Hesselgrave offers the narrow definition: "The primary mission of the Church and, therefore, of the churches is to proclaim the gospel of Christ and gather believers into local churches where they can be built up in the faith and made effective in service, thereby planting new congregations throughout the world."[3] Elsewhere he writes: "'Great Commission' mission is uniquely ours and requires us to make disciples by preaching, baptism, and teaching the peoples of the earth."[4]

Part of the challenge of choosing between narrow and broad is that both sides appeal to biblically informed intuitions. The narrow

---

1. John Stott and Christopher J. H. Wright, *Christian Mission in the Modern World*, updated and expanded (Downers Grove, IL: InterVarsity Press, 2015), 44.

2. Italics original, ibid., 38–39.

3. *Planting Churches Cross-Culturally: A Guide for Home and Foreign Missions* (Grand Rapids: Baker, 1980), 20.

4. *Paradigms in Conflict: 10 Key Questions in Christian Missions Today* (Grand Rapids: Kregel, 2005), 348.

definition appeals to the intuition that there must be *some* distinction between what the whole church must do and what I as an individual Christian must do. We wouldn't tell the whole church that its mission is to love its spouse. That doesn't make sense. And we don't ordinarily refer to planting trees as "church work." That somehow sounds strange. The broad-definition camp, however, appeals to the sensibilities that suggest that words without deeds aren't worth much. And what pastor would ever stand in front of a congregation on Sunday and say, "It is *not* your mission, church, to love God and neighbor"?

I suspect I was chosen for this four-views volume to represent the narrow camp. Yet I will actually argue that we should affirm both a narrow mission and a broad mission, each for its part, as predicated on two different jobs that God has given churches to do. Those who argue for *just* the narrow or *just* the broad easily miss one of those jobs. Still, it's probably fair to label me as the book's fundamentalist, since my pastoral and programmatic sympathies lie with the narrow camp and I will throw more elbows in the direction of the broad camp. Hopefully, however, I can keep my grouchiness in check and acknowledge good on both sides.

In order to argue for broad and narrow simultaneously, a number of themes could be traced on this knotty topic. But two strings I want to untangle and then properly tie together again are the nature of salvation and the nature of the church's authority. What do we need to be saved from? And whom has God authorized to do what? These two questions get tangled up due to the fact that God's plan of salvation transpires in two steps, corresponding with Christ's first and second coming. Writers point to what God's salvation will ultimately accomplish after Christ's second coming to argue for a "holistic salvation" or a "holistic gospel." From there they conclude, "If our salvation is holistic, then the church's mission must be holistic or broad." But wait a second! Preachers of the prosperity gospel promise health and wealth now, and then program their churches accordingly ("Give money for my jet and be blessed!"). But the real gospel promises some things now and other things later. And if the benefits of salvation will arrive in two stages, corresponding to Christ's first and second comings, shouldn't the church's present task list reflect this fact? That it can do some things now but not others?

Here is where the topic of church authority becomes crucial. Church authority is not a popular topic, I understand, partly because it divides good Christians. But the mission of the church conversation suffers from giving it insufficient attention. Whatever God *sends* a people to do, he must *authorize* them to do. It makes no sense to say the church was sent to do something for which it possesses no authorization. Sending and authorizing are tied together. If you therefore want to know what the mission of the church is, ask whom has God authorized to do what. What we will discover is that God has authorized the church as an organized collective with a priestly authority to do a priestly job, while he has authorized every member of the church with a kingly authority to do a kingly job.[5] The first yields a narrow mission; the second yields a broad one.

My answer to the question—what is the mission of the church?—is to point to these two different jobs, which correspond to two different moments in the church's life. Broadly, God sends every member of a church to do what Adam failed to do: represent him in kingly fashion as his dominion-establishing, God-imaging "sons." This broad mission roots in how Christ authorizes every son and citizen of his inaugurated kingdom. (Unlike subjects/slaves, citizens/sons possess authority.) Narrowly, God sends the church-as-organized-collective to make disciples or citizens, not just with words but with a particular kind of priestly words—adjudicatory declarations of binding and loosing. This narrow mission roots in how Christ specifically authorizes the apostles and the churches in Matthew 16, 18, and 28.

In a phrase, the broad mission is *to be* disciples or citizens, and the narrow mission is *to make* disciples or citizens. It's worth keeping these two jobs distinct for a number of reasons that I will list toward the close of this chapter. But a first reason is that it makes sense of two different ways we use the word "church," and a second reason is that it yields significant pastoral and programmatic consequences. Sometimes we use the word "church" to refer to all of the members: who they are and what they do throughout the week. Sometimes we use it to refer to those members as an organized collective, capable of doing certain things together that they cannot do apart. And typically, a church's general programming (the weekly liturgy, membership decisions, pastoral care,

---

5. The priestly and the kingly cannot be fully separated, but just as we can shift our weight onto one foot or the other, so any given set of tasks can require us to lean into either the priestly or the kingly aspects of imaging God.

any administrative work) corresponds with the latter usage. If you ignore or erase the line between these two different uses of the word church, the organized collective suddenly becomes responsible with pastoral time and budgetary monies for what the members do all week. Thankfully, even the strongest broad-mission advocates instinctively know better than to let this get too out of hand by transforming churches into soup kitchens or job training centers. Yet the question we should ask is, is the organized collective with a priestly mandate actually authorized to undertake the kingly work of its individual members? Or might something get lost if we devoted our gatherings and communion plate dollars to tree-planting and our elders' job descriptions to something other than teaching and oversight?

Part of the challenge with introducing church authority into the conversation is that advocates of an episcopalian or presbyterian form of church government view the authority of the church-as-organized-collective differently than a congregationalist. For a congregationalist like me, the narrow and priestly tasks of the organized collective belong to the gathered church. For the advocate of an episcopalian or presbyterian structure, however, the organized collective ordinarily acts through the officers, not through the gathered church. If you want to trick an advocate of a broad mission to provide a narrow answer, you might ask him or her about "the mission of the church's officers." Possibly, you will hear what some of us call the *church's* narrow mission.

Still, if we temporarily set aside our differences over the precise location of church authority, whether it's exercised by the gathered congregation or the officers, I think advocates of all three forms of church government can agree upon both the distinction between *church-as-organized-collective* and *church-as-its-members*, and that each of these possesses a distinct authorization. And if that's the case, then I would encourage us to refer to the narrow mission of one and the broad mission of the other.

To see this, we will begin by asking what humanity needs saving from, and then whom has God authorized to do what.

What Does Humanity Most Need Saving From Right Now?

At this moment of redemptive history, what does humanity most urgently need to be saved from?

Nineteenth-century theologian B. B. Warfield asked this question to begin his discussion of Christ's work of atonement. If you believe that humanity's greatest problem is ignorance, or misery, or the guilt of sin, Warfield observed, then you will point to a doctrine of atonement that offers the matching solution—whether enlightenment, or happiness, or forgiveness, respectively.[6]

We can ask the same question for a discussion on the church's mission, though we might offer a slightly different set of comparisons: at this moment in redemptive history, does humanity most urgently need salvation from the judicial, spiritual, and relational consequences of sin or from the physical, economic, vocational, and otherwise material consequences of sin?[7] Our answer will impact what we think the church is sent *to do*.

These days it's common to talk about a "holistic" gospel because "God isn't content to save souls; God wants to save bodies too," as well as "economic systems and social structures."[8] Heaven is not some cloud in the sky where disembodied souls play harps, these writers insist. God will make all things new, not all new things, as one observer put it. Not only that, but we might think about the Exodus, that remarkable picture of salvation in the Bible and one of the main archetypes for understanding salvation in the New Testament. The people were saved not just "spiritually" but in every sense of the word: physically, politically, economically, and socially.

From this holistic or broad salvation, it is argued, follows a holistic or broad mission. Christians believe that Jesus is king over "every square inch" of creation. Therefore we must dispense with any talk of a secular/sacred divide. If God cares about trees, architecture, and fair mortgage-lending practices, so should churches. Everything is sacred for the Christian who affirms Christ's Lordship. There is no secular. The calling of the parent, the lawyer, the plumber, the athlete, and the

---

6. B. B. Warfield, "Modern Theories of the Atonement," in *The Works of Benjamin B. Warfield, vol. IX, Studies in Theology* (Grand Rapids: Baker, 2000), 283.

7. To be sure, it is difficult to completely disentangle these two sides of things from each other, just like soul and body are difficult to disentangle. But the fact that a person can be reconciled to God in this life *and* still die suggests we have to make some type of distinction between what God does *now* and what God will do upon the consummation of our salvation. I'm happy for others to provide better language for drawing out this distinction.

8. Cornelius Plantinga, *Engaging God's World: A Christian Vision of Faith, Learning, and Living* (Grand Rapids: Eerdmans, 2002), 96–97; see also, 110–11.

artist, in that sense, is just as sacred or holy as the calling of the pastor or missionary. They are equally sacred in that all are "unto Christ" and performed for his holy purposes.

I recall sitting in a restaurant booth with a close friend who is a Christian and a lawyer. "Do you think your work is more important than mine?" he asked since I work in full-time Christian ministry. He only asked because he wanted to answer it himself: "No way." His work was as sacred as mine.

For my part, I have never actually encountered someone who argued for a disembodied heaven other than the *Tom and Jerry* cartoon from my childhood, where a hapless cat frequently concludes the program floating in the celestial ether after another bungled attempt to catch the mouse. Might there be a strawman in some of these critiques given by the holistic camp? Still, the positive point being made is fair enough. God will indeed ultimately save both souls and bodies together, rescuing us from sin, death, and all the present manifestations of death in their many forms. And we should care about trees and tax rates.

Ruling as Sons—A Kingly Storyline

As with the view briefly sketched above, Scripture also tells a kingly story that affirms this holistic or broad salvation and broad mission. Those who merely affirm a narrow mission would do well to recall it.

Creation. God created Adam and Eve in his image in order to image or represent God. How? By ruling on his behalf and according to his character and law. Like a son who acts like his father and follows in his father's professional footsteps (Gen. 5:1ff; Luke 3:38), men and women are designed to represent God's character and rule over creation (Gen. 1:28). Adam and Eve are "sons" and "kings," crowned with God's glory and honor (Ps. 8:5).[9]

Fall. Adam and Eve rejected God's rule and go to work ruling on their own behalf. God then banished them from his presence and cursed the serpent, child-bearing, and the ground—in effect, all creation (Rom. 8:22–23). Yet the sentence offers an ironic mercy: it has them experience

---

9. Note: I'm going to use the biblical word "son/sons" inclusively for men and women through much of this chapter instead of the gender-neutral "children" (i) in order to trace Scripture's "son" theme which culminates in the beloved Son and in our union with Christ as fellow heirs; and (ii) to retain the king-and-implied-prince resonance that the word "son" possesses, indicating rule, which "children" does not possess.

the symptoms of death—pain, frustration, and futility—before death itself, giving them and their children the opportunity to repent. In the meantime, they still image God's rule, but it's a distorted image and rule, as one's portrait appears in a wavy carnival mirror. They use authority for selfish ends.

Israel. God, in his mercy, had a plan to both save and use a group of people for his original purposes for creation—to rule on his behalf and display his glory. Where he commanded Adam, "Be fruitful and multiply," he promised Abraham and his descendants, "I will multiply you and make you fruitful." God himself will fulfill among a special people what he commands of all people, so that the special people might display God's own character and rule. To that end, Abraham and his children would be a blessing to all nations as they "keep the way of the LORD by doing what is right and just" (Gen. 18:19). God eventually called these descendants a "son" (Ex. 4:22–23), and gave them a law so that they might know the way of righteousness and justice. He also gave the son a line of kings who were to read all of God's Word and rule according to it (Deut. 17:18–20), thereby modeling what kingship looks like. Remember, sons look like their dads and train to rule whatever their father rules.

To make a long story short, both Israel and its kings chased after other images and failed to display God's own righteousness, justice, and love. So God cast them out of his presence and land. The question left lingering at the conclusion of the Old Testament: Is there no son of God who will rule on God's behalf and in God's way? Adam failed, Noah failed, Abraham and Israel failed. Anyone?

Christ. Gratefully, God sent another son, Jesus. He let this son be tempted by Satan, just like Adam. But this son—this capital "S" Son—did what Adam and Israel didn't do. He perfectly obeyed God's Word and in so doing recapitulated redemptive history. He redid it, fulfilling the commission given to Adam "to subdue and rule, to multiply and create and to fill."[10] In his life, Jesus anticipated a complete dominion over everything from taming wild animals to binding the satanic strong man. In his death, he produced not children of the flesh but "offspring" of the promise. In his resurrection, he became the "firstfruits" of a new creation anticipating the day when he destroys every rule, authority, and

---

10. Gregory K. Beale, *A New Testament Biblical Theology: The Unfolding of the Old Testament in the New* (Grand Rapids: Baker, 2011), 386, also 479.

power and "delivers the kingdom to God the Father" (1 Cor. 15:23–28 ESV). Christ was the perfect image of God (Col. 1:15).

Like Father, like Son. Adam's perverse-imaging problem—solved!

Church. After ethnic Israel's failure, Jesus evicted them as "sons of the kingdom" (Matt. 8:12; cf. 3:9) and designated another group with the title (Matt. 13:38), namely, those who would be poor in spirit, would hunger and thirst for righteousness, and would be peacemakers (5:3–10). These people, the church, God predestined "to be conformed to the image of his Son, in order that he might be the firstborn among many brothers" (Rom. 8:29, ESV). "Because [they] are his sons, God sent the Spirit of his Son into our hearts, the Spirit who calls out, 'Abba, Father'" (Gal. 4:6). No longer are they slaves but possess the full rights of sons (v. 7). They are citizens of heaven (Eph. 2:19; Phil. 3:20). The democracy of kings established in creation begins to be restored.

Thus, the Risen Son commissioned these many sons to go into all nations for his purposes (Matt. 28:18–19a), where they will give honor but remain unintimidated by the governors of this world since "the sons are free" (Matt. 17:26, ESV).

What does God call the church to do? To be sons. To be God's restored images. To rule like God rules. To display the character and likeness and image and glory of the Son and the Father in heaven! The Father's a peacemaker, so the church should consist of peacemakers. The Father loves his enemies, so the church is to love its enemies. The Father and Jesus are one, so the church is to be one. The Father is perfect, so the church is to be perfect. The Father sent Jesus, so Jesus sends the church.

Like Father, like Son, and like sons.

Glory. These sons are promised that, just as they "have borne the image of the earthly man," so they shall also "bear the image of the heavenly man" (1 Cor. 15:49; also 1 John 3:2). Not only this, but they will also reign with God in eternity (in 2 Tim. 2:12; Rev. 20:6—literally, "be kings with").

In short, God authorizes his church, in some sense of that word, to be his citizens and sons. Citizens are different from subjects, say the political scientists,[11] in that they possess authority. So with sons as

---

11. I discuss the distinction between "subject" and "citizen," which is common in political science literature, at length in *Political Church: The Local Assembly as Embassy of Christ's Rule* (Downers Grove, IL: InterVarsity Press, 2016), 121–26.

opposed to slaves, says the apostle Paul (Gal. 4:1–7). And God sends these citizens and sons, whether gathered or scattered, to accomplish his creation purposes—displaying his wise, holy, and loving image for all the world to see. To rule like Christ. The church's work is an image-recovery work. It is to live as the transformed humanity. Peter Leithart captures this when he writes, "The church's first mission is to be the church, to embody the justice of God in her own life together in the Spirit."[12]

In other words, the kingly story suggests that the church possesses a broad mission: to image God in everything; to live as just and righteous dominion-enjoying sons of the king. Therefore, it's no good to argue, as critics of a broad mission sometimes do, that "all sorts of organizations work for justice and sponsor mercy ministry; we should focus therefore on what we alone as the church can do—making disciples." In fact, God tasks the church with modeling the righteousness, justice, and love that he has required of all humanity since Adam. Throughout the week and in our Lord's Day gatherings, our words and lives demonstrate for the nations, "Here is what God requires of *you*," some of which, by God's common grace, they already do.

Mediating God's Judgments—A Priestly Storyline

But Scripture's storyline of salvation is more complicated than that. First, there is another character, the priest, whose task is to deal with the fact that the people often don't do what they should do. Second, there is a wrinkle in the timeline which the seminary folk call inaugurated eschatology. And if advocates of the narrow mission need the kingly story, advocates of a broad mission may need reminding of the priestly story. To retell the same six episodes from this storyline . . .

Creation. God didn't just give Adam and Eve the job of king; he also gave them the job of priest, called to "work" and "watch over" the garden, two activities that would one day occupy Israel's priests in the temple (Gen. 2:15 CSB; Num. 3:7–8; 8:26; 18:5–6).[13] A priest works to keep the place where God dwells consecrated to God, which he does by

---

12. Italics mine. Peter J. Leithart, *Delivered from the Elements of the World: Atonement, Justification, Mission* (Downers Grove, IL: InterVarsity Press, 2016), 231.

13. Greg Beale, *The Temple and the Church's Mission: A Biblical Theology of the Dwelling Place of God* (Downers Grove, IL: InterVarsity Press: 2004), 66–87.

pronouncing what belongs to God and what does not. "Keep the holy place a holy place, Adam. Watch out for lying serpents! And teach Eve everything I told you." Along these lines, God tells Adam to name the animals, an activity that a later priest named Noah would inherit, only this later priest would be required to name which animals were clean and which were unclean.

Fall. Speaking of Noah, the priestly office evolved after the fall. God told Noah to separate clean and unclean so that the holy could remain separate, marked off, and distinct in an unholy world. Plus, Noah enacted and so pronounced God's judgment through a sacrifice "whose aroma pleased" the Lord, intimating some kind of reconciliation between God and at least Noah and his family.

Why is a Lord-pleasing sacrifice necessary? It is not that God is ill tempered. It is that God is good and will punish assaults on his person, throne, and law, assaults which divide people from him, from one another, and even from the earth as they begin to exploit it. Humanity's most urgent problem, in other words, is not death and the material consequences of the fall. It is human rebellious hearts, the vertical and horizontal separation resulting from sin, the guilt and shame we bear, and most crucially, the promise of God's wrath we earn.

Israel. God called Abraham and illumined the substitutionary nature of sacrifices by offering a ram to sacrifice in lieu of his son Isaac. God illumined the fact that a sacrifice causes his judgment to *pass over* a people when he rendered judgment on the false gods of Egypt, and that it saves by tying it to the Exodus. He illumined a sacrifice's work of atoning for sin by tying it to the sin offerings and Day of Atonement. God calls the whole nation a "kingdom of priests" (Ex. 19:6), but he highlights the nature of priestly work by establishing a line of priests who mediate God's judgments through performing sacrifices, protecting the ritual purity of God's dwelling place in the temple, separating clean and unclean, and teaching the people God's law.

Like the kings, the priests forsook God and desecrated the temple. But now the centuries' worth of spilt blood and sacrifice, repeated day after day and year after year, make the Old Testament's lesson plain: humanity cannot atone for its own sins; we need both a perfect high priest as well as a sinless substitute whose blood offers an aroma pleasing to the Lord, that he might pass over his people's sin.

Christ. Good news: Jesus came as that savior and perfect high priest who declares and enacts the judgments of God. He also comes as the Passover Lamb who paid the price for sin by shedding his own blood. The king rules as a king by being a priest and lamb. He solved not just humanity's perverse imaging problem, but also its guilt, shame, and separation problem. At the cross Christ forgave his people's trespasses by canceling "the charge of our legal indebtedness, which stood against us and condemned us; he has taken it away, nailing it to the cross" (Col. 2:13–14). Not only that, he became the curse of death (Gal. 3:13) and then conquered the curse by rising from the dead. All this he did that we might be redeemed from under the law and "receive adoption to sonship" (Gal. 4:4–5).

Church. Christ unites these people to himself through the new covenant in his blood. This covenant grants them forgiveness; it grants them the Holy Spirit so that they might walk according to God's law; and it "democratizes the priesthood" once more (see Jer. 31:31–34).[14] In fact, these people, this church, become the "temple" where God dwells, as well as a "kingdom of priests" (1 Cor. 3:16; 1 Peter 2:5, 9). As with Adam and Eve in the garden and the priests in the tabernacle, these people are to keep God's holy space—*themselves*—consecrated to the Lord, commanded to "come out from them and be separate. . . . Touch no unclean thing, and I will receive you" (2 Cor. 6:17).

To this end, Christ may have authorized his people to go like conquering kings into all nations, but he also authorized them to make priestly judgments as they go. Wielding what Jesus called the keys of the kingdom, which we'll discuss further below, God's people once more must draw a line between the holy and the unholy. They do this by preaching the gospel and marking off Christ's holy people through baptism and the Lord's Supper. The two ordinances both picture Christ's sacrifice as well as constitute the visible church, publicly naming who belongs to Father, Son, and Spirit and thereby showing the nations who is "in" and who is "out." As with the Old Testament priests, this task of making disciples also involves teaching everything Christ had commanded.

Glory. One day every knee will bow and every tongue will confess that Jesus Christ is Lord, either as celebrating citizens or as conquered

---

14. Beale, *A New Testament Biblical Theology*, 733–34, 737–40.

subjects (Phil. 2:10–11). Priestly and kingly work alike will be consummated in the new heavens and earth where a redeemed humanity, who gave their lives as sacrifices of praise, will rule together with Christ on his behalf once more (Rom. 12:1; 2 Tim. 2:12; Heb. 13:15).

In short, God has authorized churches to mediate his judgments in the declaration of salvation and in the separation of a people unto himself in spite of all their sin and rebellion. Narrowly speaking, then, the mission of the church, in some sense of that word, is to make disciples by declaring or mediating God's judgments, which it does through gospel proclamation, baptism and the Lord's Supper, and instruction.

Doing all this addresses humanity's guilt and shame problem, reconciles people to God (Eph. 2:1–10), and reconciles them to one another (Eph. 2:11–20).

An Eschatological Wrinkle

If the church has both the broad kingly and the narrow priestly work to do, why don't we therefore simply affirm a so-called broad mission? Doesn't the broad include the narrow?

It is critical to keep these two things distinct based on a wrinkle in the timeline of redemptive history: the Bible spreads God's work of salvation in Christ across two comings. The first inaugurates salvation; the second consummates it. Presently, we live inside the overlap of two ages, the age of creation and new creation, like this:

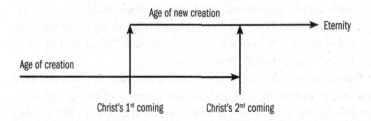

Jesus came as both priest and king in his first coming, but only those with Spirit-filled eyes could "see" that Jesus was a king. His identity as a sword-wielding, curse-removing king won't be publicly revealed until his second coming. Meanwhile, everyone, regenerate and unregenerate, could "see" his priestly work—the sacrifice—at the first coming. His priestly work was in that sense foregrounded.[15] Further, Christ may rule over every square inch, but at this moment so does God's Genesis 3 curse. Everything still dies. Everything under the sun remains futile. All our work, politics, art, romance, and engineering projects remain Sisyphean. Push the stone up the hill and down it rolls. Is Jesus really in charge here? I can't see him.

It is important to recognize this timeline wrinkle for at least four reasons. First, the fact that Jesus placed his priestly work in the visible foreground in the first coming suggests that humanity's most immediate and pressing problem is the problem which the forgiveness-granting, obedience-empowering, people-forming, new-covenant-giving priest must solve, not the problem the curse-removing, sword-wielding king will eventually solve. It suggests that the judicial, spiritual, and relational consequences of sin are more urgent, even more profound, than the physical, economic, vocational, and otherwise material consequences of sin. To draw the circle a little tighter, the threat of God's eternal wrath is the most urgent matter of all. And what Jesus foregrounded in his first coming, the church should also foreground.

The point here has nothing to do with souls versus bodies and everything to do with the eternal versus the temporal. Jesus warns about the One who will throw both soul and body into hell, after all. And trees and whales need not worry about hell. It's surprising, then, to observe that the indexes of so many recent books on mission or the church's mission contain almost no references to hell. Where did hell go? Hell is a difficult topic to grapple with, to be sure, but we could almost short-circuit the mission of the church conversation by asking every reader to stop and consider very honestly with him/herself: "What do I think of hell? Is it real? Is it eternal? Who is it for?"

But not only is eternity weighty, God is as well. Let's turn our gaze from hell to heaven by asking: "Is it the prospect of being with God that delights me most about eternity, or is it everything else? Is God himself my 'gospel'?" (borrowing from John Piper). The weightiness of God should yield certain emphases and priorities in the conversation. If God is the greatest good, the greatest joy, the greatest love, and the right object of all our love, such that even our love for our neighbor is no love

---

15. Which is not to deny the fact that he showed himself a king by being a priest (e.g., Mark 10:37, 42, 45), nor is it to say that everyone received his death as a sacrifice of atonement.

at all unless given with respect to love of God, as Augustine said,[16] then it would seem that directing people's hearts and minds to God is the most important thing a church can do, and the singular activity around which everything else hangs.

Growing in maturity means growing a longer and longer time perspective. Wisdom follows a matter through to its end, after all. So shouldn't the saints always measure the *now* by the eternal *then*? Unfortunately, our fallen hearts are not eternally calibrated but are rather what Proverbs calls foolish. We want heaven on earth now, and to live by sight. Immediacy has always been the temptation of God's people, from the complaining Israelites in the wilderness to the cheering crowds on Palm Sunday. Likewise, liberal Christianity promises the universal brotherhood of man or liberation for the poor. Its less-educated cousin, the prosperity gospel, promises a beautiful spouse or a car with leather seats. How easy it is to encourage people with the news, "God's kingdom has come"! How hard to say, "You are a sinner who needs forgiveness."

But if eternity really is that long and God really is that good, doesn't disciple-making possess a special importance? I love my four daughters by providing for them in all the physical, social, and emotional ways that I can. But I love them best by pointing them to the wicket gate of conversion and the narrow path of salvation, where they can run toward God and the world of love that is heaven (borrowing from Jonathan Edwards[17]). "Christians care about all suffering, especially eternal suffering," says John Piper. "Else they have a defective heart or a flameless hell."[18] There is no "either/or" in this quip, but there is an "especially." One wonders how each of these chapters will sound to us in ten thousand years. What if we were to write them from that perspective?

Second, the problem with taking our eyes off the eternal "not yet" is not only that it jeopardizes the so-called next life; the loss of an eternal measuring stick diminishes the value of everything in this

---

16. E.g. Augustine, *On Christian Doctrine,* trans. D. W. Robertson (Indianapolis: The Bobbs-Merrill Company, 1958), 3.10.16; 1.23; see also discussion in Jonathan Leeman *The Church and the Surprising Offense of God's Love: Reintroducing the Doctrines of Church Membership and Discipline* (Wheaton, IL: Crossway, 2010), 82–84.

17. See "Lecture XVI: Heaven, A World of Charity or Love," in Jonathan Edwards, *Charity and Its Fruits: Christian Love as Manifested in the Heart and Life* (Carlisle, PA: Banner of Truth Trust, 1969), 154f.

18. Twitter, 01/21/2011.

world. Read Camus's *The Stranger.* Contrary to popular belief, the most heavenly minded person often does the most earthly good. She is freed from the selfish ambitions of this world in order to pour herself out for others. Robert Woodberry's award-winning article, "The Missionary Roots of Liberal Democracy," suggests as much.[19] The article compares African nations visited by conversionary Protestant missionaries in the nineteenth and twentieth centuries to those visited by Roman Catholic or state-church missionaries. Woodberry demonstrates with data that "conversionary Protestants were a crucial catalyst initiating the development and spread of religious liberty, mass education, mass printing, newspapers, voluntary organizations, most major colonial reforms, and the codification of legal protections for nonwhites."[20] Not only that, but these nations had comparatively stronger economies, healthier people, lower infant mortality, less corruption, and more education, especially among women. A strong doctrine of conversion helps us to live generous, productive, and loving lives. Never mind those who call conversion intolerant.

Third, recognizing the timeline wrinkle should temper how we talk about the church's mission. We rightly dismiss the secular/sacred divide, but we cannot dismiss the regenerate/unregenerate or Spirit-restored/under-the-curse divide. Only the Spirit can regenerate and remove the effects of the curse. Christians cannot. Unless someone wants to argue that the curse rolls back from creation gradually—and a few people do—churches only sow eschatological and soteriological confusion by talking about "redeeming" creation or "transforming" culture, which is popular language these days. Might Ecclesiastes be worth re-reading? The church cannot redeem and transform anything. It can only point to the One who does. The kingdom of God goes no further than God's life-giving Spirit. A regenerated person might build a house with Spirit-given ambitions, but eventually the inhabitants will die, the house will crumble, the foundation will sink, and all will be forgotten. Remember the mighty rule of Shelley's "Ozymandias."

Fourth, the timeline wrinkle helps us to recognize that a church, in one sense of that word, does a different kind of work than anything else.

---

19. Robert D. Woodberry, in *American Political Science Review* 106 (May 2012): 244–74.
20. Ibid, 244–45.

And this will help us transition to our next question about whom God has authorized to do what.

We are born, live, work, marry, have children, and die on the lower "Age of Creation" line. Here we parent, lawyer, build, farm, and paint. If we become Christians through repentance, faith, and the regenerating work of the Holy Spirit, however, we do *all those same things* on the upper "Age of New Creation" line. Or at least what Paul calls the "new man" in us begins to.

What about the local church and its officers, or the church-as-organized-collective? In a way, its work doesn't properly belong to either horizontal line. It wasn't possible before Christ's first coming and it won't be possible after his second. Instead, the local church was uniquely designed and established for this stage of redemptive history to do "elevator work." Its goal is to get as many people as possible, starting with themselves, off the lower "creation" floor and onto the upper "new creation" floor—not just to change peoples' status, but to change their whole way of living. Weekly teaching helps the "new man" battle against the "old." As in the priestly storyline above, the church and its officers work to mediate God's judgments and make disciples through proclaiming Christ's sacrifice, separating the holy from the unholy through the ordinances and teaching.

A job assignment chart might look like this:

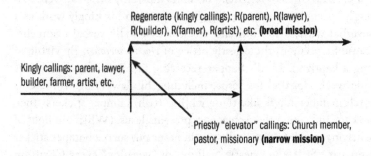

Regenerate (kingly callings): R(parent), R(lawyer), R(builder), R(farmer), R(artist), etc. **(broad mission)**

Kingly callings: parent, lawyer, builder, farmer, artist, etc.

Priestly "elevator" callings: Church member, pastor, missionary **(narrow mission)**

Notice also how the horizontal and vertical lines correspond respectively to the broad mission as defined in the kingly narrative (ruling on God's behalf as princely sons) and the narrow mission as defined in the priestly narrative (making disciples).

Both kinds of labors, vertical and horizontal, priestly and kingly, are crucial. Without the regenerate kingly, the elevator workers have no model to present. Without the elevator workers, no one gets onto the upper floor.

Furthermore, every Christian does both kinds of work because the priestly and kingly can never be fully separated. Every Christian is a priest-king. So go back to the restaurant conversation with my friend. He maintained that, insofar as lawyering and pastoring for a Christian are both sacred (which I agree with), they are equally important. It's true there are no "extra points" in heaven for someone in full-time vocational ministry. Still, we need to do more than give all the kids a first-place blue ribbon so that everyone feels good about themselves, as in Garrison Keillor's mythical Lake Woebegone "where all of the children are above average." It's better to acknowledge that lawyering and pastoring, or parenting and missions, are apples and oranges. They play different roles in the kingdom of Christ and the economy of redemption. It's true that pastors sometimes get paid to pastor, and in that sense pastoring serves the creation and kingly purposes of providing food and shelter for the pastor and his family. So in one regard pastoring can be compared to any other occupation. But that shouldn't obscure the fact that, from a kingdom standpoint, pastoring and being a missionary are unlike other occupations because their primary purpose is the priestly one of helping people get inside the elevator.

That said, my lawyer friend occupies a priestly office as well. His "kingly" occupation is lawyering. But he can do his kingly work as a nonverbal witness to God and as an occasionally verbal evangelist because he occupies the priestly office of *church member*. By virtue of being a baptized, Lord's Supper–receiving member of a church, his whole week "speaks" for Jesus, including his lawyering work. Our church membership is like those ichthus (fish) bumper stickers stuck onto cars, indicating that someone represents Jesus. (Which, in light of my driving, is why I personally would never put such a bumper sticker on my car.) Still, the priestly "calling" or "vocation" every Christian possesses (or should possess) as a church member obligates and shapes our kingly work of representing Jesus in all of life.

Ultimately, the Bible's story of salvation calls for a broad and narrow mission. But the eschatological wrinkle suggests that the narrow mission deserves special attention. To downplay or diminish the narrow mission of the local church and its officers effectively downplays or diminishes the need for all humanity to get inside of that elevator—to get saved and sanctified. It also wrongly relieves our kingly work of the priestly demands. It blurs the line between the world and the church, damnation and salvation. It risks misidentifying the unholy as holy. It treats the two horizontal lines of creation and new creation as if they are not that separate, or as if everyone is saved, or as if an unbeliever can participate in kingdom work merely by doing good things (as some liberation theologians have taught).

So how do we give special attention to the narrow mission?

Whom Has God Authorized to Do What?

God specially highlights the church's narrow mission by giving the church-as-organized-collective an authority that he does not give to every individual member. And it is a distinctly priestly authority in this way: it mediates the judgments of God through proclaiming Christ's sacrifice; through uniting a people to a baptismal and eucharistic picture of that sacrifice, thereby separating the holy from the unholy; and through teaching Christ's law.

Overrun by individualism, consumerism, and a preoccupation with marketing methods, many Protestants have little room left in their thinking for a conception of the church's authority. Yet the first few centuries of Protestants understood quite well that the local church as an organized collective possesses an authority that the individual Christian or church member does not possess. Specifically, churches possess the authority to pronounce binding judgments on the *what* and the *who* of the gospel—confessions and confessors. In everyday terms, they possess the authority to write statements of faith and to preach so as to bind the consciences of their members as well as to add or remove names from the church's membership. Think of Paul telling the church in Corinth to remove a man from their fellowship who is engaged in unrepentant sin (1 Cor. 5:2, 5). He says to them, "Is it not those inside the church whom you are to judge?" (v. 12, ESV). Or think of how Paul tells the churches in Galatia to treat as cursed anyone who preaches a gospel other than the gospel he preached to them (Gal. 1:6–9).

The Authority of the Keys

The biblical basis for the church's collective authority can be found in Matthew 16, 18, and 28. Briefly, Jesus hands Peter and the apostles the keys of the kingdom to bind and loose on earth what's bound and loosed in heaven after Peter offers a right confession of who Jesus is (Matt. 16:13–20). A couple chapters later Jesus hands those keys to a church for the express purpose of church discipline (18:17–18).[21] So if Matthew 16 speaks of employing the keys of the kingdom to bind or loose the *what* of right confessions, Matthew 18 employs them for binding and loosing the *who* of right confessors.

What then does it mean to bind and loose? Commentators diverge, but I think it's helpful to recognize that the rabbis used the language of "binding and loosing" to describe both their work of interpreting Moses's law, and then applying those interpretations as a judgment to particular cases. For instance, they would debate what Moses said about divorce. And then, based on their interpretive decisions, they would judge whether a particular man could divorce his wife. They concerned themselves with a *what* and a *who*.

Similarly, whoever holds the keys of the kingdom to bind and loose has the authority of a judge. A judge does not make the law what it is, nor does he or she make someone actually guilty. A judge is always under the law, and his or her authority derives from it. Still, the judge has an authority to interpret the law and then pronounce judgment with the "Bam!" of a gavel: "guilty" or "not guilty." The judge's speech is a special kind of speech. It imparts information, like a law professor's lecture imparts information. But more distinctively, a judge's speech binds or looses.[22]

Likewise, a church does not have the authority to *make* the gospel.

---

21. People often overlook the significance of the authority to discipline or to exclude. Whoever possesses the authority to discipline or to exclude an individual from any given body politic possesses the highest or final authority in that body politic. It gives all other decision making *force*, or the ability to ensure sanctions are carried out. For instance, the fact that the state possesses the power of "the sword" to exclude someone from the body politic through punishment (e.g., Gen. 9:5–6; Rom. 13:1–7) means that it can unilaterally enact its decisions in every other area of the nation's life. It can raise your taxes, conscript you into the army, or make you drive on whichever side of the road it pleases. Likewise, if a congregation, presbytery, or bishop can exclude you from membership, it can also receive or deny you from membership, rewrite a church's statement of faith, or do anything else. This is not to deny that whoever possesses the sword or the keys are under God's Word; it's simply to affirm that the Word delegates this final, unilateral, earthly authority to enforce the nation or church's decisions to *some* party. The power of the sword or keys, in word, is the power of enforcement. In a church, that authority can be used not just for discipline but "about anything they ask" (Matt. 18:19). The word "anything" in verse 19 is a courtroom word.

22. It's worth observing how Jesus invokes the language of a courtroom in Matthew 18:16, 19, and 20, just as Paul does in 1 Corinthians 5:4 and 12 in the context of excommunication.

It is under God's gospel and Word. And a church cannot *make* someone a Christian *ex opere operato*, or from its own action. Only the Word and the Spirit can do this. Still, Jesus authorizes churches to interpret Scripture and declare God's binding judgments through preaching and the ordinances. A church's preaching says, "You must believe *this* to be and walk as one of God's people. This is true doctrine and this is false doctrine." And a church's giving or withholding of the ordinances declares, "Member of Christ's body" or "Not a member."

Such declarations, furthermore, are a special kind of speech. As with a judge's speech, the church's speech binds or looses both the conscience and one's inclusion or exclusion from the visible church on earth. The speech might be in error. Its binding of the conscience is relative or *prima facie* (never absolute or *ultima facie*), as is the case with all God-established, mediating human authority figures. (For example, a child should feel conscience-bound to obey his or her parents, but that doesn't mean the parents can require sin). Individuals must defy a church if they are convinced its adjudications contradict God's Word. Still, with these qualifications firmly in place, the speech represents or mediates or "speaks on behalf of" the kingdom or rule of heaven, just as a judge speaks for a government.

In that sense, a church that says, "This is the gospel" is actually doing something more than my lawyer friend who evangelistically says to his colleagues, "This is the gospel," even if they use the exact same words. Both speak with and under the authority of the Word. And both speak like ambassadors (a church member is a passport-carrying citizen of heaven, after all). But the church also speaks with the adjudicating authority of the keys—again, like a judge.

I recognize all this provides a too-brief introduction to a complicated topic. Readers who wish to dig deeper can turn to what I have written elsewhere, whether for academics,[23] church leaders,[24] or church members.[25]

---

23. Jonathan Leeman, *Political Church*, 168–70; 332–65.

24. Jonathan Leeman, *Don't Fire Your Church Members: The Case for Congregationalism* (Nashville: B&H Academic, 2016), 19–22, 25–28; 70–81; 97–108; also *The Church and the Surprising Offense of God's Love*, ch. 4.

25. Jonathan Leeman, *Understanding the Congregation's Authority* (Nashville: B&H, 2016), 29–41; *Church Membership: How the World Knows who Represents Jesus* (Wheaton, IL: Crossway, 2012), 52–66.

Making Disciples

Strangely, Christians often read Matthew 28:18–20 in isolation from Matthew 16 and 18, but the text itself suggests that Jesus had his words about the keys in mind. Presumably, it is the one with all authority in heaven and on earth who can authorize the church to bind and loose on earth what's bound and loosed in heaven (16:19; 18:18). Presumably, it is the ones who gather in Christ's name who possess the authority to baptize into Christ's name (18:20; 28:19). And presumably, it is the people with whom Christ dwells now that he will dwell with always (18:20; 28:20).

Jesus commands his disciples to "make disciples" by baptizing and teaching. And the context of chapters 16 and 18 suggests that this commission is not for isolated individuals but for churches. Individuals will "go," but fundamentally Great Commission work is church work. Baptism represents an exercise of the keys and is a church ordinance. Where no church exists, as with the Ethiopian eunuch, then an individual must be baptized outside the context of a church. Or we might say that the first two who gather to baptize and be baptized are the constitutive beginning of a church (Matt. 18:19–20). A missionary faith must allow for this. But ordinarily baptism is a church ordinance because in baptism, not only does the baptizee profess unity with Christ, but the baptizer formally affirms a person's union with Christ. Leaving aside any differences we might have over infants, we can at least agree that, for adults, baptism involves two parties speaking. One party says, "I am a Christian." The other party says, "We believe you are, and are happy to name you as such before the nations and powers."

Further, baptism in the New Testament is ordinarily into church membership (see Acts 2:41) and participation in the Table (again, leaving aside differences over infants).[26] The Lord's Supper is not an individual ordinance for friends at home or the couple in a wedding. It is a key-exercising church ordinance, teaches Paul: "Because there is one loaf, we, who are many, are one body, for we all share the one loaf" (1 Cor. 10:17). The one bread demonstrates and reveals that we are one body. The Supper is a church-*revealing* meal. It shows who the people of

---

26. See Bobby Jamieson, *Going Public: Why Baptism Is Required for Church Membership* (Nashville, TN: B&H Academic, 2015).

God are. Therefore, Paul encourages participants to "[discern] the body" before they eat (11:29), and he could not be more practical with his counsel: "When you gather to eat, you should all eat together" (11:33).[27]

The nations of the earth knew who belonged to the kingdom of Israel through the covenant signs of circumcision and Sabbath keeping. And eventually they would know because Israel became identified with a land. But how do the nations of the earth know who belongs to the kingdom of Christ? How do you exercise border patrol in a kingdom with no borders? How do you make membership in the Spirit-indwelling, invisible new covenant visible? Answer: through the local church. Churches are embassies of Christ's kingdom, representing the kingdom of Christ not across geographic space but across eschatological time. Jesus says he is "there" (Matt. 18:20), not meaning that he hovers like a mystical fog in the room, but that these gatherings represent and speak for him. Here is where his national flag flies. And like embassies, churches possess the authority not to *make* someone a citizen, but to affirm a person's citizenship through the ordinances, as if handing out passports. Through the ordinances and the preaching of the gospel, the church, these people of Christ's kingdom, become visible on planet Earth.

Citizenship language like this might sound kingly, but remember who adjudicated citizenship matters in ancient Israel, declaring people as clean or unclean, holy or unholy: the priests. Priests, like Adam, were to protect the holy place where God dwelled. Not surprisingly, then, Paul picks up cultic temple language to exhort the whole church: "What agreement is there between the temple of God and idols? For we are the temple of the living God. As God has said: 'I will live with them and walk among them, and I will be their God, and they will be my people.' Therefore, 'Come out from them and be separate, says the Lord. Touch no unclean thing, and I will receive you'" (2 Cor. 6:16–17).

The church-as-organized-collective has been authorized to preach a message of reconciliation, to separate holy from unholy by identifying repenting sinners with God, and to teach them. Making disciples requires not only the speech of courtrooms and embassies, it also requires priests. (If you think I'm mixing metaphors, just remember how many

---

27. For two excellent and basic resources on the ordinances, see Bobby Jamieson, *Understanding Baptism* and *Understanding the Lord's Supper*, both published by B&H in 2016.

metaphors Paul uses to describe the church!) As a biblical theological inference, I think we can say that the exercise of authority by the church-as-organized-collective is priestly.[28]

What Is the Mission of the Church?

What then is the mission of the church? Answering that requires defining what we mean by the "church." Theologians make distinctions between the universal and local church, the invisible and visible church, the institutional and organic church, or the gathered and scattered church. For our immediate purposes, I'm not interested in any of these distinctions.

The distinction we need is similar to an old Presbyterian division between the elders' "joint" and "several" power. They say elders are authorized to do some things together or "jointly," like excommunicate, and other things independently or "severally," like teach. I don't expect to revive the language of "joint" versus "several," but that is the distinction we need for thinking about the church's mission. Recall what I said earlier: ascertaining what the mission of the church is requires us to ascertain whom God authorized to do what. To rephrase "joint" and "several," then, I think we can say that God authorizes a *church-as-organized-collective* one way and a *church-as-its-members* another way.[29]

Broadly, Christ authorizes a church-as-its-members with a kingly authority to represent him as God-imaging sons and citizens, whether gathered together or scattered apart. That's not to deny there is also something priestly about a church-as-its-members. We're priest-kings, after all. But I do mean to put the accent on the kingly authority of ruling here.

Narrowly, God authorizes a church-as-organized-collective with a distinct priestly authority to publicly separate sinners from the world and to reconcile them to himself and his people through renaming and teaching.

---

28. Gregory Beale agrees: "Christ establishes himself as having an authoritative position in the new temple in Matthew 16:18 and then extends his priestly authority to his disciples, who also have priestly authority. Matthew 16:19, in light of 18:15–18 and John 20:23, says they express what would appear to be their priestly task by declaring who is forgiven and who is not" (*The Temple and the Church's Mission*, 188).

29. Notice, then, I am not making the institutional/organic distinction of Abraham Kuyper. Both sides of my distinction involve authority or an institutional element. I, as an individual Christian, represent Christ on Monday to Saturday at home and at work because I am a baptized, Lord's Supper–receiving member of Capitol Hill Baptist Church. The so-called institutional church is right there with me at the dinner table or in the office all week by virtue of my participation in the ordinances.

Very plainly, then, what is the mission of the church? The narrow mission of a church–as-organized-collective is to *make* disciples and citizens of Christ's kingdom. The broad mission of a church-as-its-members is to *be* disciples and citizens of Christ's kingdom. The narrow employs judge-like or priestly words of formal separation, identification, and instruction. The broad rules and lives as sons of the king, representing the heavenly Father in all of life's words and deeds. The narrow protects the holy place where God dwells, which is his temple, the church. The broad pushes God's witness into new territory, expanding where his rule is acknowledged. For illustration purposes, we might say the narrow mission is to be an embassy, while the broad mission is to be an ambassador.

	Narrow mission of a church-as-organized-collective (the church jointly)	Broad mission of a church-as-its-members (the church severally)
Biblical themes:	Priest (or kingly priest)	King (or priestly king)
Authorization:	Mediate heaven's judgments (binding/ loosing)	Rule as sons
Actions:	Speak judge-like words of formal separation, identification, and instruction	Live as witnesses in word and deed
Primary domain:	The gathering where Christ specially dwells	Both the gathering and the nations
Illustration:	Embassy	Ambassador
Summary	Make disciples/citizens	Be a disciple/citizen

In the congregationalist conception, seeing how the two sides of the ledger work together is quite simple. Every church member, by virtue of his or her salvation, is a priest-king. Therefore every member is put to work mediating God's judgments with the gathered church and ruling on God's behalf whether gathered or scattered. To ask a member of a congregationalist church about the mission of the church requires specifying which hat you mean for him or her to wear: the whole-church-together hat or the church-member hat? In the presbyterian or episcopalian conception, the priestly and kingly roles work together similarly, but a greater place is given to the church officers in the "narrow mission" column for acting on behalf of the whole church.

That's why I suggested earlier that some advocates of the broad mission might look at the "narrow" column and regard that as the mission of the officers.

Why is it important to maintain the distinction between the church's broad and narrow mission? First—believe it or not—for the sake of clarity. It satisfies our conflicting intuitions. When someone asks me, "What's the mission of the church?" or "Is caring for creation church work?" or "Does the church's work center on words or both words and deeds?" or "Is the church's mission to care for the poor?" I need to know whether the questioner means the church as a corporate actor or the church as its individual members.

Second, the distinction protects the pastoral and programmatic priority the church-as-organized-collective should give to the narrow mission since that is its job. Several friends run a website that states in one place, "Christian churches must work for justice and peace in their neighborhoods through service." If by that they mean that my church, Capitol Hill Baptist Church, "must" hire staff members to do political engagement or mercy ministry, then I vehemently disagree. That would bind where Scripture does not bind. If they mean that the members of Capitol Hill Baptist "must" seek justice and peace through serving others, each according to their callings and stewardships, then I entirely agree. At the moment of this writing, in fact, I am teaching a Sunday School class called Christians and Government in which I am teaching just that.

Third, maintaining a broad mission for the church severally is critical for *obeying* everything Jesus commanded his followers to do. It is critical for cultivating "integral" (a useful word I learned from Christopher Wright)[30] Christian lives and for warding off hypocrisy and nominalism. It keeps us from imposing a false line between the secular and the sacred for the Christian. My loving, feeding, teaching, and evangelizing my children is all of one piece.

Fourth, maintaining a narrow mission focused on adjudicatory words for the church jointly is critical for identifying the saints, equipping the saints, maintaining the existence of the local church, and maintaining the line between the church and the world. The individual Christian or

---

30. Stott and Wright, *Christian Mission*, 47–48, 54.

church member is not authorized to do everything the whole church is, and the individual Christian needs the whole church to do its specially sanctioned work in order for the individual to identify as a Christian and to live the Christian life that God intends.

Fifth, keeping one eye on the narrow mission keeps us eschatologically honest. Christ has come, but the curse remains. We cannot "transform" or "redeem" anything from which the curse has not been lifted. At its worst, transformationism is a kind of disillusionment-promising prosperity gospel. Yes, the kings of the earth will bring their glory into the New Jerusalem (Rev. 21:24), as so many transformationalists today point out. But is this verse talking about Genghis Kahn, Margaret Thatcher, and Donald Trump, or about the sons of the kingdom, the saints? Either way, why not encourage Christians in their vocations through the many passages commending faith and working unto Christ, rather than speculating on one verse from apocalyptic literature? The church's goal is not to transform the world but to live together as a transformed world, and to invite the nations in word and deed to the Transformer.[31]

Sixth, by the same token, the distinct narrow mission reminds us to calibrate everything in our broad vocation according to the eternal possibilities of heaven or hell, destinies with much biblical support. And it gives urgency to our evangelistic witness in word and deed.

Seventh, the narrow mission of the church jointly both shapes and "brands" the whole Christian life. The average church member should not think that evangelizing their neighbor comes before caring for their own children or building good houses or being honest lawyers. But it does mean their parenting, lawyering, and building should be performed for Christ and one's witness to Christ, as if everything we did had a fish bumper sticker on it.

Eighth, maintaining the distinction both preserves the existence of the local church and properly situates the individual Christian to a church. No one would try to blur the distinction between the law school's mission and the lawyer's mission. Each needs the other. Many Christians today, however, underestimate the role and distinct authority of the local church. They fail to see that the individual Christian life

---

31. See John C. Nugent, *Endangered Gospel: How Fixing the World Is Killing the Church* (Eugene, OR: Cascade, 2016), 192, 194.

should equal the church member's life and should be lived in submission to the church's affirmation, oversight, and discipleship. When a believer harbors these mistaken assumptions, a broad mission won't require otherwise, even if making disciples is "prioritized." One can fulfill a broad mission apart from membership in a local church so long as one finds fellowship (with Christian friends on the golf course or at the gym), good teaching (favorite podcast preachers), songs of praise (car karaoke with Christian radio and my wife), the Lord's Supper (with a friend over dinner or at the annual Christian conference), and doing good to all people (occasional volunteering at the local soup kitchen or voting in elections?). The only thing that formally requires believers to join a local church as a matter of obedience—above and beyond pragmatic considerations—is the fact that the church-as-organized-collective possesses an authority the individual Christian does not possess. Take away that distinct authority and mission, and at best the local church becomes optional. If submission to the local church is a "good" but not "necessary" thing, we also have to say the existence of the local church itself is a good, not necessary thing. Lest all this sounds hyperbolic, those advocating for an undifferentiated broad mission should realize that a decent-sized swath of less careful American "Christians" adopt precisely this optional approach to "church."

On the other hand, too many so-called Christians today have learned that "church" and even "Christianity" is a one-day-a-week affair, and so nominal Christianity abounds both in the state-churches of Europe and the revivalistic and seeker churches of America. And when that's the case, the narrow definition alone will more likely appeal to them. "Leave me alone. I was baptized and prayed a prayer!"

All this is why I want to keep these two missions or jobs distinct, and then to insist that both the church-as-organized-collective and church-as-its-individual-members each do their God-assigned jobs. We need both the narrow and broad definition of the church's mission, and we need to maintain them distinctly. Losing the broad definition tempts the Christian to separate Sunday from the rest of the week. Losing the narrow definition tempts us to let go of the local church, to downplay the significance of verbal witness, and to blur the line between regenerate and unregenerate. Both errors will lead to Christian nominalism, ethical complacency, and eventually the death of churches.

Practical Takeaways

What are some practical lessons church members and pastors can take away from this discussion about the church's mission? Here are nine.

1. The first step of the Christian life is to be baptized into membership in a church. The Christian life is the church member life. If you're not at the family dinner table, how do I know you belong to the family?

2. Acting together as a church, we must pastorally and programmatically prioritize making disciples through preaching and teaching, celebrating the ordinances, and receiving and disciplining members.

3. Churches should carefully practice church membership and discipline.

4. Churches must preach about heaven and hell, the new creation, and eternal condemnation.

5. Churches should sing and pray often about heaven and the new creation.

6. While there are certainly important conversations to have about contextualization, what's most important about a local church is what it shares in common with every other church in every other time and every other place, whether the society is comparatively favorable or unfavorable toward Christianity: reading the Word, preaching the Word, singing the Word, praying the Word, and seeing the Word through the ordinances (borrowing from Ligon Duncan).

7. Christians should live together *as* the church not just on the Lord's Day but every day (Acts 2:42–46). It's in our life and love for one another that they will know we are Christ's disciples (John 13:34–35). We should represent King Jesus as the transformed humanity and a model body politic before the nations, where the righteousness, justice, and love of God reign.

8. Church members should share the gospel and call people to repent and believe.

9. Churches don't just need a mission, they need missions and boundary-crossing missionaries.

RESPONSE TO JONATHAN LEEMAN

CHRISTOPHER J. H. WRIGHT

I cannot speak for John Stott, of course (though he would probably permit me to!), with whom Jonathan Leeman connects me in our view of mission, but I feel we may well be closer to Leeman's own position than he thinks. There is much to agree with in his essay, not least of which is the way he insists that what he defines as "narrow" and "broad" mission tasks are all *included within* his full understanding of mission. While he regards the distinction as important, he does not *confine* the range of what is legitimately included within the church's mission to the primarily Word-based ministries of evangelism and teaching. In that respect Leeman's position is different from that of Kevin DeYoung and Greg Gilbert, who do wish to limit the concept of mission to the latter activities on the grounds that these activities constitute all that God sends the church, *as church*, into the world to do. Good works in the world are assuredly the responsibility and duty of individual Christians in the world in obedience to Christ, they affirm, but these good works are not part of the mission of the church.

Leeman makes the same distinction as do DeYoung and Gilbert between the church as a gathered collective on the one hand, and individual Christians in their lives out in the world on the other hand; but he includes *both* dimensions of the church's life ("narrow" and "broad," his terms) within its mission. Our mission as a whole church is to *be* disciples (broad definition), and to *make* disciples (narrow definition). This nuance seems preferable to DeYoung and Gilbert's position, arguing that the Great Commission mandates only the latter through the tasks of evangelism and discipling—a view I find rather illogical, given that the Great Commission includes "teaching them to obey all that I have commanded you." Surely those who evangelize and disciple others must themselves be obeying Jesus's commands, modelling what they teach. The Great Commission embraces and implies obedience to all

Christ's commands, not only proclamation and teaching. That is why John Stott could write in 1975:

> It is not just that the Commission includes a duty to teach baptized disciples everything Jesus had previously commanded (Matthew 28:20), and that social responsibility is among the things that Jesus commanded. I now see more clearly that not only the consequences of the Commission but the actual Commission itself must be understood to include social as well as evangelistic responsibility, unless we are to be guilty of distorting the words of Jesus.[1]

Or in Leeman's helpful phrases, *being* disciples and *making* disciples must be held together as integral parts of our overall mission, even if, in his argument, they need to be "maintained distinctly."

Second, I appreciate Leeman's strong ecclesiology (something often lacking in evangelical thinking and practice in mission), which echoes in some respects the similar emphasis in Peter Leithart's essay. We need these reminders of the proper authority and functions of Christ's church, in its own order and function and in relation to the world.

Now a fairly obvious difference exists between the church-as-collective and the church-as-members scattered in their various callings out in the world. However, I wonder if Leeman makes too much of that difference, creating a dichotomy that might be hard to sustain biblically. It is easy to point out that the church collectively is not commanded to love my wife, as I am. Would it not be more appropriate to say that the Bible envisages the church-collectively as a *community characterized* by husbands who love their wives (etc.)—such that my obedience to that command (among others) is the manner in which I personally "walk" in ways that are consistent with belonging to that community, with its "calling" in the world for the sake of the gospel? My ethical behavior (in that and other realms of personal obedience) is an integral part of "being" the new humanity that God has created the church to be, and

---

1. John Stott, *Christian Mission in the Modern World*, updated and expanded, with Christopher J. H. Wright (Downers Grove, IL: InterVarsity Press, 2015), 22–23. Stott explains and illustrates this conviction in pp. 23–33, and I comment on how that argument has been developed among evangelical missiologists in recent decades on pp. 41–54.

the mission that flows therefrom. I obey those commands individually precisely as part of sharing in the quality of life that the communal mission of the church demands.

I wonder if it would be more helpful to concentrate on the relationship between the church-*gathered-for-worship* and the church-*scattered-in-the-world*. That is a distinction reflected in Paul's letters. From what he writes to the churches in Corinth and Colossae, and to Timothy and Titus, Paul clearly envisages Christians gathering together for worship, singing, praying, eating together, sharing the Lord's Supper, reading Scripture, receiving edifying words of prophecy, apostolic teaching, and mutual admonition and encouragement together with practical sharing and financial giving. But the immediate outcome of such gathered living, loving, and learning together is transformed lives in the wider community of family and society. That certainly is the flow in Colossians. Paul prays initially that they would grow "with the knowledge of [God's] will . . . *so that you may live a life* worthy of the Lord and please him in every way: *bearing fruit in every good work*" (Col. 1:9–10, emphasis added). Then, after his warm description of the church's gathered activities (Col. 3:15–17), he immediately goes on to individual instructions to wives and husbands, children and parents, and slaves and masters. The latter especially refers to "church-scattered-in the world"—since these would be slaves of non-Christian masters, yet Paul says that, right there in their pagan workplace, they are "working for the Lord . . . It is the Lord Christ you are serving." Is that not mission in the world? Is that not mission having been taught and nourished by the inner life of the church-gathered-for-worship?

And that in turn illuminates the missional dimension of what happens "in church," especially through the ministry of pastor-teachers. For according to Ephesians 4:11–13, their ministry is to equip the saints for *their* "works of ministry," which I believe did not mean only service within the church but also all forms of *diakonia* in the world. It is the saints out in the world who are on the front line of mission, and it is part of the role of the gathered church and its pastors to equip them for that challenging responsibility. Significantly, Paul's instructions about ministry and maturity within the church immediately flow on to the practical missional ethic of living out the life of the "new humanity."

In these ways, there is a missional dimension to *both* the life of the gathered church *and* the life of believers out in the world, with the former equipping the latter for that role. In the combination of these dimensions, Paul sees the church as a whole—as that new humanity in Christ—proclaiming the "manifold wisdom of God" to "the rulers and authorities in the heavenly realms" (Eph. 3:10). The church is the cosmic showcase of the victory of God through Christ, and every dimension and intention of its mission—gathered or scattered—must serve that purpose.

Third, I appreciate Leeman's helpful discussion of the kingly and priestly dimensions of the life and work of God's people in the world. These are very much neglected theological concepts in much missiology and there is a rich seam of biblical truth connected to them. I am also very encouraged by the way he traces both themes through the six acts of the great biblical drama. He is determined, as I am, to draw our missional theology from the whole Bible, not just one or two prominent texts to which we give the titles like "Great Commission," etc. And it is excellent to see a strong affirmation of the "kingly" role—as a God-authorized missional role of "image-recovery"—that we have in all our engagement with creation in multiple areas of our daily work in the world. That was a major emphasis of John Stott that has sadly fallen on many deaf ears within evangelical circles. Leeman's stress on this is very welcome.

However, once again, I wonder if Leeman goes too far in assigning the priestly role primarily to the church-as-organized-collective, and the kingly role to the church-as-all-its-members out in the world. Leeman himself is a little uncomfortable with making this allocation too sharp, since church members have priestly roles too, bearing witness to Christ in the course of their kingly role in the public arena. I would add (a point Leeman does not make) that the church-as-organized-collective can surely act in a "kingly" role (or perhaps we might want to suggest, in a "prophetic" role, to complete the triplet), when it acts or speaks with a single voice unified in the public square. Are there not times when the church (whether as a single local congregation or a national or international communion) is biblically justified in taking action to expose injustice, or to help the victims of human evil (such as war refugees), or to respond to creational disorder, etc.? This is not *instead of* its work of proclaiming the gospel and making disciples, but integrated with that central task in ways that authenticate words with deeds. In that sense, so-called holistic mission is for the whole church—"joint and several," collectively and individually.[2]

Once again, I struggle to find in the New Testament the sharp distinction Leeman advocates. Rather, in the text that most emphatically speaks of both the kingly and priestly role of God's people, 1 Peter 2:9–12, the two seem combined. The "you" of the whole passage is plural. Peter assigns the identity of Old Testament Israel (from Ex. 19:4–6) to all those who, in Christ, have had their exodus experience. It is a collective identity, yes, but it immediately issues in the twin tasks of *both* proclaiming the praises of our redeemer God *and* living out such good lives there in the world "among the nations" that our witness brings others to glorify God. And immediately, like Paul, he goes on to significant instructions for life in the public and domestic arenas (2:13–3:7). The "joint and several" identities and responsibilities seem wholly integrated in this passage.

Fourth, I fear there is a confusing collapse of the "already but not yet" nature of the New Testament's portrayal of the kingdom of God into (adapting Leeman's terms) the "some now . . . more later" of the promises of the gospel. I agree that we cannot promise to believers *now* all that will only ultimately be true for us in the new creation (a major theological weakness of many forms of prosperity-gospel teaching as well as old liberal "social gospel").[3] I also agree that we cannot redeem or transform the world—that is God's, not ours, to accomplish. Nevertheless, even

---

2. It would be impossible to illustrate this without multiple examples of such integrated missional outreach. Suffice it to say that, for example, in Lebanon there are both church congregations (collectively) and many believers (individually) reaching out in "good works" of mercy and love, with food, clothing, and assistance of all kinds, to Muslim Syrian refugees. Large numbers of the latter attend those churches, hearing the gospel for the first time, with many coming to faith. The churches themselves become, in Newbigin's terms, "the hermeneutic of the gospel," embodying the good news they share in word and deed. According to DeYoung and Gilbert, the first action of these churches is not mission; only the second is. According to Leeman, the first is "broad mission" and the second "narrow mission." To my mind, the whole outreach and its impact is simply "mission"—integrated and effective.

At one point, Leeman refers to the compelling historical evidence that Protestant conversionist missionary work in many countries led to all kinds of positive social benefits in those cultures. The evidence also shows that those missionaries did not *only* engage in preaching for conversion but also deliberately multiplied enormous efforts in educational and medical work, in opposing corruption and other social evils. They probably did not think of their combined efforts as priestly and kingly, but in Leeman's definitions, they certainly were.

3. I have written on this in *Salvation Belongs to Our God: Celebrating the Bible's Central Story* (Downers Grove, IL: InterVarsity Press, 2008), ch. 6, "Salvation and the Sovereignty of God."

though all our "kingly" mission in the world remains partial and provisional, I cannot accept Leeman's pessimism that it "remains futile" (in an Ecclesiastes sense), when Paul explicitly says that, because of Christ's resurrection, it is not (1 Cor. 15:58).

"All our work, politics, art, romance, and engineering projects remain Sisyphean," says Leeman. "Push the stone up the hill and down it rolls. Is Jesus really in charge here? I can't see him." I have to disagree. The gospel of the resurrection and of the new creation subverts precisely that Greek myth of ultimate futility. To say that all our work now is *partial* and interwoven with the sin and fallenness of the world is not to say that it "remains futile." Rather, we discern and participate in the *reality* of the kingdom of God *already* present in this world, though in hidden and small ways, like yeast and mustard seed as Jesus told us, and not yet fully revealed. In ways only God can accomplish through his purging and redeeming power, our work will contribute to the new creation in which God will reign and we will reign with him.

To the question, "Is Jesus really in charge here?" We have to answer with John in Revelation 4–7 and Paul in Ephesians 1:20–21 (note: "in the present age"), and Jesus himself in the opening words of the Great Commission, "Assuredly Yes!" Christ is (now, not just in future) "the ruler of the kings of the earth" (Rev. 1:5). We do not "see him" with the eyes in our heads, but it is surely at the heart of biblical faith to affirm and "see with the eyes of faith" the "already here" reign of God in the midst of the fallen, cursed realities of our world—and to align our mission efforts with that discernment as we "seek first the kingdom of God and his righteousness/justice." So the partiality, ambiguity, and vulnerability of our "kingly" mission is no reason to relegate it to secondary and even somewhat "futile" status.

Fifth, I applaud Leeman's words on the urgency of evangelism, something that my own position has never questioned (as my essay's commitment to the centrality of the gospel makes clear). I would simply want to add that the urgency is not only (though truly) because of the reality of the wrath of God and eternal destruction (2 Thess. 1:8–9), but because evangelism is telling the *good* news of all that God has done and promises to do in the present and future. We are not only saved *from* the consequences of our sin, but *for* the glorious task of kingly and priestly service in this world and the new creation.

Finally, one brief caution. In his historical survey Leeman writes, "After ethnic Israel's failure, Jesus evicted them as 'sons of the kingdom' (Matt. 8:12; cf. 3:9) and designated another group with the title." This could be heard as simple supersessionism or "replacement theology"— the superficial view that God simply replaced the Jews with the church. A more careful rendering of the biblical fulfillment language would be that God expanded Israel (as he had always promised and intended) to include the Gentiles, so that even though some unbelieving "branches" were cut off, there remains the indestructible promise and calling of God for "all Israel." Too complex for here, but it is an issue that needs careful expression.

JOHN R. FRANKE

Jonathan Leeman's essay is shaped by a distinction he develops between the narrow mission of the church-as-organized-collective to *make* disciples and the broad mission of the church-as-its-members to *be* disciples. The narrow mission is connected to the priestly function of the church while the broad mission is connected to the kingly function. He makes clear that these two aspects of the church's mission, the priestly and kingly, can never be fully separated—that every Christian is called to involvement in both kinds of work as a "priest-king."

What I appreciate about his framing of the mission of the church is the generous way it seeks to integrate two approaches to mission that Leeman views as frequently at odds with each other. While he admits that it is fair to identify him as the "fundamentalist" contributor to the book since his "pastoral and programmatic sympathies lie with the narrow camp," he nevertheless maintains that we should affirm both the narrow and broad elements of mission and acknowledges the good on both sides. This is a welcome approach to engaging with theological and ecclesial differences.

Having said that, I do not think we should divide the mission of the church in the way Leeman proposes. While I agree that making disciples and being disciples are basic parts of the mission of the church, articulating them as "narrow" and "broad" aspects of mission is problematic. From my perspective the two are inextricably linked and should not be separated. Now in one sense, Leeman does not disagree; he is clear that both must function in the mission of the church and that they should be distinguished. However, on my reading of his essay he is also clear that what he labels the narrow mission of the church has priority over the broad mission of the church because of his understanding of an "eschatological wrinkle" in redemptive history that leads to the greater urgency for the narrow mission. He provides a coherent statement of this rationale in the development of the Bible's "kingly" and "priestly" storylines by making it clear that Christ's priestly work is "foregrounded," because while only those with "Spirit-filled eyes" could perceive Jesus as a king, everyone, "regenerate or unregenerate," could still see his priestly work of sacrifice.

Based on the two narratives and the eschatological wrinkle, Leeman concludes that the most immediate and pressing problem concerns "the judicial, spiritual, and relational consequences of sin" and that these are more "urgent" and "profound" than the "physical, economic, vocational, and otherwise material consequences of sin." In positing the greater urgency of the narrow mission of the church, this prioritizes the "spiritual" and "eternal" consequences of sin over the "physical" and "temporal."

While this sort of approach has been common in the tradition of the church, it suffers from the difficulty of not being faithful to the witness of Scripture. While Scripture certainly addresses the spiritual consequences of sin, it does not prioritize them over the physical and temporal consequences of sin. In fact, the biblical writings are much more focused on the immediate consequences of sin and unfaithfulness to the ways of God in the present situation of life in the world than they are on those consequences in the eternal future. Even a cursory reading of the Bible will confirm this. It is not that the spiritual concerns are absent, but that they do not take precedence in the texts over temporal concerns.

Now I suspect that Leeman would not disagree with this. He clearly knows his Bible and would, I think, acknowledge the preponderance of scriptural engagement with present, earthy concerns. If that is the case, then why posit greater urgency regarding the spiritual implications of sin? The answer for Leeman, it seems to me, is based on the application of a particular sort of logical and systematic reading of the texts rather than a strictly biblical one. A particular approach to systematic theology is developed based on supposed logical inferences of various texts, and then this overarching approach is imposed on the texts as the correct way to interpret the Bible.

From my perspective, this is precisely what occurs in Leeman's understanding of the church's mission. Even though the distinction he wants to make in prioritizing the spiritual and eternal consequences of sin over the physical and temporal is not found directly in the texts, he asserts that the spiritual and eternal consequences of sin are "more urgent" in the church's mission. But this is a deeply mistaken approach that draws Christian communities away from embracing the fullness of their vocational calling to be the good news of the gospel for their neighbors whatever their religious convictions. As much as I appreciate Leeman's embrace of what he calls the "broad" mission of the church, I fear that his prioritizing of the "narrow" mission will inappropriately circumscribe the practice of the broader mission.

Of course I am aware that Leeman's approach to the mission of the church and the systematic theological means he employs to articulate it, are well established in the church, and particularly within evangelical communities. I have come to be deeply dissatisfied with this way of thinking, especially with respect to the prominence it appears to give to systematic theology and when it does not forthrightly acknowledge its contextual and provisional nature. The critiques of biblical scholars across the theological and ideological spectrum regarding this way of reading texts abound. In addition, the majority world scholars are often resistant to the discipline of systematic theology because it does not comport well with their own cultural intuitions about reading texts and doing theology. They see in it a form of a Western theological hegemonic colonialism that attempts to impose particular perspectives and structures for reading the Bible on them that are foreign to their contexts and particular ways of thinking. An evangelical African theologian once said to me: "We (African Christians) do not want or need the systematic theologies and doctrinal formulations of the West to do our work. The canon of Scripture and the traditions of our people are sufficient." Let the Bible be the Bible, acknowledge its manifest plurality, resist the impulses of imposing theologies, and trust the Holy Spirit to lead the whole church into truth.

The difficulty with allowing theology to exercise this kind of role in reading the Bible is simply that theology is not a universal language. It is situated language that reflects the goals, aspirations, and beliefs of a particular people, a particular community. No statement of theology can speak for all. Throughout history the consequences of concluding that a particular theology is a universal theology for all people have been devastating, resulting in injustice and indifference to the humiliation and suffering of others. I believe that the practice of theology that is faithful to the mission of the church calls on us to surrender the pretensions of a universal and timeless theology. Where we are unwilling to do this, we propagate forms of cultural, ethnic, and racial imperialism under the guise of religion and theology and then link these forms of imperialism to the divine. Once this link has been forged, the results are catastrophic. To be clear, I'm not saying Leeman is intending this; I don't think he is. But I believe that his theological approach will lead in this direction in spite of his intentions to the contrary.

Of course, in saying all of this I have to acknowledge a couple of significant theological differences I have with Leeman that likely enable me to take a more open and flexible position on the issues being discussed in this volume. Leeman notes that many recent books on the mission of the church "contain almost no references to hell." He wonders where hell went in discussions of the mission of the church and asks: "Is it real? Is it eternal? Who is it for?" I agree that these are important questions that are consequential for the mission of the church and I am happy to provide straightforward answers.

I believe that hell is real and that its consequences are eternal. However, I do not believe in the notion of eternal conscious punishment. I affirm the position of conditional immortality or annihilationism. At the end of the age all will face divine judgment and God will destroy those who are incorrigible in their evil ways. They will cease to exist. I have been persuaded by the study of Scripture and the arguments of evangelical leaders such as Philip Hughes,[1] John Stott,[2] Clark Pinnock,[3] and Edward Fudge.[4] This position is held by an ever increasing number of those committed to biblical authority and believe that annihilationism represents the best understanding of the biblical texts. The destructive consequences of hell are thus fully eternal, they are everlasting and are not reversible, but they do not entail ongoing and never-ending

---

1. Philip Edgcumbe Hughes, *The True Image: Christ as the Origin and Destiny of Man* (Grand Rapids: Eerdmans, 1989).

2. David L. Edwards and John Stott, *Evangelical Essentials: A Liberal Evangelical Dialogue* (Downers Grove, IL: InterVarsity Press, 1989).

3. Clark H. Pinnock, "The Conditional View" in William Crocket, ed. *Four Views on Hell* (Grand Rapids: Zondervan, 1997), 135–166.

4. Edward William Fudge, *The Fire that Consumes: A Biblical and Historical Study of the Doctrine of Final Punishment*, 3rd ed. (Eugene, OR: Wipf & Stock, 2011).

punishment or torment. When I read through the texts of the New Testament that address the consequences of a negative divine judgment without the Hellenistic assumption of the inherent immortality of the soul, it seems to me that the position of annihilationism is the most natural conclusion.

I have already offered an answer to Leeman's question, "Who is hell for?" It's for the incorrigibly evil, those who are unrepentant in their determination to work against God's intentions for creation. This assertion often leads people to ask, who are the incorrigibly evil? And it particularly leads to questions about those who are not Christians in general and those who practice other religions in particular. My view on this follows that of Lesslie Newbigin who articulated his position along the following lines: exclusive in the sense of affirming the unique truth of the revelation in Jesus Christ, but not in the sense of denying the possibility of salvation to those outside the Christian faith; inclusive in the sense of refusing to limit the saving grace of God to Christians, but not in the sense of viewing other religions as salvific; pluralist in the sense of acknowledging the gracious work of God in the lives of all human beings, but not in the sense of denying the unique and decisive nature of what God has done in Jesus Christ.[5]

The coming of the kingdom of God is good news for all people, even those who may not believe in it. It is the mission of the church to bear witness to this kingdom by living God's love and becoming the gospel as a provisional sign, instrument, and foretaste of God's intentions for all creation. While I appreciate Leeman's willingness and desire to affirm the "broad" mission of the church, I fear that his interpretation of a "narrow" mission and his prioritizing of it as more "urgent" and "profound" will undermine the nature and fullness of all that the church is called to be and do.

---

5. Lesslie Newbigin, *The Gospel in a Pluralist Society* (Grand Rapids: Eerdmans, 1989), 182–3.

PETER J. LEITHART

Jonathan Leeman thinks he was invited to contribute to this volume to represent a "narrow" understanding of mission. As he says, that would not be an accurate characterization of his views. Rather, like many before him, he sees the mission of the church in a double frame—one narrow, one broad. The narrow mission is the "priestly" work of "making disciples"; the broader mission is the "kingly" labor of "being disciples" in the world. Christians gather as priests to be dispersed as kings. As Leeman puts it:

> Broadly, Christ authorizes a church-as-its-members with a kingly authority to represent him as God-imaging sons and citizens, whether gathered together or scattered apart. . . . Narrowly, God authorizes the church-as-organized-collective with a distinct priestly authority to separate sinners from the world and to reconcile them to himself and his people through renaming and teaching.

Leeman roots this distinction partly in an already/not yet eschatological scheme—"an eschatological wrinkle"—where the age of new creation has already come but is not yet consummated. As a result, the church carries on its mission in a world under the curse of Genesis 3, which will not be removed until Jesus returns. This eschatological scheme underscores the priest-king distinction: Jesus's first work was priestly, culminating in the sacrificial offering on the cross, which dealt with "humanity's most immediate and pressing problem." He will not be unveiled as a "curse-removing, sword-wielding king," however, until his final coming. That Jesus is first priest, then king, suggests that "the judicial, spiritual, and relational consequences of sin are more urgent, even more profound, than the physical, economic, vocational, and otherwise material consequences of sin." In the interim between advents, Jesus calls the church as gathered people to the priestly work of proclaiming and applying his saving death, and the dispersed church to the kingly work of dominion in the world.

Leeman thinks this distinction is essential for many reasons (he closes the essay with a list of eight). It "protects the pastoral and programmatic priority of the church-as-organized-collective," and "keeps us eschatologically honest" and modest, recognizing that "we cannot 'transform' or 'redeem' anything from which the curse has not been lifted."

At a certain level of generality, Leeman's distinctions are unobjectionable. It is true that the church lives by a systolic rhythm of gathering *and* dispersal, and also true that these two things are not the same. Priests are not kings, nor vice versa. When we get down to specifics, though, his priest/king, gathered/dispersed distinctions begin to unravel. Unsurprisingly, I will argue that Leeman's missiology needs to be spiced with liturgical and sacramental seasoning. On the way to that conclusion, let me highlight what I see as several weaknesses in his presentation.

Leeman is aware that the distinction between priestly and kingly activity and realms is not absolute. He knows that "the priestly 'calling' or 'vocation' every Christian possesses . . . as a church member obligates and shapes our kingly work of representing Jesus in all of life," and admits "there is also something priestly about church-as-its-members." Leeman does not explicitly say, however, that the distinction is porous from the other direction, that there is something royal about our gatherings. His silence is first puzzling, then disquieting, then suggestive of a truncated liturgical theology.

What happens when the church gathers for worship as a community of priests? We offer a sacrifice of praise, we are taught, we pray. And *what* do we pray for? Among other things, we pray for kings and all who are in authority, deliverance for persecuted brothers and sisters, and, if we are praying as the Psalms direct us, we ask the Lord to break the teeth and arms of predatory oppressors. We call on the Father to exalt his King on Zion so that the nations will be wise enough to kiss the Son. In other words, much of our "priestly" work aims to affect the world of "kingly" activity outside. Priestly worship reaches out to the "kingly" realm, and the fruits of our royal activity flow into the priestly gathering. Most historical liturgies include an offertory, when church members give their goods to God to be distributed in the church's various ministries. Economic life does not stop at the door of the church, any more than political life does. We bring it all in and lay it before the Lord.

We lay it before the Lord because he is *King*. We may gather as priests, but we gather before the king as royal advisors who form a royal council. In ancient Israel, the temple was a *heykal*, the "palace" of the high King to whom the Davidic kings paid homage. In the innermost room of the temple was the ark of the covenant, the throne where Yahweh sat above the wings of the cherubim. When John ascends into the heavenly temple, a throne is front and center (Rev. 4). Gathered worship is a *political* act, *the* political act of acknowledging the King of Kings. Priestly action is infused with kingliness. If the church is, as Paul says, a temple, it is a place for priestly service directed to King Jesus.

Of course, there was a distinction between priest and king. King Uzziah became leprous when he tried to take over the priestly privilege of offering incense (2 Chron. 26:16–10).[1] But the distinction existed within a matrix of collaboration and interpenetration. Leeman's use of the distinction seems to be a more modern projection of church-culture relations than one that arises from the biblical text. In a word, Leeman should reflect on the fact that "pastor" means "shepherd," and shepherds are primarily *royal* figures in Scripture (e.g., Jer. 23; Ezek. 34).

Traditional as it is, Leeman's treatment of the coming of Christ and its effect on the curse is mistaken in several respects. If Jesus was coming for priestly *and not* kingly work, why was his message "Repent, the *kingdom* of God is at hand"? Why does Psalm 2 figure so prominently in apostolic preaching? Psalm 110 rivals the second Psalm for frequency, and it is a Psalm about a priest. But the priest of Psalm 110 is the priest-king Melchizedek, an enthroned priest.

Leeman would acknowledge all this, no doubt. He agrees that

---

1. Leeman misconstrues the distinction of priest and king in the Bible. He acknowledges that the use of "citizenship" language in the New Testament "might sound kingly," but he keeps his distinction intact by claiming that priests "adjudicated citizenship matters in ancient Israel" by distinguishing between holy and unholy, clean and unclean. Not so. Clean and unclean, holy and profane have nothing to do with citizenship but only with access to the sanctuary. In some cases, priests did participate in judicial proceedings, but the king and elders handled most judicial business, including adjudication of citizenship (if such a thing existed!).

Jesus is king over all things, but he would presumably argue that what first-century Jews saw was not a king but a priest, not a royal act of sword-wielding but a priestly act of self-sacrifice. But he, like many, focuses on a single dimension of sacrifice. Animals were not merely killed at the temple; they were killed and dismembered in order to be transformed to smoke that could ascend to Yahweh. Noah offered sacrifice after the flood in a "priestly" capacity, but the sacrifice marked his ascension to kingship. So too Jesus's sacrifice does not stop with his substitutionary death but climaxes in his resurrection and ascent. This is most obvious in John's gospel, where Jesus is "lifted up" on the cross, his death the beginning of his return to the Father. The cross is a manifestation of glory, *royal* glory. Leeman's distinction of priestly sacrifice and kingly rule once again projects modern categories onto the gospel and thus neutralizes the gospel's political impact. If the divine King offers himself for his people *as king*, then kingship is not what we thought it was. If we confine the cross to priesthood, we risk giving brutes and tyrants a pass: of course our rulers are not self-sacrificing; they are kings, not priests.

Like his distinction of priest and king, Leeman's eschatological scheme works at a certain level of generality. We are certainly between the times, in the *saeculum* of the present age. But Leeman minimizes the impact of the already (perhaps due to his minimization of the kingly dimension of Jesus's first coming). Pain in childbirth, recalcitrant soil, thorns and thistles, and death are, of course, still with us. Yet, if the kingdom has indeed already come in any sense, then that should have *some* impact on the curse's reign. Is soil as recalcitrant as it used to be? Have we not developed ways to curb the pain of childbirth for those who want it? In a fundamental way, the curse has been reversed already. As Leeman says, after Adam and Eve sinned, "God . . . banished them from his presence." That banishment continued, with some qualifications, throughout the old covenant. At the cross, Jesus overcame that exclusion, tearing the veil that separated the holy and most holy and making a way into the presence of God. We are no longer *outside* Eden but are invited in. We know this because we gather without veils to feast on the fruit of the Tree of Life, Jesus Christ himself.

Leeman's distinction between "judicial, spiritual, and relational" consequences of sin and the "physical, economic, vocational, and otherwise material consequences" is problematic. If I am an opium addict, is it a "spiritual" or "physical" affect of sin? If I clash with an employer or employee, or have trouble supporting my family, does that qualify as a relational or as an economic/vocational problem? If my guilt over past wrongs and failures paralyzes me, evacuates joy from my life, and leaves me with a dusty taste in my mouth, is that a judicial or a material issue? The two sides of his distinction interpenetrate so completely as to be indistinguishable.

Leeman helpfully points to the role of "ordinances" in the church's life, but a stronger, more expansive sacramental theology would help resolve some of the weaknesses of his position.[2] The theology of the Supper is especially relevant. At the Lord's table, we participate in the body and blood of Christ (1 Cor. 10:16–17), and so are joined more intimately to him. We are assured of our standing with God because he invites us to be his table companions. But the Supper is simultaneously a covenant meal that knits individuals into one multimembered body: "We are one body because we partake of the one loaf." This "spiritual" and priestly meal displays the aim and goal of all "kingly" economic and vocational effort—namely, to be shared with joy and thanksgiving in the presence of God. The theology of the Supper does not permit a facile distinction between spiritual and physical, since it is a physical meal by which we receive Christ as food by the Spirit (as Calvin says).

A missiology attentive to the material/spiritual, royal/priestly work of the liturgy would be more inoculated against the misleading dualisms that mar Leeman's view.

---

2. I do not mean a "higher" sacramental theology, only a sacramental theology that plays a more prominent role in missiology.

PARTICIPATORY MISSION:
THE MISSION OF GOD'S PEOPLE REVEALED
IN THE WHOLE BIBLE STORY

CHRISTOPHER J. H. WRIGHT

Who Are We? And What Are We Here For?

Those two simple questions may be a good place to start as we try to articulate the mission of the church. It is often pointed out that "mission" is not a biblical word, and yet, like "Trinity," it is a *needed* word to summarize some core and essential biblical teaching. "Mission" is a way of saying that the Bible defines what the church *is* by making clear what the church is *for*. We cannot biblically answer the question "What is the church?" (its identity) without paying attention to the purpose for which the church exists (its mission)—the reason why, according to the Bible, God has called this people into relationship with himself through his sovereign grace in election, redemption, and covenant. And by that phrase, "according to the Bible," I mean, according to the Bible as a whole in both testaments. The New Testament makes it very clear that there is an organic continuity between Israel, the people of Yahweh in the Old Testament, and the multinational community of believing Jews and Gentiles who, according to the New Testament, are united through faith in the Messiah Jesus.

Peter combines the identity and the mission of the church in thoroughly scriptural terms in 1 Peter 2:9–12. First he quotes from Exodus 19:6, where God had given Israel the role of being his royal priesthood and holy nation amidst all other nations on earth, as the Exodus text states. Secondly, he draws in Isaiah 43:21, applying to his Christian readers the purpose for which God created Israel—namely, that they should "proclaim my praise"[1]—the praise of the God who, in effect, recreated the exodus for them in bringing them "out of darkness into his wonderful light." Thirdly, he uses Hosea 1:9 and 2:23 to make the point that, as Gentiles, his readers had once had no place among God's people but have now become God's people (a text Paul uses to make the same point in Romans 9:24–26). Finally, he emphasizes the meaning of being a "holy nation" in terms of practical, ethical distinctiveness: "Keep your conduct among the nations good."[2] The words ("see your good deeds") echo Jesus (Matt. 5:16), but the expectation of God's people being so visibly different from the surrounding nations that the nations would notice was also first entrusted to Israel (Deut. 4:6–8; cf. Lev. 18:1–4; 19:2).

This rich combination of texts and allusions, in a passage intended to remind Christian believers of their identity and mission (who they are, why they are what they are, and how they should then live), does two things relevant to our purpose here. First, it integrates the church of Jesus Christ with Israel of the Old Testament, just as Peter had done since his opening verses (1 Pet. 1:1–2).[3] Jews and Gentiles who are believers are one people, created by God for the same reason and purpose. Secondly, it integrates words and deeds. The purpose for which God called us into existence as his people (by the exercise of his saving grace and mercy) is that we should bear witness to the wonderful truths of who God is and what God has done (his "excellencies"), *and* that we should live in such a way that the nations will come to glorify our God. There are things to be said and there are deeds to be done. This integrated duality had been fully woven into the identity and role of Old Testament Israel and is

---

1. Peter makes use of the LXX translation of Isaiah 43:21 here, both in the term "belonging to God," and in the use of the word *tas aretas*—"excellencies." The expression does not merely mean the act of praising God in worship; it also means declaring/proclaiming wonderful truths about God in the public arena. See Psalm 96:1–3 for a graphic portrayal.

2. *en tois ethnesin.* Though the word is translated "pagans" or "Gentiles," referring to the life of the Christian community in the midst of unbelievers, the term's OT background is the "nations"—the nations in the midst of which Israel was to live as God's priestly, holy people.

3. Note that I did not say "replaces" or "supersedes" Israel with the church. There is a vast difference between the idea that the church replaced Israel (supercessionism), and the view that Israel itself expanded (as God always intended) to include the Gentiles—people from all nations incorporated through faith in the Messiah Jesus into the one olive tree of God's covenant people. The Bible teaches, in other words, not "replacement theology" but "fulfillment theology."

now laid, as a privilege and responsibility, on those who in the Messiah Jesus have entered into that inheritance and are to live "for the praise of his glory" (Eph. 1:12).

If we are to understand the mission of the church, then, we must understand the overarching biblical narrative within which the church participates as, on one hand, the people of God in the present era between the first and second coming of Christ and, on the other hand, the people of God in spiritual and theological continuity with Old Testament Israel: in short, as those in Christ and thereby also in Abraham.

> The people of God are those from all ages and all nations whom God in Christ has loved, chosen, called, saved and sanctified as a people for his own possession, to share in the glory of Christ as citizens of the new creation.
>
> The Church from all nations stands in continuity through the Messiah Jesus with God's people in the Old Testament. With them we have been called through Abraham and commissioned to be a blessing and a light to the nations. With them, we are to be shaped and taught through the law and the prophets to be a community of holiness, compassion and justice in a world of sin and suffering. We have been redeemed through the cross and resurrection of Jesus Christ, and empowered by the Holy Spirit to bear witness to what God has done in Christ.
>
> *The Cape Town Commitment*, I.9 and 10.a

The great biblical narrative has been described as "the drama of Scripture,"[4] and it is the essential foundation of all great themes of biblical theology, including the identity, role, and mission of God's people in both testaments. It is this narrative that generates both the great *indicatives* of biblical faith (i.e., truths the Bible affirms about God as creator and redeemer, about creation, about humanity, and the relationships between all three), and the great *imperatives* of biblical responsive living. How *we* are to live, and what *we* are mandated to do as God's people in the world, are constantly rooted in the facts of who *God*

---

4. See Craig G. Bartholomew and Michael W. Goheen, *The Drama of Scripture: Finding Our Place in the Biblical Story*, 2nd ed. (Grand Rapids: Baker, 2014). Their work is a helpful popularization of the hermeneutical perspectives of Kevin Vanhoozer and N.T. Wright.

is and what *God* has done. This is as true of the Ten Commandments and the two commandments that Jesus calls the first and second greatest in the law (all predicated on affirmations about Yahweh), as it is of the Great Commission (Matt. 28:16–20), which begins with the affirmation of the universal Lordship of Jesus Christ over all creation. The Great Commission, therefore, cannot be isolated or elevated in ways that disconnect it from the rest of the story wherein it fits, whether looking back to all God had done and taught in the life of Old Testament Israel, or looking forward to all God purposes in Christ for the whole creation.

Bartholomew and Goheen propose that the "drama of Scripture" proceeds through six acts: (1) creation; (2) fall; (3) redemption initiated (OT Israel); (4) redemption accomplished (in the life, death, resurrection, and ascension of Jesus Christ); (5) the mission of the church (from Pentecost to the *parousia*); and (6) redemption completed (in the new creation). I find this a helpful outline on which to "peg" what I regard as key components of a biblical theology of mission.

God's Good Creation, Spoiled by Sin: Acts 1 and 2 of the Bible Story

The Bible begins with creation. Its opening chapters present a triangle of relationships between God as creator, the earth (as that part of the wider creation where we live), and human beings. Made in the image of our creator, humans were entrusted with God's delegated authority to exercise both kingly rule over, and priestly service for the benefit of, the rest of earth's creatures and resources (putting together the verbs of ruling in Genesis 1:28 with those of serving and keeping in Genesis 2:15). Those mandates within creation have been radically impacted by our sin, the consequent curse on the ground, and Adam and Eve's expulsion from the garden context. But there is no rescinding of the basic function and mission of our humanity—responsible and godly stewardship of, and care for, the creation of which we are part. Inasmuch as we do not cease to be human when we become Christians (indeed, our humanity is being restored in the perfect image of God that is Christ), we may find a legitimate place for creation-care within the scope of a biblical understanding of our missional responsibilities (more on this later).

But the story of creation (Act 1) quickly flows into the story of the great rebellion and its consequences (Act 2). God's good creation has been invaded by evil and sin, causing enormous disruption and fracture at every level of human life (personal, spiritual, intellectual, physical, and social) and within wider creation. This part of the Bible story confronts us with The Big Problem, to which the rest of the Bible story will provide God's ultimate solution.

What is the nature and scope of that problem? Clearly there is a massive fracture between humans and God. Disobedience and sin have brought exclusion and death. This happened because of human collusion with the evil presence symbolized in the serpent in Genesis 3, an evil that God promises will eventually be crushed (Gen. 3:15). However, the early chapters of Genesis build two other dimensions of the problem around that fundamental human alienation that calls for God's saving solution. Human alienation from God is not the only issue at stake.

The first is the curse on the earth. The longing for that curse to be lifted is expressed very early in the post-Eden narrative. Lamech (in the line of Seth) names his son Noah, in hopes that "he will comfort us in the labor and painful toil of our hands caused by the ground the LORD has cursed" (Gen. 5:29). Noah did not eliminate the curse (that comes at the very end of the entire biblical story—Rev. 22:3), but he does become the focus of a new release of blessing into creation through God's covenantal commitment not only to humanity but to all life on earth. The earth is simultaneously under God's curse and the beneficiary of God's covenant. Creation matters to God.

The second other dimension of the problem is the confusion and scattering of the nations from the tower of Babel. The enmity between brothers in Genesis 4, which escalated to the "corruption and violence" of all human society that precipitated the flood (Gen. 6), finally engulfs the nations, whose arrogance in refusing God's intention that they should fill the earth results in their being scattered anyway in confusion (Gen. 11:1–9). It is against this background of the problem of the nations that God's call and promise to Abraham arrives in Genesis 12. The language of blessing that had embraced the outcome of the story of Noah now embraces the future of this people, the descendants of Abraham. To Noah, God promises blessing for all life on earth. To Abraham, God promises blessing for all nations on earth.

So, the opening twelve chapters of the Bible set in motion a grand narrative that will see God redemptively addressing The Big Problem that binds together all human beings as sinners, the divided nations, and the cursed earth. It is not for Adam, or Noah, or Abraham, or his descendants, to solve this vast problem by themselves. Only God can put things right in the end—and God will. Psalm 96 pictures even the inanimate features of the earth rejoicing when God comes to put things right ("judge the earth"). Psalm 148 calls on all creation—angelic, inanimate, creaturely, and human—to praise the Lord God. Revelation portrays multitudes of redeemed people from all nations, all angels, and all creatures in heaven, earth, and sea, as a collectively unified, reconciled, and worshipping creation, redeemed and ruled by the Lamb of God (Rev. 5). The closing vision of the Bible corresponds to its opening narratives.[5] And it is the mission of God that accomplishes the ultimate transformation from Act 1 and 2, to Act 6, as we shall see. The Bible is God's story, a story in which God has chosen to include the participation of a people for his own possession and his own purposes. In whatever way we fill in the details of our conception of the mission of the church, we must start by locating it within this overarching biblical narrative framework.

The Mission of Old Testament Israel: Act 3 of the Bible Story

In speaking about "the mission of Israel," we are not enquiring as to whether Israel sent out missionaries to other nations, or believed that they, as a nation, were commissioned to "go to the nations," however that would occur. Although some argue that Israel should have understood that God intended them to do that, I do not see strong evidence for a "missionary mandate" in the modern sense of that phrase (sending out missionaries across cultures to proclaim a message from God) as an expectation on Israel within the historical period of the Old Testament.

By enquiring about "the mission of Israel" in the Old Testament, I

---

5. I prefer to see these dimensions of the problem (and its solution) in this integrated way, rather than the strongly separate and isolated emphasis that Kevin DeYoung and Greg Gilbert put on the problem of human guilt in the presence of the Holy God: "One question . . . stands at the very heart of the Bible's story: *How can hopelessly rebellious, sinful people live in the presence of a perfectly just and righteous God?* . . . *The prime problem that the Bible sets up in its first three chapters is the alienation of man from God.* . . . [The other problems—alienation from one another and from creation] are symptoms of the underlying problem" (*What Is the Mission of the Church?: Making Sense of Social Justice, Shalom, and the Great Commission* [Wheaton, IL: Crossway, 2011], 69, 73–74; italics original). There is no doubt that human sin is the root cause, but when considering the rest of Gen. 4–12, and the resonance of Rev. 5 and 21–22, it is inadequate to consider the brokenness of creation and the nations as only "symptoms." God's salvation and God's mission address all three areas: human guilt and alienation, international strife and enmity, and creational disorder—and God has accomplished redemption, and reconciliation in all three areas through the cross and resurrection of Christ.

am asking what the Bible tells us about the purpose for which God created that people, in relation to what the Bible as a whole shows clearly to be the ultimate purpose of God, namely to bring about a new creation—liberated (Rom. 8:21), reconciled (Col. 1:20), unified (Eph. 1:9–10), and inhabited by people redeemed from every nation, tribe, and language (Rev. 7:9–10), through Christ's cross and resurrection. Where does Old Testament Israel fit in that great plan?

Why did God create Israel? We could rally texts such as Isaiah 43:7–21: for his own glory (v. 7); this involves their being witnesses among the nations to the unique revealing and saving power of Yahweh (vs. 8–13); which would in effect proclaim Yahweh's praise (v. 21). Such a role is connected to the only possible hope for the nations of the world, that through and beyond divine judgment they should ultimately turn to Yahweh, the God and Savior to whom all humanity will one day bow (Isa. 45:20–25). Israel's existence, then, as the people of this unique and universal God, is connected to blessing of the rest of the nations through experiencing Yahweh's saving power. These texts show us God's *ultimate* intention for the nations, and God's *instrumental* intention for Israel in relation to the nations.

This harkens back to Israel's emergence as a nation in the biblical text—although still in Abraham's loins. God promises Abraham that his descendants will become "a great nation," being blessed along with Abraham, and in some unexplained way be the conduit of divine blessing for all families/nations on earth. One of the texts connects that expectation not only to God's sovereign purpose in Abraham's election but also to the ethical quality of life that God would require of Abraham's people. Here is God's mission defining Israel's mission.

> Abraham will surely become a great and powerful nation, and all nations on earth will be blessed through him. For I have chosen him, so that he will direct his children and his household after him to keep the way of the LORD by doing what is right and just, so that the LORD will bring about for Abraham what he has promised him (Gen. 18:18–19).

God's stated goal in verse 18 summarizes Genesis 12:1–3 in a double promise: that Abraham will become a great nation and that through him all nations on earth will be blessed. The last clause of verse 19 repeats that promise as the reason why God chose Abraham in the first place (notice the strong intentionality in the verse through the twofold "so that"). But in between comes God's expectation of the people who would emerge from Abraham. They were not to set off in all directions to somehow bless the nations. Their responsibility was simply to "keep the way of Yahweh by doing righteousness and justice"—a powerfully ethical agenda standing between election (19a) and mission (19c).

The mission of Old Testament Israel was not to *go* to other nations but to *be* the nation God called them to be, to live as Yahweh's people, and in the combination of their *worship* and the ethical quality of their *social life* (Deut. 4:6–8), to bear witness to the identity and character of Yahweh their God in the midst of nations that knew him not as yet.[6] That explains why the prophets saw so clearly that when Israel fell into idolatry (betraying covenantal worship) and injustice (betraying covenantal ethics), they ended up betraying their mission to be a visible model ("a light to the nations") and were instead a scandal and curse among the nations.

At this point I find DeYoung and Gilbert's critique of my use of the Abrahamic covenant misplaced. In their desire to stress the importance of Matthew 28:16–20, the Great Commission, as *the* key text on which to build a valid understanding of the church's mission, they survey a few other texts that "are sometimes pushed forward as offering a different and fuller mission identity for the church," among them Genesis 12:1–3. In critiquing my exegesis of this text and its emphasis on blessing for all nations, they argue that it did not commission Abraham or his descendants to go out and engage in "a community blessing program." Abraham's obedience is only constituted by his going and leaving, his circumcising his household, and his willingness to sacrifice Isaac, so "we should not take Genesis 12:1–3 as a moral agenda[7] or as another Great Commission." Abraham's "obedient going is not going out to serve Amalekites and help them grow crops and learn to read."

---

6. For my full discussion of this ethical dimension of mission, including its connection to election, redemption and covenant in OT and NT, see my *The Mission of God: Unlocking the Bible's Grand Narrative* (Downers Grove, IL: InterVarsity Press, 2006), ch. 11.

7. A comment which overlooks the powerful moral agenda contained in Genesis 17:1; 18:19, and God's own endorsement of Abraham's life in Genesis 26:4–6, in ethical terms that anticipate the Torah.

Abraham did not take his call "as a commission to go find ways to bless the nations."[8]

In response, this is a very superficial dismissal of a major biblical theme and misreads my treatment of the Abrahamic covenant in relation to mission.[9] I do not "push Genesis 12:1–3 forward" as an alternative to the Great Commission, but rather seek to show that the Great Commission is a climactic part of the whole biblical story of God's mission, wherein Jesus himself draws on the Abrahamic language of "all nations"—as does Paul in the definition of his mission as bringing about "the obedience of faith among all nations" (Rom. 1:5; 16:26). From Abraham to the Great Commission there is a massive arch of biblical texts and themes that need to be held together in providing our mission mandate, not set in competition with each other.

I nowhere imagined that Abraham or Israel were to go out on "community blessing" missions to the nations, and to suggest that idea seems drawn from an exclusive definition of mission as "sending people out on a task or project." I offer an extended survey of what blessing meant in Old Testament terms and how it must ultimately be Christocentric in the gospel, as Paul insists. For me, however, the prime reason for stressing the missiological importance of Genesis 12:3 and the equivalent texts is not so much the "blessing" element (massive though that is in the context of sin and curse) as the *universality* of the repeated "all families/nations on earth." That is the truly missional freight of the Abrahamic covenant. The God who calls childless Abram and Sarai promises that, through them, blessing will reach to all nations, to the ends of the earth.[10]

To be fair, DeYoung and Gilbert give a fuller survey of the Old Testament story—including creation, fall, Abraham, Moses and the exodus, the law, and King David. They rightly see the need to involve the whole Bible in understanding our mission today. However, two features of their presentation reduce the missional impact that the Old Testament (Act 3 of the Scriptural Story) might otherwise have.

---

8. *What Is the Mission of the Church?*, 30–33.

9. *The Mission of God* chs. 6–7 trace the Abrahamic theme through the whole Bible, OT and NT.

10. That is the theme—God's plan for the nations, clearly a fundamental missiological thread within the Bible but sadly often neglected in biblical theologies—to which I devote chs. 14–15 in *The Mission of God*.

First, they persistently see the thrust of the Old Testament as exposing the problem of how sinful humans can live with a holy God, showing that we need a mediator and sacrifice to deal with that problem and pointing forward to the One who would fulfill that role. All of which is undeniably true. However, to present the story and the message of the Old Testament purely and predominantly in that way overlooks the enormous body of teaching, truth, exhortation, instruction, wisdom, worship, warning, and encouragement that fills the Old Testament. The fact that Jesus could take the two travelers to Emmaus through each section of the canon and point out the things concerning himself does not mean that the Hebrew Scriptures have nothing else to tell us.[11] Paul knew that they have a wider function (2 Tim. 3:15–17), part of which is missional—to shape God's people for lives they must live in the world.

Secondly, DeYoung and Gilbert's treatment of the law of Moses is particularly disappointing. They write: "In the story of Moses and the giving of the Law, the central problem being addressed is how a sinful and rebellious people can live in the presence of a holy God."[12] But this confuses *the story in which the giving of the law is set* (which was indeed one of constant sin and rebellion in spite of the redemptive act of the exodus), and *the purpose for which the law was given*, which has a wide horizon. Israel's sinfulness was indeed a problem and needed to be met with God's remarkable patience and forgiving grace, and with the ministrations of the sacrificial system. But there is a great deal more in the law than the sacrifices. To present the law as "addressing a central problem" seems to get us off on the wrong foot. The law was not given to "solve a problem" but to shape a people and at an individual level, to give blessing, security, guidance, comfort, and joy to the believer's life (see Ps. 1, 19, 119). Not just the sacrifices but the *whole* law is a gift of God's grace intended for a wholesome, life-giving purpose, to enable God's people of that era to live as a whole community of contrast and witness in response to the grace of their redemption.

When Israel was first called to respond in covenant obedience to

---

11. I am totally committed to the hermeneutical principle that we must read all of Scripture in the light of Christ and adopt a Christotelic understanding of the OT as a whole, while at the same time resisting distorting this principle into trying to "read Jesus" into or out of every OT text. I discuss this in *Preaching and Teaching the Old Testament For All It's Worth* (Grand Rapids: Zondervan, 2016), chs. 3–5.

12. *What Is the Mission of the Church?*, 83.

the law God was about to give them at Mount Sinai, the reason why they should do so is explicit and gloriously positive. If they would obey, then they could *be something* for God—his priestly kingdom and holy nation—in their role as his "special possession" in the midst of all the nations in the earth (Ex. 19:4–6). Motivations for obedience to the law abound in Deuteronomy, including long life in the land "for your own good," and the ever-present reminder of God's redeeming grace in the exodus. But a significant motivation in the programmatic Deuteronomy 4 is that obedience to God's law would show something *to the nations* about Israel and their God (Deut. 4:6–8). A similarly universal horizon comes among the blessings for obedience in Deuteronomy 28:9–10. And it is recalled at the dedication of the temple when Solomon anticipates the spreading fame of Yahweh among the nations if only Israel would be committed to keeping his law (1 Kings 8:60–61).

In other words, while it is undoubtedly true that the Old Testament law exposes sin and drives its subjects to the need for God's mediatorial grace in the gospel, there is also a strongly positive purpose to the law in the Old Testament—to shape God's people for their role in the world, by living according to the character and ways of Yahweh their redeemer. That missional dimension of Old Testament law, in relation to God's purpose for his people in that era, needs to be included in a fully biblical understanding of the mission of God's people. For Israel to be Yahweh's witness in the midst of the nations, they were called *both* to proclaim his name, glory, salvation, and mighty acts in their worship, *and* to walk in his ways, in righteousness and justice, in their life as a people.[13] That, in my understanding of the Bible's grand narrative, was the mission of Old Testament Israel. And that dual calling and responsibility is not cancelled out by the more centrifugal "sending" dimension of New Testament mission, but rather subsumed within it, as our opening study of 1 Peter 2:9–12 makes clear.

God's Mission Accomplished: Act 4 of the Bible Story

Of course, Israel failed—*as God knew they would!* Deuteronomy, for all its emphasis on God's redeeming grace and its hearty motivations

---

13. Exploring multiple dimensions of the paradigmatic missional identity and role of Israel and their land within God's purposes for the nations and the earth has been a major preoccupation of my research and writing, now contained in *Old Testament Ethics for the People of God* (Downers Grove, IL: InterVarsity Press, 2002) and *The Mission of God*.

to respond to God's love by obedience to God's law, is a book that begins and ends in failure. It opens with the exodus generation's failure, through fear and unbelief, to take the land. And its scorching conclusion (chs. 29–32) portrays the anticipated failure of the generations to come that would unleash the threatened curses and drive the nation to virtual extinction but for the saving and restoring grace of God once more.

The point is, therefore, that we should not imagine that the sending of God's Son was some kind of Plan B. Israel's failure did not surprise God nor did it derail his plans. On the contrary, as Paul would understand with reverent amazement and insight into the thrust of Deuteronomy 32, God built Israel's failure into his redemptive plan for all nations, including Israel!

In fact, God accomplished his mission through the paradoxical *double* significance of Israel. On one hand, Israel was God's chosen vehicle for his plan of salvation for all nations. On the other hand, Israel was as fallen and sinful as any human nation and in many ways had replicated and amplified all the sin of humanity since the garden of Eden—as the prophets clearly perceived.

Matching the first dimension of Israel's identity, Jesus came as Israel's Messiah, their representative and king, the one true faithful and obedient Israelite, to fulfill Israel's mission and open the gate of blessing to all nations. Matching the second dimension, empirical Israel embodied the rebellion that humanity has always shown towards God by rejecting the Son of God himself. But, in the mystery of God's sovereign will, Israel's rejection of Israel's Messiah actually accomplished both Israel's mission and God's.

What was the full scope of God's accomplishment through the cross and resurrection of Christ?[14] And what does that imply for our mission? We need to see the accomplishment of the cross and resurrection within the breadth of all that the Bible reveals as the mission that God set out to achieve. We need, therefore, both a God's-mission-centered theology of the cross and a cross-centered theology of our mission.

A mission-centered theology of the cross, focused by key texts referring to the cross, highlights at least the following dimensions of

---

14. On the importance of keeping cross and resurrection together, see Ross Clifford and Philip Johnson, *The Cross Is Not Enough: Living as Witnesses to the Resurrection* (Grand Rapids: Baker, 2012).

God's mission: to deal with the guilt of human sin (1 Peter 2:24; Isa. 53:6); to defeat the powers of evil (Col. 2:15); to destroy death (Heb. 2:14); to remove the barrier of enmity and alienation between Jew and Gentile (Eph. 2:14–16), and to heal and reconcile his whole creation (Col. 1:20—the cosmic mission of God). All of these huge dimensions of God's redemptive mission are set before us in the Bible and connected to the cross. God's mission was that

- Sin should be punished and sinners forgiven.
- Evil should be defeated and humanity liberated.
- Death should be destroyed and life and immortality brought to light.
- Enemies should be reconciled to one another and to God.
- Creation itself should be restored and reconciled to its creator.

All of these together constitute the mission of God. *And all of these led to the cross and resurrection of Christ.* The cross was the unavoidable cost of God's total mission, of God's will being done—as Jesus himself accepted, in his agony in Gethsemane: "Not my will, but yours be done." This leads in turn to a theology of mission that is cross-centered, showing the cross as both the unavoidable cost of *God's* mission as well as the unavoidable center of *our* mission. All Christian mission flows from the cross, which stands as the source, power, and defining scope of mission. It is vital that we see the cross as central to every aspect of holistic, biblical mission, and that we do everything we do in the name of the crucified and risen Jesus.

It is fundamentally mistaken, then, to suggest that, while evangelism should center on the cross (as of course it must!), our social engagement and various forms of practical mission and service work should have some alternative theological basis or grounding. Rather, in all forms of Christian mission in the name of Christ we are confronting the powers of evil and the kingdom and chains of Satan and their impact on all dimensions of human life. By what authority? With what power? Only through the power of the cross and resurrection of Jesus Christ.

The fact is that sin and evil constitute bad news in every area of life on this planet. The redemptive work of God through the cross of Christ is good news for every area of life on earth, all of which has been infected by sin. Bluntly, we need a holistic gospel because the world is in a holistic mess. And by God's incredible grace we have a gospel big enough to redeem all that sin and evil has invaded and spoiled. And every dimension of that good news is good news utterly and only because of the blood of Christ shed on the cross.

Ultimately, all that will exist in the new, redeemed creation will be there because of the cross and resurrection. Conversely, all that will not be there (suffering, tears, sin, Satan, sickness, oppression, corruption, decay, and death) will be absent because it will have been defeated and destroyed by the cross and resurrection. This is exceedingly good news, and the foundation of all our mission.

So it is my passionate conviction that holistic mission must have a holistic theology of the cross and resurrection. That includes the conviction that the cross must be as central to our social engagement as it is to our evangelism.[15] There is no other power, no other resource, no other name through which we can offer the whole gospel to the whole person and the whole world than Jesus Christ crucified and risen.[16]

God's Mission Consummated: Act 6 of the Bible Story[17]

All five of the great accomplishments of the cross and resurrection of Jesus will be brought to their ultimate consummation at the *parousia*, the "appearing" of Jesus Christ in glory. All of those dimensions of God's mission will be gloriously real and eternal. John's climactic vision pictures them all. There will be an uncountable multitude of people from every nation who will have been redeemed and cleansed of their sin by

---

15. For this reason, I disagree with the labels DeYoung and Gilbert attach to their broader and narrower perceptions of "the gospel" in the NT. They rightly point out that the word "gospel" is used both to describe the good news of God's reign having arrived, with personal, social, and cosmic dimensions—the "big story"—and also to describe the more individual and spiritual good news of forgiveness of sin and the assurance that goes along with that for each believer. But it is a mistake to call the first "the gospel of the kingdom" and the second "the gospel of the cross." They rightly insist that you can only have the gospel of the kingdom when it includes the gospel of the cross, and that there is only one gospel. So to use the two separate phrases leads to a false dichotomy and the tendency to associate the cross only with the individual and spiritual dimension of God's saving work—which the above texts counteract. All the work of the kingdom, and all the work of our mission, must have the "gospel of the cross" at its heart.

16. A fuller exposition of the preceding section can be found in *Mission of God*, 312–16.

17. At this point in our journey through the Bible story, I outline Act 6 before coming to Act 5. This is to see the outer framework of the biblical gospel "from beginning to end," as it were, before focusing on our penultimate mission mandate in Act 5.

the blood of the Lamb who was slain. All evil powers, Satan, and all that the beasts represent will be defeated and destroyed eternally. Death itself will be hurled into Hades and "there will be no more death." The nations and kings of the earth, which have rampaged in oppression, violence, and persecution according to the book of Revelation, will "walk by the light" of the glory of God and the lamp of the Lamb, and will bring their own "glory," no longer into the idolatrous city of Babylon but cleansed and purged to become the city of God. And the earth itself will be united with heaven in a renewed creation in which God, Immanuel, will dwell with his redeemed humanity forever, and "no longer will there be any curse." That is the Bible's great ending—and new beginning—of the story it told from Genesis 1. It is the climax of "mission accomplished."

Our Mission Mandated: Act 5 of the Bible Story

The consummation of the ages will be then, but here we are now. What then, is the mission of God's people between the ascension and the return of Christ? That is the penultimate act of the great Bible story— the penultimate era between Pentecost and *parousia*, launched in the book of Acts and continuing through generations including our own. It is known as the day of grace or the day of mission. God calls and sends his people into the world, driven, guided, and motivated by all that God has done in Acts 1–4 and drawn forward in hope by all that God will bring about in Act 6 of the Scriptural Story. We are to live within the Bible's own story and participate in its great unfolding drama. Mission is not merely a matter of obeying God's commands (such as, for example, the Great Commission—vitally important as that is), but of knowing the story we are in and living accordingly, bearing witness to the mighty acts of God (past and future), as Israel was told and as Jesus repeated to his disciples.[18]

What was it that made Christianity a missionary faith from the very start? What made the very first followers of Jesus so passionately, courageously, and unstoppably committed to telling the world about him? It was not merely that Jesus *commanded* them to go, but that they knew

---

18. It is surely significant that Luke ends his gospel (Luke 24:48) and begins Acts (1:8) with Jesus entrusting his disciples with the same role that Yahweh had given to Israel in Isaiah 43:10–12—the task of being witnesses to the identity and acts of Yahweh/Jesus. The difference is that that role will now involve actually going out to the nations, to the ends of the earth.

the scriptural story so far, they understood that the story had just reached a decisive moment in Jesus of Nazareth, and they knew what the rest of the story demanded.[19]

The imperative of mission is contained within "what the rest of the story demanded." Of course mission is a matter of obedience to the commands of Jesus (and nothing I have said or written ever minimizes that mandate), but the point here is that those commands were not something new and unprecedented *in principle* (they were the logical outcome of the scriptural story of God with Israel). But they were radically new in *scope and direction*. The completion of the Abrahamic promise, now made possible through the death and resurrection of Christ Jesus, required the missional people of God (a people whose reason for existence was to serve the purpose of God *among the nations*) to become also a missionary people (sending and being sent *to the nations*).[20]

The apostle Paul embarked on his mission to the nations before the canonical Gospels provided the written record of the Great Commission. But his own summary of his apostolic mission, emphatically positioned at the beginning and end of Romans, is fully coherent with the mandate that Jesus had given the other apostles before Saul of Tarsus was added to their number—namely, "to bring about the obedience of faith for the sake of his name among all the nations" (Rom. 1:5 ESV; cf. 16:26).

That definition of Paul's mission is thoroughly Abrahamic in at least two ways: most obviously in the reference to "all nations," but also in the genitival combination of faith and obedience (binding the two together as a single integrated objective), since Abraham is the model of both. "By faith Abraham . . . obeyed" (Heb. 11:8). Paul affirmed that practical obedience demonstrated in good works was an indispensable accompaniment of saving faith. The gospel was a message to be believed that had implications to be obeyed.[21]

Both of those aspects of Paul's missionary consciousness reflect key elements of the Great Commission. Paul's phrase, "the obedience of faith," summarizes two lines of Jesus's instructions. "Baptizing them . . ."

---

19. *Mission of God's People*, 35–36.

20. Significantly, it is the *risen* Jesus who insists that the *messianic* fulfillment of the OT story must lead on to the *missional* fulfillment of the OT promise for the blessing of all nations (Lk. 24:45–48).

21. Rom. 15:18; 16:19; 1 Thess. 1:3; 2 Thess. 1:8; Eph. 2:8–10.

presupposes that people have responded to the good news in repentance and *faith*.[22] "Teaching them to obey all that I have commanded you," presupposes that those who "go and make disciples" are themselves living out their faith in practical *obedience* to Jesus, and then instructing those they have brought to faith to live out their discipleship by doing the same. Faith and obedience are as integral to the Great Commission as they are in Paul's missiology.

The Great Commission reveals its roots in the Old Testament in other ways too. It begins and ends with the God of creation and covenant. It begins with the affirmation of the lordship of Christ over all creation (echoing Deut. 4:35, 39) and ends with the promise of the presence of Christ to the end of history, echoing the covenant words of God to the patriarchs, Moses, Joshua, and Israel as a whole (Isa. 43:1–2). All our mission takes place within the creation over which Christ is Lord and within the history where Christ's covenanted presence is forever with us. Furthermore, the echo of Deuteronomy continues in Jesus's instruction, "teaching them to *observe all that I have commanded you*"—words spoken again and again by God or Moses in Deuteronomy, drawing attention to the ethical imperative that was part of belonging to God's covenant people. As I said earlier, there is certainly a newness in the centrifugal dynamic of mission here in the New Testament—*going out* to disciple all the nations.[23] But the mandate that the crucified and risen Messiah of Israel, having accomplished the work of redemption, gives to his disciples is nothing less than participation in the mission of earth's creator, Israel's covenant Lord, and the nations' hope. When we see the Great Commission in the light of this whole-Bible context, then, it takes on a breadth of content, either directly commanded or biblically implied. It is a command that is saturated with the claims, assumptions, and demands of the whole drama of Scripture.

How, then, can we define the mission of the church? One helpful proposal was produced by the Anglican Consultative Council in 1984. Conceived as a mission statement for the worldwide Anglican Communion, it was adopted by the Lambeth Conference of bishops

---

22. As was the case in the preaching of John the Baptist, Jesus, and Peter (Matt. 3:2; Mark 1:15; Acts 2:38).

23. We should note, however, that this too is anticipated in the OT, which not only speaks poetically of Yahweh's name, salvation, and glory going forth to the ends of the earth, but also of God's eschatological sending of his emissaries to accomplish that (Isa. 66:19).

in 1988 as the "Five Marks of Mission" and goes a great distance in understanding holistic/integral mission. It stated this:

The mission of the church is the mission of Christ

1. To proclaim the good news of the Kingdom
2. To teach, baptize and nurture new believers
3. To respond to human need by loving service
4. To seek to transform unjust structures of society
5. To strive to safeguard the integrity of creation and to sustain the life of the earth.[24]

These could be summarized in a few words: evangelism, teaching, compassion, justice, and care of creation. It is a remarkably comprehensive list having deep roots in the whole Bible, and having generated additional literature.[25] All five "marks of mission" can also be linked (directly or indirectly) to the Great Commission and integrated together around it—*provided* (and this is an utterly crucial *provided*) we put at the center of all of them the opening affirmation of the Great Commission: the Lordship of Christ over all creation.

All of those five dimensions of mission depend on the Lordship of Christ displayed in the following ways:

• In evangelism—we proclaim the good news that Jesus Christ is Lord, King, and Savior.
• In teaching—we bring people into maturity of faith and discipleship in submission to Christ as Lord.
• In compassion—we follow the example of the Lord Jesus, who "went about doing good."
• In seeking justice—we remember that the Lord Jesus Christ is the judge of all the earth and all justice flows ultimately from his throne.
• In using and caring for creation—we are handling what belongs to the Lord Jesus Christ by right of creation and redemption.

---

24. Bonds of Affection-1984, ACC-6, p. 49; Mission in a Broken World-1990 ACC-8, p. 101. See: http://www.anglicancommunion.org/ministry/mission/fivemarks.cfm.

25. E.g., Andrew Walls and Cathy Ross, eds., *Mission in the Twenty-First Century: Exploring the Five Marks of Global Mission* (Maryknoll, NY: Orbis, 2008).

I find it simpler to group these five dimensions together in a way that generates three larger domains:

1. *Cultivating the church* through evangelism and teaching, colaboring with Christ to see people brought to repentance, faith, and maturity as disciples of Jesus Christ.
2. *Engaging society* through compassion and justice, in response to Jesus's commands and example, to love and serve, to be salt and light, to be "doers of good."
3. *Caring for creation* through the godly use of the resources of creation in economic work along with ecological concern and action.

CHURCH, SOCIETY, CREATION

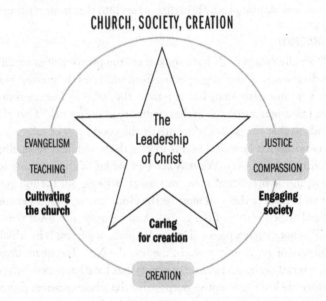

This triple scope of mission is fully biblical. *The Cape Town Commitment* recognizes that all three need to be held together in a truly holistic and integrated understanding of mission.

> Integral mission means discerning, proclaiming, and living out the biblical truth that the gospel is God's good news, through the cross and resurrection of Jesus Christ, for individual persons,

and for society, *and* for creation. All three are broken and suffering because of sin; all three are included in the redeeming love and mission of God; all three must be part of the comprehensive mission of God's people.[26]

Cultivating the Church (Evangelism and Teaching)

"Make disciples, baptizing them . . . and teaching them."

This flows immediately and directly from the Lordship of Christ. For if Jesus of Nazareth is truly Lord and God, then we are summoned to *become* disciples by submitting to him in repentance and faith, and we are sent to *make* disciples by bringing others into that same relationship.

1. Evangelism

Traditionally evangelicals have spoken of "the primacy of evangelism." They do so because, they argue, evangelism addresses the greatest human need. I do not deny that, but it frames the issue in human-centered terms. I now prefer to speak of the "centrality of the gospel." That phrase reminds us that the gospel is essentially the good news of *what God has done* in witnessed historical events to save the world, and evangelism is the telling of *that* story. We may do a whole lot of things, quite legitimately, in the breadth of many missional callings, but the integrating heart and center of them all must be the God-centered, God-generated, and God-willed reality of the gospel. And we must also insist that "the gospel" is not merely a personal insurance plan, or a formula by which we can be sure of going to heaven. In the way the New Testament uses the term, it is rather the declaration of events that have happened—the cosmic story of God's redemptive purpose for the whole creation, promised in the Old Testament and accomplished by the death and resurrection of Jesus Christ. It is in evangelism that we *tell that story*. And it is from that story (only)—that central gospel good news—that all our mission flows.

So when I speak of the centrality of the gospel, and the evangelistic task of telling that good news, I do not mean a center that makes everything else peripheral—marginal and secondary, out there, far off from

---

26. *The Cape Town Commitment*, I.7a (italics in original).

the center. Rather I mean central in the way that a hub is central to a wheel—connecting and integrating everything else around itself. A wheel is an integrated functioning object, with a rim or tire connected to the road. But the full orb of the rim must be connected at every point to the hub through the spokes. In that sense the hub is the integrating center of all that the wheel is and does. And the hub is connected to the engine, transmitting its power to "where the rubber hits the road."

In this analogy for integrated mission, the engine is the dynamic power of the biblical gospel ("the power of God for salvation," *what God has done in Christ to save the world*). The hub is our sharing of that good news. The rim/tire is the *embodiment* of the gospel in the world, through our life and work and all our engagement with the context and culture (the road). To engage in integral mission, one needs integration between the *historical facts* of the gospel, the *declaration* of that in evangelism, and the *embodiment* of it in social and contextual engagement with society and creation.

The Cape Town Commitment seeks to capture this integrated understanding of mission in the following statement:

> *The integrity of our mission.* The *source* of all our mission is what God has done in Christ for the redemption of the whole world, as revealed in the Bible. Our evangelistic task is to make that good news known to all nations. The *context* of all our mission is the world in which we live, the world of sin, suffering, injustice, and creational disorder, into which God sends us to love and serve for Christ's sake. All our mission must therefore reflect the integration of evangelism and committed engagement in the world, both being ordered and driven by the whole biblical revelation of the gospel of God.[27]

2. Teaching

". . . teaching them to observe all that I have commanded you."

Churches need not only to be planted through evangelism but also watered through teaching. Both are Great Commission mandates. God

---

27. *The Cape Town Commitment*, I.10b.

is at work not only bringing people to faith in Christ but also bringing them to maturity in Christ through the work of the Holy Spirit within them, with his gifts, power, and fruit in their lives. The task of teaching within the church is participating in the process by which God himself brings his people to the fullness of maturity and Christlikeness. It is another way in which we share in the mission of God.

When we look at Paul, we notice that teaching was integral to his whole life as a missionary church planter. For nearly three years he stayed in Ephesus. While he was there, we read that he had taught them not only all that was helpful for them but "the whole counsel of God"—which almost certainly means the whole scriptural revelation of God's great plan and purpose (Acts 20:20, 27; cf. Eph. 1:9–10). And when Paul could not personally do the teaching, he ensured that it was done by others who were part of his missionary team, like Timothy and Titus. Then there was Apollos (from Africa), who was learned in the Scriptures, a gifted teacher, who gained further theological education at the home of Priscilla and Aquila (in Asia) and then went to Corinth (in Europe), where he systematically engaged in teaching that included Old Testament hermeneutics, Christology, and a kind of apologetics (public debate and defense of the gospel; Acts 18:24–28). Later, when the Christians in Corinth divided into factions boasting loyalty to Paul or Apollos, Paul wouldn't allow it. Yes, Paul was the evangelist church-planter. Yes, Apollos was a theological church-teacher. But they shared a *common mission*. Paul insists that the evangelist (planter) and the teacher (waterer) have "one purpose"—that is to say, a single mission (in Greek, "they are one"; 1 Cor. 3:5–9).

So teaching within the church in all its forms, including what we would now call theological education, is an intrinsic part of mission. It is not merely ancillary to "real mission." Teaching is an essential part of our obedience to the Great Commission. Once again *The Cape Town Commitment* is emphatic on this point:

> The mission of the Church on earth is to serve the mission of God, and the mission of theological education is to strengthen and accompany the mission of the Church. Theological education serves *first* to train those who lead the Church as pastor-teachers, equipping them to teach the truth of God's

Word with faithfulness, relevance and clarity; and *second*, to equip all God's people for the missional task of understanding and relevantly communicating God's truth in every cultural context. Theological education engages in spiritual warfare, as 'we demolish arguments and every pretension that sets itself up against the knowledge of God, and we take captive every thought to make it obedient to Christ' [2 Cor. 10:5]

Those of us who lead churches and mission agencies need to acknowledge that theological education is *intrinsically* missional. Those of us who provide theological education need to ensure that it is *intentionally* missional, since its place within the academy is not an end in itself, but is intended to serve the mission of the Church in the world.[28]

Engaging Society (Through Compassionate Service and Justice)

Where is that in the Great Commission? it might be asked.[29] I see it plainly implied in what Jesus says in verse 18: ". . . teaching them to observe *all that I have commanded you*." For it is certain that Jesus had plenty of words to say to his disciples about compassion and justice. As the Deuteronomic echo in his very words recalls, he built his teaching on the constant call of the Old Testament Scriptures for Israel to be like God by showing compassion and seeking justice for the poor and needy, for the homeless, the family-less, the land-less—just as God had done for Israel in their need. In the same way and, I'd like to think, in the same tone of voice, Jesus says to his disciples, "Your mission is to make disciples and to teach them to obey what I have commanded you, which aligns with all that God has commanded his people from the beginning."

Even if we only look back through Matthew's gospel, we find this note again and again (e.g., Matt. 5:6; 6:33). Jesus says that the really weighty matters of the law are "justice, mercy and faithfulness"

---

28. *The Cape Town Commitment*, IIF.4.

29. In putting the question this way, I do not concede the view that elevates this single text (the Great Commission) as the only, all-sufficient biblical text for the content of our mission. I am arguing rather for a whole-Bible understanding of the identity and mission of God's people, such that even if social engagement were not legitimately found or implied in the Great Commission, that would not invalidate its inclusion in a biblical theology of mission. My *ad hominem* point is rather that *even if* the Great Commission were to be taken as the supreme governing text for mission, it actually *does* require obedience to all that Jesus taught, which certainly included teaching about works of love, compassion, and justice.

(Matt. 23:23). It is likely he has in mind the similar triplet found in Micah 6:8: "What does the LORD require of you? To act justly and to love mercy and to walk humbly with your God." Or the one in Zechariah 7:9: "Administer true justice; show mercy and compassion to one another."

Out of this shared scriptural background comes Jesus's astonishing word to his disciples, 'You are the light of the world' (Matt. 5:14–16). Did he mean that they would be preachers of the truth of the gospel that would bring light to people in the darkness of ignorance and sin? Undoubtedly Jesus would have included that in the overall task of the apostolic mission—as Paul explains using the same metaphor in 2 Corinthians 4:4–6. But what Jesus actually stresses when he explains what he means by "light" is "Let your light shine before others, that they may see *your good deeds* and glorify your Father in heaven." They did have a message to preach—of course they did. The good news of the kingdom of God must be shared. But when Jesus talks about "light" he is speaking of *lives* that are attractive[30] by being filled with goodness, mercy, love, compassion, and justice.

Once again Jesus is drawing on a strong Old Testament tradition. God had called Israel to be a "light to the nations," which included the quality of their lives as a society. "Light" had a strongly ethical and social meaning, with "light" and "righteousness" combined in Isaiah (58:6–8, 10). Light shines from people committed to compassion and justice. And, as Isaiah would continue, such light, because it reflects the light of God's own presence and glory among his people, will draw the nations—it is missionally attractive (Isa. 60:1–3). It will bring people to glorify the living God, which is exactly what Jesus said.

So then, in the Old Testament, God commanded Israel to be a people committed to practical, down-to-earth exercise of compassion and justice in ways that would reflect and embody God's own commitment to those things. Jesus both endorsed that mandate for his disciples (and radically deepened it), and then in the Great Commission commanded them to pass it on to the new disciples they would make ("teaching them to obey all that I have commanded you"). Both in their own life as a community of disciples, and in their mission of making disciples, they

---

30. The word translated "good" is *kalos*, which also means "beautiful," not just morally upright.

must reflect the character of the God who cares for the poor and needy, who defends the cause of the widow and orphan.

And they did.

We know, of course, about the exciting story of the mission of the early church, spreading in all directions through evangelism and church planting. But we should not overlook how the apostles and those first little communities of believers showed a strong commitment to this other dimension of the Great Commission—obeying what Jesus himself had taught about social and economic compassion and justice.

Luke tells us twice that the earliest community of Jesus-followers in Jerusalem sought to give their spiritual unity practical outworking in economic mutuality (Acts 2:44–45; 4:32–38). They did not believe there should be any poor persons among them while they had the ability to do something about it. Whether consciously or not, they were fulfilling another word of God in Deuteronomy (Acts 4:34 is almost word-for-word the same as the Greek translation of Deut. 15:4).

Paul's first missionary journey with Barnabas was actually not when they were sent by the church in Antioch to preach the gospel in Asia Minor (Acts 13), but when they were sent earlier by that same church to bring famine relief to needy believers in Jerusalem (Acts 11:27–30). That memory must have been part of the reason for Paul's sustained effort to raise funds among the Gentile churches in Greece for the support of the poor in Judea. Clearly Paul had taught those new disciples that responsibility, such that they even pleaded for the privilege of sharing in it (2 Cor. 8–9). In fact, at a most significant moment in Paul's missionary career, when he was granted acceptance ("the right hand of fellowship") among the Jerusalem apostles for the gospel message he was preaching, he adds this revealing comment, showing that Paul included care for the poor as an integral part of his missionary work:

> All they asked was that we should continue to remember the poor, the very thing I had been eager to do all along (Gal. 2:10).

That emphasis on practical economic and social compassion echoes elsewhere. The following passages speak for themselves and leave us in no doubt about the importance of this kind of obedience: 1 Timothy 6:17–19; James 2:14–17; 1 John 3:17–18. Jesus and the apostles would all have agreed with the simple affirmation of Proverbs 29:7: "The righteous care about justice for the poor, but the wicked have no such concern." We are called to the integration of faith and works, of word and deed, of the proclamation and demonstration of the gospel.

Caring for Creation

We could have started with creation, since it's where Jesus starts in the Great Commission. "All authority in heaven and earth is given to me." That combination "heaven and earth" is the typical scriptural way of referring to the whole of creation. It's not only where Jesus starts, it's also where the Bible starts (Gen. 1:1), and where the Bible ends, with a new heaven and new earth—the new creation of Revelation 21–22. The whole mission of God in the Bible story runs from creation to new creation, and Jesus stands at the center of it, claiming to be Lord over it all. Jesus is not just "up in heaven." Jesus is Lord of heaven *and earth*.

Whatever our mission may include as we obey the Great Commission in multiple ways, it presupposes that Jesus is Lord of creation, that the earth belongs to him, that he is the landlord and we are his tenants. The earth is his property and we are stewards of it, accountable to him for what we do on and with it. Wherever we go among the nations, we are walking on Christ's property under his authority.

Paul expands this cosmic, creational truth about Christ in one of the most amazing passages he ever wrote—Colossians 1:15–20. Notice how many times Paul refers to "heaven and earth" or to "all things"— another Jewish way of referring to the whole created universe. The whole universe, including our planet Earth, was created by and for Christ, is sustained in existence by Christ, belongs to Christ as his inheritance, and has been reconciled to God by Christ through the cross. And God wills that earth and heaven will be renewed, for God's glory and ours (Rev. 21–22).

So if the earth we live on is the property of Jesus, belonging to him by right of creation and redemption, we cannot separate our personal submission to Jesus as Lord from how we think about, and how we act upon, the earth. Godly use and careful stewardship of the resources of the earth, along with specific ecological advocacy and action, are legitimate dimensions of Christian mission. Christian mission cannot exclude our primal human mission, which was to exercise godly rule over creation by serving and keeping it (Gen. 1:26–28, combined with Gen. 2:15). *The Cape Town Commitment* puts it this way:

> The earth is created, sustained and redeemed by Christ [Col. 1:15–20; Heb. 1:2–3]. We cannot claim to love God while abusing what belongs to Christ by right of creation, redemption and inheritance. We [as Christians] care for the earth and responsibly use its abundant resources, not according to the rationale of the secular world, but for the Lord's sake. If Jesus is Lord of all the earth, we cannot separate our relationship to Christ from how we act in relation to the earth. For to proclaim the gospel that says 'Jesus is Lord' is to proclaim the gospel that includes the earth, since Christ's Lordship is over all creation. Creation care is thus a gospel issue within the Lordship of Christ.
>
> *Such love for God's creation* demands that we repent of our part in the destruction, waste and pollution of the earth's resources and our collusion in the toxic idolatry of consumerism. Instead, we commit ourselves to urgent and prophetic ecological responsibility. We support Christians whose particular missional calling is to environmental advocacy and action, as well as those committed to godly fulfillment of the mandate to provide for human welfare and needs by exercising responsible dominion and stewardship.[31]

It is baffling to me that there are so many Christians, including (and especially, sadly) those who claim to be evangelicals, for whom this matter of creation care, or ecological concern and action, is weak and neglected at best, and even rejected with hostile prejudice at worst. It seems to me that the reason for this is a very defective theology of creation among contemporary evangelicals. To put it bluntly, some people seem to have damaged Bibles, in which the first two and last two pages have got mysteriously torn off. They start at Genesis 3, because they know all about sin. And they end at Revelation 20, because they know all about the day of judgment. And they have their personal solution to the sin problem and their personal security for the day of judgment, provided by the death and resurrection of Jesus. Praise God, I believe all

---

31. *The Cape Town Commitment*, I.7.a.

that too. But the Bible has a wider story from Genesis 1–2 to Revelation 21–22, the story of the whole creation, within which our personal salvation fits. And the Lordship of Christ spans the whole story. So I need to see Christ as Lord of my physical environment as well as my spiritual salvation, and behave as his missionally obedient disciple in relation to both. This is precisely the rationale that makes creation care an essential feature displayed within the full spectrum of Christian mission.[32]

Conclusion

The mission of God's people is the correlate of the mission of God as revealed in the whole overarching narrative of the Bible. "God's people" includes both Israel in the OT and the church of Christ in the NT and today. For although the *nature* of mission has changed (between Act 3 and Act 5, outlined above), the fundamental reason for our existence as God's people has not. God has called into existence a people, in the midst of all the nations of the earth, to participate with God in his purposes for the world—"coworkers with God," as Paul put it. This does not mean that we do everything God does. God is God, we are not. But it does mean that our understanding and practice of mission must reflect in some way, however imperfectly and provisionally, the comprehensiveness of God's biblically revealed actions, concerns, commands, promises, and intentions.

The church exists for the sake of God's mission.[33] It is not so much the case that God has a mission for the church (to be carried out ordinarily by a few church-paid professionals), as that God has the church for his mission. The church is, in that sense, missional by definition because the whole church is called to participate in the mission of God.

In this regard, Lesslie Newbigin made a very helpful distinction between missional *dimension* and missional *intention* in the life of the church. Because the church exists for the sake of God's mission, its

---

32. See *The Mission of God*, ch. 12; *Old Testament Ethics for the People of God*, ch. 4; and *The Mission of God's People* (Grand Rapids: Zondervan, 2010), ch. 3. See also Colin Bell and Robert S. White, eds., *Creation Care and the Gospel: Reconsidering the Mission of the Church* (Peabody, MA: Hendrickson, 2016).

33. I mean this statement in the context of the church's life in this fallen world and within the story of God's redemptive work in history. In eternal perspective, the church will continue to exist within the new creation to worship and glorify God, to serve and enjoy God, and to exercise human kingship and priesthood forever within creation. That relational reality of the church's "ontology" is not overlooked here. But in terms of our *mission within history*, I believe the Bible supports the view of the church's mission affirmed here.

whole life (worship, fellowship, pastoring, teaching, outreach, etc.), has a missional dimension, simply because that is why and how the church is meant to be. Everything the church is and does should be connected in some way to our very reason for existence as the people of God in the first place, which is to serve the mission of God for the ultimate glory of God. Church activities should be evaluated in terms of what the church exists for. Are they, as we say, "fit for purpose?" That is the missional dimension of all church life.

But the church also acts with missional intention. It engages in specific actions and initiatives that are planned, resourced, and carried out with deliberate intention of bearing witness, in word and deed, to the good news of the kingdom of God, and of fulfilling the broad range of commitments found in the Great Commission and expounded through the whole Bible story. These are summarized, but certainly not exhausted, by those "five marks of mission."

Newbigin's distinction helps us overcome the fallacy of that much-abused saying, "If everything is mission, nothing is mission." That slogan arises from a fear that if everything a church does is *described* as "mission," then there will be no special category left for evangelism and sending out missionaries for church planting. The assumption inherent in the slogan is that *that* (i.e., sending missionaries to evangelize) is what "real" mission is. I hope it is clear from what I said above about the centrality of the gospel and the non-negotiable evangelistic responsibility of proclaiming it, that I am utterly committed to the importance of evangelism and cross-cultural missionary church-planting. But they simply are not the *whole* of what I believe the Bible includes in the mission of the church, which rather uses "mission" in the sense of all that God has called the church into existence for and all that God has sent the church into the world to do. It would be more accurate, biblically, to simply say, "Since everything is mission (because we are God's people for God's mission), then yes, *everything* is mission (in terms of all the dimensions and intentions of the church's life and work)."[34]

---

34. To illustrate the point, we could say that there is a ministry *dimension* to all that a church does—for we are engaged in serving Christ, one another, and society in multiple ways. But there is also a ministry *intention* about specific forms, callings, giftings, and orders of ministry that Christians undertake, within and outside the church. To affirm the first does not deny the second. Or in other words, it would be equally nonsensical to say, "If everything is ministry, nothing is ministry."

JONATHAN LEEMAN

It was a Sunday school class on biblical theology. I was teaching on the relevance of Old Testament law to New Testament believers and used an absolutely splendid analogy I thought of the night before. Then a member of the class raised his hand and asked a question which demonstrated that my analogy was not so splendid after all. The question highlighted the continuities between the biblical covenants, and I realized that my analogy swerved too hard toward the discontinuities.

Such is the challenge of rightly rendering the many-colored woven cloth that is Scripture. Faithfully retelling a story requires not just the right data, but the right emphases.

Christopher Wright rightly asserts that we best discern the church's mission through the storyline of the whole Bible. All four authors in this volume have attempted to do this. But don't be fooled by all the biblical theologians who, for several decades now, have regularly dismissed the old-school proof-texting preachers as "missing the big picture." The interpretive stories of biblical theologians are just as subject to imbalances, biases, and agendas. Some of the good ol' proof-texters have better judgment about the comparative weight of things than the highly degreed storytellers. When the lawyer asked Jesus about the greatest commandment, Jesus proof-texted with just the right proof texts.

I like Wright's retelling of the biblical storyline; it gets a lot of things right. But I don't share all his judgments about how much things "weigh." Like everyone else, his retelling leans, shades, interprets. At its best, his chapter should help church members feel an elephantine burden to integrate words and deeds in their lives. At its worst, the topics of conversion, the local church, even hell look awfully emaciated.

In plainer language: the chapter demonstrates too little concern for the salvation of sinners from the wrath of God and an eternity of darkness.

Creation (Act 1)

Wright's emphases on the image of God and our kingly and priestly roles in creation match my own. And God never rescinds these purposes post-fall.

Fast forwarding to the church, then, I expected him to say that the church's mission consists of displaying the image and righteous rule of God in all of life, whether the mother nursing her child by faith or the mechanic so wielding his wrench. Franke's chapter does this well. I also like Greg Beale's observation that the Great Commission is "the renewal of the Gen. 1:26–28 commission to Adam."[1] What surprised me, however, is how much Wright narrows that Adamic commission for the church. He jettisons the idea of imaging Christ in the whole of our lives, and adopts instead a threefold summary of an Anglican bishops' statement: the church's mission is to cultivate the church, care for creation, and engage society through compassionate justice and service. I don't disagree that church members should be interested in all three things, but where's most of what it means to be human? Where are faith-filled acts of children-feeding, wrench-wielding, picture-drawing, teeth-brushing? Why privilege creation care and doing justice? To my own parochial ears, these sound like the emphases of center-left Christian politics. Wright says, "Everything is mission," but apparently "everything" doesn't mean everything.

The Fall and Israel (Acts 2 and 3)

Let's move to his discussion of the fall and Israel. Again, I like much of the material here. Yes, Adam and Eve's sin precipitated a three-way break with God, others, and creation. And Israel's moral-law-shaped life together—their ethics—was crucial to their worship and witness (from Deut. 4:6–8). Wright the integrationist serves his readers throughout this discussion.

That said, some of what he chooses to emphasize or deemphasize confuses me. For instance, Wright objects to the way Kevin DeYoung and Greg Gilbert argue that the problem of sin is at "the very heart of the biblical story." Wright concedes that sin may be "the root cause,"

---

1. G. K. Beale, *A New Testament Theology: The Unfolding of the Old Testament in the New* (Grand Rapids: Baker Academic, 2011), 423; see also pp. 57, 390–91.

but "it is inadequate to consider the brokenness of creation and the nations as only 'symptoms.'" He wants us to weigh all three equally. I confess I don't understand the logic here. If sin is the "root cause," why is it "inadequate" to treat the brokenness of creation and the nations as "symptoms"? Isn't that how causes and effects work? God curses the ground *because* humanity has put itself in the place of God. Cain kills Abel *because* Cain has put himself in the place of God. All sin is fundamentally against God (Ps. 51:4).

Part of the problem here, it seems to me, is Wright's hermeneutic. He has a good appreciation for covenantal continuity but a less developed sense of discontinuity. The progressive nature of revelation means that, sometimes, later biblical authors will identify certain problems more clearly than earlier authors. They'll turn up the dimmer switch, and different emphases will move to the forefront. Looking at the Pentateuch, for instance, Wright argues that Israel's mission was "*both* to proclaim [Yahweh's] name, glory, and salvation . . . *and* to walk in his ways." He says this in response to DeYoung and Gilbert's emphasis on the law's role in exposing sin, which he calls "particularly disappointing." If we're looking at just the Pentateuch, surely Wright is correct. But what if we let later authors turn up the dimmer switch, particularly in light of Israel's mission failure? Paul, for instance, says that the law was added "because of transgressions" and to keep Israel "captive" (Gal. 3:19, 23). He says elsewhere that it came "to increase the trespass" (Rom. 5:20). So, yes, the Mosaic law's proximate Old Testament purpose was to shape Israel's life, but its ultimate canonical purpose was to expose Israel to itself (and, by extension, us to ourselves).

When Jesus turned up the dimmer switch on "the Law of Moses and the Prophets and the Psalms," what did he emphasize? His death, resurrection, and the preaching of forgiveness and repentance (Luke 24:44–47).

Wright gets a lot of the Old Testament details right, like someone with excellent visual acuity. But DeYoung and Gilbert get the emphases right. They possess better depth perception.

Christ (Act 4)

Wright's discussion of the cross and the work of Christ is good. We can only understand the Christ event in light of the Old Testament, which means we need a theology of fulfillment, not replacement. Building on the Old Testament, then, we see that Christ came to forgive sin, defeat evil, destroy death, reconcile enemies, and restore creation. His death and resurrection should be at the center of our mission.

Wright's holism comes out in full force here. A "holistic mess" requires a "holistic gospel," which in turn requires a "holistic mission" built upon a "holistic theology of the cross and resurrection." I agree with this, basically. I am concerned, however, about the lack of nuance anytime people talk about a holistic mission. Again, we must not smother the discontinuities of redemptive history, particularly the already/not yet nature of our salvation. The gospel will ultimately accomplish everything, but it doesn't accomplish everything right now. Wright acknowledges that this salvation will not be complete until the consummation of the ages, yet nothing in this chapter concretely discourages a thoroughgoing transformationalism.

Yet think of how Satan tempted Jesus: with bread, with a public spectacle, and with an instantaneous crown. Just this past Sunday my pastor observed that those are precisely the things the occupied Jewish nation was clamoring for. Satan often tempts us with the immediate and visible.

As I argued in my chapter, we rightly dismiss the secular/sacred divide, but we cannot dismiss the regenerate/unregenerate or Spirit-restored/under-the-curse divide. Yes, let's do good in love. But only the Spirit can regenerate and remove the effects of the curse. The church cannot redeem and transform anything. It points to the One who does.

Part of me wonders if Wright has for so long dedicated himself to fighting against fundamentalists to his right that he forgets to warn against transformationist utopianisms to his left.

Consummation (Act 6)

Wright jumps ahead to the end of all things with the glorious vision of earth uniting with heaven in a renewed creation. No more curse. Hell makes a cameo, though I find Wright's discussions of hell not just brief but a bit abstract and impersonal. Evil powers, Satan, and the beast will be destroyed eternally, he says. But will people be there? It's not entirely clear from this chapter or his books on the mission of God or the church. Instead, his discussions of judgment emphasize the purging and cleansing elements of judgment, as in Roman Catholic ideas about purgatory.

Perhaps the most surprising line in this section of the chapter is his claim that the very nations and kings "which have rampaged in oppression, violence, and persecution" will now walk among the redeemed of heaven. Presumably, he means those who have repented and believed? Or not?

Church (Act 5)

The same emphases and trends already mentioned continue in Wright's final section on the mission of the church. For instance, he wants to reapportion the weight between the church's evangelism and everything else. The gospel "is not merely a personal insurance plan." It's "a cosmic story for God's redemptive purpose for the whole creation."

That's true, of course. But we need to combine this kind of canonical awareness with institutional sensitivity to the discontinuities of redemptive history, especially (again) between the now and the not yet. Sticking with his insurance metaphor for a moment, consider the insurance agent who says to a person standing inside a burning house, "Good news! Your policy covers fire. We'll build you a whole new house!" Okay. That *is* good news. But the most pressing news the person inside the house needs—right now—is where the door to the outside is. Wright deserves high marks for reading the whole insurance policy, even the fine print. Yet what grade shall we give for spotting the most crucial clauses? I assume most contracts say you need to survive the fire in order to get money for a new house.

Wright does try to emphasize the role of making disciples with a useful metaphor likening gospel proclamation to the hub of a wheel and our obedience and embodiment of that gospel to the rim. The metaphor is good, and, in my mind, affirms DeYoung and Gilbert's point that our sin against God is the "heart" (aka, hub) of our problem. But the metaphor is no good if we don't do anything concrete or programmatic with the integrated but asymmetrical roles of "hub" and "rim," leaving them only in the realm of theological ideas and on the pages of books. How in "real life" does Word ministry do its job as a *hub*? And deed ministry as the *rim*?

I think Scripture's programmatic answer is very simple: it establishes local churches and charges them narrowly with making disciples through preaching and administering the ordinances. The existence of the local church *as an organized collective* makes the hub-ness of Wright's meta-phor very concrete. And its narrow disciple-making mission addresses the urgencies of the "now" versus the hope of the "not yet." Strangely, the preaching, baptizing, Lord's Supper–receiving local church never really shows up in Wright's chapter. Indeed, he doesn't really distinguish insti-tutionally "the church" from "God's people." All this seems undeveloped in his proposal. It's possible that the local church *as an organized collective* is what he has in mind when he whittles his mission down to the big three (cultivating the church, societal engagement, creation care). But I doubt he would say that offering plate dollars should be used to hire political consultants and arborists. Either way, his big three strike me as simultaneously too narrow (as I've already said) and too broad.

If Wright were to add the local church to his chapter and assign it with the narrow disciple-making priorities enumerated in my chapter, then his wheel metaphor would—I think—work splendidly.

JOHN R. FRANKE

Christopher Wright's essay is an admirably concise statement of what he has written elsewhere at considerable length. His work has become a standard bearer for evangelical conceptions of mission and missional hermeneutics in which he has provided detailed and compelling accounts of the mission of God and the mission of God's people.[1] I am appreciative of his work, particularly his emphasis on the holistic nature of the church's mission and the robust affirmation of creation care as an integral part of that mission. I do not have any major differences with Wright on his summary of the basic components of the church's mission as involving evangelism, teaching, compassion, justice, and care of creation, though I suspect we would have some significant differences on theology and epistemology. But in general, I agree with him on the big picture.

In light of that, I'd like to focus some attention on the question of hermeneutics and theology as it relates to his narration of the biblical story. Lesslie Newbigin envisioned a mission-shaped theology as one that emerged from an ongoing interaction between the gospel, culture, and the church. For Newbigin the dynamic and situated nature of this inter-action served as a constant reminder of the contextual and local character of all theologies, gospel proclamations, and accounts of the biblical story. He observes that while the ultimate commitment of a Christian theolo-gian is to the biblical story, all would-be theologians are also participants in a particular social setting, which consciously and unconsciously shapes their entire outlook and thinking. He goes on to observe that while these cultural models cannot be absolutized without impairing the ability to properly discern the teachings and implications of the biblical narrative,

---

1. See Christopher J. H. Wright, *The Mission of God: Unlocking the Bible's Grand Narrative* (InterVarsity Press, 2006) and *The Mission of God's People: A Biblical Theology of the Church's Mission* (Grand Rapids: Zondervan, 2010).

we are so shaped by our cultural situatedness that we are not able to see many of the numerous ways in which we take for granted and absolutize our own socially constructed cultural assumptions.

In response to this Newbigin maintains that Christians must find ways of expressing the biblical story which make use of particular cultural models (so they will be understood) without being controlled by them. Newbigin concludes that this can only be done if we are "continuously open to the witness of Christians in other cultures who are seeking to practice the same kind of theology."[2] Newbigin's perspective invites an important amendment to standard notions of evangelical hermeneutics that see the process as an interaction between a reader and the biblical text. Following Newbigin, hermeneutics must involve a third group of interlocutors—Christians from other cultures who read and engage the biblical texts in different ways. This intercultural approach significantly alters the shape of the hermeneutical process as well as the contours of a missiology and theology that emerges from that process.[3]

Following the insights of a contextual, intercultural, and pluralist approach to biblical interpretation and theological construction, I suggest three features of a missional theology that I believe to be central to the mission of God in the world and the mission of the church. Missional theology should be: (1) open and committed to, or angled toward, others; (2) beyond foundations; and (3) against totality. I will briefly comment on each of these.[4]

Openness to the plurality and difference of others calls on us to recognize the limitations of our own perspectives and experiences and invites a life lived for the sake of others as the means by which we can be delivered from the prison of our own imaginations and begin to experience something of the reality made known by God in Jesus Christ. This reality exceeds our particular language, thought forms, and experiences; yet from the perspective of the Christian biblical tradition,

---

2. Lesslie Newbigin, "Theological Education in a World Perspective," *Churchman* 93 (1979): 114–15.

3. For a recent account of intercultural hermeneutics, see Henning Wrogemann, *Intercultural Theology: Intercultural Hermeneutics*, trans. Karl E. Böhmer, Missiological Engagements (Downers Grove, IL: InterVarsity Press, 2016).

4. For a fuller discussion, see John R. Franke, "Intercultural Hermeneutics and the Shape of Missional Theology," in Michael W. Goheen, ed., *Reading the Bible Missionally*, the Gospel and Our Culture Series (Grand Rapids: Eerdmans, 2016), 86–103.

it has come near to us in the person of Jesus Christ, who is the embodiment of the Way, the Truth, and the Life. This posture of openness and commitment to others and the corresponding commitment to plurality for the sake of faithful Christian witness forms the positive agenda of a theology that serves the mission of the church. Missional theology is also shaped by two closely related formal concerns that function to clear space for the flourishing of a community truly open and committed to others for the sake of the gospel and the sake of the world—it is beyond foundations and against totality.

In keeping with its commitment to otherness, contextuality, and plurality, missional theology affirms the theological and philosophical critique of enlightenment foundationalism and the quest for epistemological certitude. It places emphasis on the local, the particular, and the practical rather than on the universal, the general, and the theoretical. A theology beyond foundations seeks to respond positively and appropriately to the situatedness of all human thought and therefore to embrace a principled theological pluralism. It also attempts to affirm that the ultimate authority in the church is only the living God revealed in Jesus Christ. This means that human beings are always in a position of dependence and in need of grace with respect to epistemic relations with God. Attempts on the part of humans to seize control of these relations are all too common throughout the history of the church and, no matter how well intentioned, inevitably lead to forms of conceptual idolatry and oppression. Missional theology seeks to nurture an open and flexible approach that is in keeping with the local and contextual character of human knowledge.

The commitment to resist foundationalism leads to a posture that is against totality. Because missional theology is positively committed to the radical contextuality of intercultural hermeneutics, it stands in opposition to claims that any particular theology or reading of the Bible is universal for all times and places. We inhabit linguistically and socially constructed worlds to which our personal identities are intricately bound. The construction of these worlds, as well as the formation of personal identity, is an ongoing, dynamic, and fluid process in which the forming and reforming of shared cultural meanings play a crucial role. To be human is to be embedded in culture and to participate in the process of interpretation and the creation of meaning as we reflect on and internalize the cultural symbols we share with others in countless exchanges that shape our ever-shifting contexts. While the cultural contexts we inhabit can often appear to be universal and objective realities, they are in fact the products of particular social constructions. This goes straight to Newbigin's concern: all theologies and gospel proclamations are shaped by a particular culture and hence cannot be absolutized without also absolutizing the cultural framings that shape them. When this is allowed to occur, mission quickly becomes colonization.

Alert readers will quickly discern the postmodern leanings that I have rehearsed here, and doubtless many will find my summary problematic, especially in the evangelical context. In most cases, if past experience can be trusted, this will be due to the sense that it compromises our epistemological confidence in the truth of the gospel. I don't believe it does, but then I do not think our confidence in the gospel should be grounded in certitude. I agree with Lesslie Newbigin that the convictional confidence proper to a Christian "is not the confidence of one who claims possession of demonstrable and indubitable knowledge. It is the confidence of one who had heard and answered the call that comes from God through whom and for whom all things are made: 'Follow me.'"[5]

My interest in postmodern thought is connected to the ways in which it explores the ethics of knowledge and offers alternatives that are more hospitable to those who do not share the outlooks and assumptions of hegemonic cultural communities. James Olthuis captures this concern succinctly: "Ethically, postmodern discourses share an alertness to plurality and a vigilance on behalf of the other. Modernist rational ethics, in its Enlightenment dream of a world increasingly controlled by a pure rationality, has shown itself not only blind and indifferent to those who are other and different, those who fall outside the dominant discourse, but violent and oppressive to them."[6]

From this perspective let me raise a couple of concerns related to Wright's narration of the biblical story. It seems to me to be highly influenced by particular notions of theology that suggest the story of the

5. Lesslie Newbigin, *Proper Confidence: Faith, Doubt, and Certainty in Christian Discipleship* (Grand Rapids: Eerdmans, 1995), 105.

6. James Olthuis, "Face-to-Face: Ethical Asymmetry or the Symmetry of Mutuality?" in James Olthuis, ed., *Knowing Otherwise: Philosophy at the Threshold of Spirituality* (New York: Fordham University Press, 1997), 135.

Bible can be summarized in a relatively neat and coherent fashion that moves forward in a fairly straight line that can be articulated in six acts. This, or something very close to it, has become standard fare in evangelical circles. But not everyone reads the texts in this way. While I believe the Bible is inspired by God, I see a set of diverse texts characterized by considerable plurality that tells different stories from different points of view. These canonical texts contain diverse law codes, chronologies, ethical assertions, theological assertions, and historical accounts. Most pointedly they contain four different gospels. Hence, it is not surprising that the communities that produced these texts were characterized by plurality and that a plurality of communities and theological perspectives have emerged from reflection on them. I see this contextually diverse plurality as an indispensable aspect of the mission of God in the world. This leads me to two questions for Wright. First, is there a place for a plurality of different readings and corresponding expressions of theology and practice in his thinking about the mission of the church? Second, how does he understand the significance of contextuality in the biblical texts themselves and in the interpretation of those texts for understanding the mission of the church?

Finally, I wonder about the coherence of his reading of the story of Scripture, which he describes as the essential foundation for the identity, role, and mission of God's people. This affirmation comes after a citation from *The Cape Town Commitment* which states that the church from all nations stands in continuity with God's people in the Old Testament who have been called to be "a blessing and a light to the nations" and to be a community "of holiness, compassion and justice in a world of sin and suffering." While I fully agree with this affirmation, I find myself wondering if this can really be justified as the conclusion of an allegedly singular biblical story as Wright seems to imply in his essay. Specifically, how does he understand the biblical narrative of the Canaanite genocide in relation to his conclusions concerning the mission of God's people? Does he think the eradication of the Canaanites was part of the mission of God? Does the story represent a faithful participation in God's mission? And if so, how does that factor contemporary accounts of mission? It seems to me that this is a question Wright needs to address in some detail given his understanding that the mission of God's people is revealed in the whole biblical story.

RESPONSE TO CHRISTOPHER J. H. WRIGHT

PETER J. LEITHART

hristopher Wright's essay has a target, but the target is not I. He takes aim at narrow construals of mission, especially as developed in Kevin DeYoung and Greg Gilbert's *What Is the Mission of the Church?*, which I also criticized in my contribution to this volume. Wright advocates a "holistic mission" that arises from "a holistic theology of the cross and resurrection." "Holism" in mission involves cultivating the church through evangelism and teaching, engaging society through pursuit of justice and compassion, and caring for the creation. Wright's expansive understanding of mission is the natural—which is to say, the *narrative*—consequence of his rich missional reading of both Testaments.

With all this I agree. What concerns me is not what he says but what he fails to say. Allow me to devote most of my response to an absence.

I have already stated the criticism in my own essay: Wright almost completely ignores the sacramental and liturgical dimensions of the life and mission of the church. The second of the "Five Marks of Mission" adopted by Lambeth in 1988 is "to teach, baptize and nurture new believers," but in Wright's account, baptism disappears: "In teaching—we bring people into maturity of faith and discipleship, in submission to Christ as Lord." Later he cites the great commission but emphasizes the need for teaching while ignoring Jesus's command to baptize. He uses baptismal imagery (perhaps inadvertently): "Churches need not only to be planted through evangelism but also watered through teaching." But the watering he mentions is an entirely *an*hydrous one.

The absence of baptism is a symptom of the larger absence of worship and liturgy in Wright's account of mission, and this has some significant consequences for his project. It somewhat distorts his reading of Israel's "mission" in the Old Testament. I can agree that the transition from Old to New is from the centripetal vocation of Israel to the centrifugal mission of the church, but attention to the liturgical life of

Israel introduces important complications. Much of Torah is devoted to describing the institutions and patterns of worship, and even with the rise of the Davidic monarchy the sanctuary remains central to Israel's life and vocation. Solomon's prayer of dedication at the temple indicates that it is intended from the beginning to be a "house of prayer for all nations." Not only distressed Israelites but also *Gentiles* are invited to pray toward the house where Yahweh has set his name, eyes, and heart (1 Kings 8:41–43; 9:3). It is only fair, since Gentiles played a significant role in the construction of the temple. Egypt contributed treasure to the tabernacle, but largely under duress. Pummeled by plagues, they were only too happy to hand over plunder to get Israel to leave. Hiram of Tyre, though, offers materials, transport, and expertise voluntarily (1 Kings 5:1–12). Between the Mosaic and the Davidic eras, Gentiles are incorporated more fully into Israel's priestly task.

It all ends in the disaster of exile, but Yahweh turns this disaster, like the scattering of Levi after the incident at Shechem (Gen. 34), into a blessing for Israel and Gentiles. Israel is scattered from the land like seed, and the seed bears fruit. Babylonian and Persian kings favor Jews like Daniel, Nehemiah, and Mordecai; Israel seeks the peace of the cities where they have been deported; and when the exile ends, Cyrus, a new and richer Hiram, oversees the rebuilding of Israel's temple. To be sure, Israel is *forced* into centrifugality, but then, so are the early Christians, who remain in Jerusalem after Pentecost until the martyrdom of Stephen leads many to flee to Samaria, Antioch, and ultimately to the uttermost parts of the earth (Acts 7–8).

This retelling of Israel's mission does more than qualify Wright's rather stark contrast of centripetal/centrifugal. Wright claims that Israel's calling was not to "go" but to "be," to "live as Yahweh's people, and in the combination of their *worship* and the ethical quality of their *social life* . . . to bear witness to the identity and character of Yahweh in the midst of the nations." When we attend to the sanctuary and liturgy of Israel, we realize that the roots of centrifugal mission are already embedded within changes in the design and liturgy of the temple.

By the same token, "being" the church is essential to the centrifugal mission of the new Israel. Wright understands that Israel's mission of worship and obedience was not "cancelled out by the more centrifugal 'sending' dimension" but "subsumed within it." Construction of the temple of God was central to Israel's mission, and it *remains* so in the new covenant. The apostles are foundation stones (Eph. 2:20) of a glorious new Jerusalem, a temple city, and Paul at least is a "wise master builder" (1 Cor. 3:10–15 KJV). Gifted by the Spirit, as Bezalel was, all the members of the church are called to "edify"—to build up—the temple of the Holy Spirit that is the church. Temples are for worship, which means that a fully biblical missional theology needs to incorporate liturgical theology as well. Adam was commissioned to rule the creation, but he began in the garden-sanctuary, the source of refreshing water that flowed out to the world. Wright, I suspect, largely agrees with this, but there is little or no explanation in his chapter.

We can make a similar point from another angle. Elsewhere in this volume, John Franke helpfully emphasizes the Trinitarian grounding of Christian mission. The church's mission is not extrinsic to the character and nature of God. It is not as if God commands the church to engage in mission "from the outside." Rather, God is himself a missionary, a sending Father with his sent Son and sent Spirit. By that Spirit, we are united to the Son and caught up in the mission of God. Wright agrees: Jesus's mandate "gives to his disciples nothing less than participation in the mission of the earth's creator."

Concretely, though, *how* are we caught up into that mission? How are we united to the sent Son by the sent Spirit? The New Testament links this incorporation to baptism. We die to the old in the waters of baptism in order to walk in newness of life, to devote the members of our body to the justice of God (Rom. 6:1–14). We commune with the missionary God at his table and are sent out to "love and serve the living God." To emphasize teaching while ignoring baptism is to risk a Pelagian missiology, which would treat the church's mission as a human effort in response to God's command. A Trinitarian and liturgical framework for mission forecloses this possibility, since the "go, you are sent" is always spoken to those who have been incorporated into the mission of God by baptism and who have participated in the body and blood of the Sent One.

Wright's essay also risks defining the church in functional terms. He states at the outset that "we cannot biblically answer the question 'what is the church?' (its identity), without paying attention to the purpose for which the church exists (its mission)." He uses similar language elsewhere. He asks "the purpose for which God created" Israel and probes "God's *instrumental* intention for Israel in relation to the nations." In his conclusion, he claims that "the church exists for the sake of God's mission." Wright would surely agree that the church exists ultimately for the glory of God, and its mission is ordered to that end. But his setup misses an equally critical point: The church *is* an end, not merely a means toward an end. The purpose of the church's mission is to realize herself as church, as the assembly of God, as the eschatological bride and body of the Son. When all is said and done, *this* will remain: the Bridal city, a reconciled humanity in a renewed creation, in eternal communion with her husband, the Lamb.

We might well say it both ways: The church exists for the sake of God's mission, but God's mission exists for the sake of the church. And in both, *soli Deo Gloria.*

CONTEXTUAL MISSION: BEARING WITNESS TO THE ENDS OF THE EARTH

JOHN R. FRANKE

But you will receive power when the Holy Spirit has come upon you; and you will be my witnesses in Jerusalem, in all Judea and Samaria, and to the ends of the earth" (Acts 1:8 NRSV). After speaking these words to his chosen apostles, Jesus was lifted up and taken from their sight. The apostles returned to Jerusalem to wait and pray. On the day of Pentecost, a strong wind came upon them and they were filled with the Holy Spirit and began to speak in other languages (Acts 2:1–4). The text goes on to say that a large and diverse gathering who were present for this phenomenon were bewildered because they each heard their own language being spoken. Those who experienced this linguistic phenomenon were reportedly amazed and perplexed and asked one another what it meant (Acts 2:5–12).

The meaning of this Pentecostal plurality is significant for understanding the mission of the church to bear witness to the ends of the earth. Of particular importance is the contextual character of Christian witness. The action of the Spirit here effectively decenters any particular language or culture with respect to the proclamation of the gospel and the mission of the church. The implication is that no single language or culture is to be viewed as the prime or inseparable conduit of the Spirit's message. Christians have sought to make the Bible available to people in different cultures by translating it into their languages rather than insisting that new followers learn the biblical languages. This principle has been a key component in the development of Christian approaches to mission shaped around the notion of contextuality. Christian historian and missiologist Lamin Sanneh contrasts this approach to mission with that of Islam, which he believes "carries with it certain inalienable cultural assumptions, such as the indispensability of its Arabic heritage in Scripture, law and religion." Sanneh asserts that, at its best, Christian witness follows the Pentecostal pattern in the Acts narrative and prefers "to make the recipient culture the true and final locus of the proclamation, so that the religion arrives without the presumption of cultural rejection."[1]

This approach to mission has led to the translation of the Bible into nearly 2,400 different vernacular languages and the establishment of a culturally and socially diverse witnessing community throughout the world. This new community is called to live out an alternative way of life in the world as every tribe and nation bears witness to the good news of God's love for all people. In this way, the church, in the diversity of its various and varied social, historical, and cultural settings, is called to be, in the words of Lesslie Newbigin, a sign, instrument, and foretaste of the kingdom of God.[2] This brief description invites a consideration of the mission of God as the context in which we are to understand the mission of the church.

The Mission of God

One of the most significant developments in the ecumenical movement in the twentieth century was the broad consensus, shared by virtually all theological and ecclesial traditions that participate in ecumenical discourse, that the mission of the church finds its rationale in *missio Dei*, the "mission of God."[3] One of the challenges of this consensus is that, while it served to inseparably link the mission of the church with participation in the mission of God, it did not lead to specification with regard to the precise nature of the church's participation in that mission.

1. Lamin Sanneh, *Translating the Message: The Missionary Impact on Culture* (Maryknoll, NY: Orbis, 1989), 20.

2. Lesslie Newbigin, *Foolishness to the Greeks: The Gospel and Western Culture* (Grand Rapids: Eerdmans, 1986), 124.

3. For a brief description of this development, see Lesslie Newbigin, *The Open Secret: An Introduction to the Theology of Mission*, rev. ed. (Grand Rapids: Eerdmans, 1995), 1–11; for a more detailed discussion, see John Flett, *The Witness of God: The Trinity*, Missio Dei, *Karl Barth, and the Nature of Christian Community* (Grand Rapids: Eerdmans, 2010), 35–162.

Attempting to provide such specification has proved controversial and prompts the need for books like this one as well as others.[4] While the connection between the mission of God and the mission of the church remained murky, this ecumenical consensus did secure two additional important points: first, that God, by God's very nature, is a missionary God; and second, that the church of this missionary God must therefore be a missionary church.

With regard to the first of these points, mission is essential to God's very nature and is expressed in the being and actions of God throughout eternity and made known by the sending of the Son and Spirit into the world. In the gospel of John, Jesus says to his disciples: "Peace be with you. As the Father has sent me, so I send you" (John 20:21). The term "mission" is derived from the Latin words "to send" (*mitto*) and "sending" (*missio*). Mission entails a sending and a being sent. The sending of the Father and the sentness of the Son point to the being and action of the triune God as both sender and sent. Mission is an attribute of God and thus descriptive of God's very nature.[5] One of the consequences of affirming that mission is an attribute of God and inherent to the divine nature is that the mission of God does not have an end point. It does not cease at the consummation of the age but instead continues into eternity as an essential aspect of the divine nature.

While the mission of God is complex and multifaceted, its central character—that from which all other aspects flow—is love. Perhaps the single most significant development in twentieth-century Trinitarian theology has been a large consensus among interpreters of the significance of relationality for providing renewed and helpful models of understanding the doctrine of the Trinity.[6] At the heart of the contemporary consensus of the divine relationality is the apostolic witness that God is love (1 John 4:8). Developing the doctrine of the Trinity in accordance with relational categories indicates how this biblical

---

4. Craig Ott, ed. *The Mission of the Church: Five Views in Conversation* (Grand Rapids: Baker Academic, 2016).

5. For a particularly helpful discussion of this idea and its implications, see Stephen R. Holmes, "Trinitarian Missiology: Towards a Theology of God as Missionary," *International Journal of Systematic Theology* (January 2006): 72–90; and Flett, *The Witness of God*, 196–239.

6. For example, see the essays employing relationality, albeit using different philosophical conceptual tools, from Thomas H. McCall and Paul S. Fiddes in *Two Views of the Doctrine of the Trinity*, ed. Jason S. Sexton (Grand Rapids: Zondervan, 2014).

assertion is to be understood. Throughout all eternity the divine life of the triune God is aptly characterized by love. When viewed in the light of relationality, it signifies the reciprocal self-dedication of the Trinitarian members to each other and provides a profound conception of the reality of God as understood by the Christian tradition. Love expressed, received, and shared by the Trinitarian persons among themselves provides a description of the inner life of God throughout eternity. In addition to enjoying the support of the biblical witness, love is an especially fruitful term as an explication of the divine life because it is a relational concept. Love requires both subject and object. Because God is triune, unity-in-plurality and plurality-in-unity, the divine reality comprehends both love's subject and love's object. The statement "God is love," then, refers primarily to the eternal relational intra-Trinitarian fellowship.

This notion that God is a loving missionary from all eternity points to the particular concerns of God in engagement with the world. As Stephen Holmes puts it: "Purposeful, self-sacrificial acts of loving concern flowing from the Father through the Son and Spirit to the world God has created are fundamental images of who God is, from all eternity."[7] For this reason, the idea of mission is at the heart of the biblical narratives concerning the work of God in human history. It begins with the call to Israel to be God's covenant people and the recipient of God's covenant blessings for the purpose of blessing the nations. The mission of God is at the heart of the covenant with Israel and is continuously unfolded over the course of the centuries in the life of God's people recorded in the narratives of canonical Scripture. This missional covenant reaches its revelatory climax in the life, death, and resurrection of Jesus Christ and continues through the sending of the Spirit as the one who calls, guides, and empowers the community of Christ's followers, the church, as the socially, historically, and culturally embodied witness to the gospel of Jesus Christ and the tangible expression of the mission of God. This mission continues today in the global ministry and witness to the gospel of churches in every culture around the world and, guided by the Spirit, moves toward the promised consummation of reconciliation and redemption in the eschaton.

---

7. Holmes, "Trinitarian Missiology," 88.

The love that characterizes the mission of God from all eternity is the compelling basis for the extension of the divine mission to the world. From this perspective, creation can be understood as a feature of the expansive love of God, whereby the triune God brings into being another reality, that which is not God, and establishes a relationship of love, grace, and blessing for the purpose of drawing that reality into participation in the divine fellowship of love. However, human beings, created in the image of God, have rebelled against the love of God. Instead of seeking the well-being of their fellow humans, they have sought their own good at the expense of others and established oppressive societies that colonize and marginalize their citizens, particularly the powerless and vulnerable. This activity, along with the dispositions of the intellect, emotions, and will that bring it into fruition, is what Scripture calls sin.

Out of love for the world, the Father sends Jesus the Son into the world: "For God so loved the world that he gave his only Son, so that everyone who believes in him may not perish but may have eternal life. Indeed, God did not send the Son into the world to condemn the world, but in order that the world might be saved through him" (John 3:16–17 ESV). The Son is sent into the world to redeem it through a cruciform life of humility, service, obedience, and death for the sake of others: "Let the same mind be in you that was in Christ Jesus, who, though he was in the form of God, did not regard equality with God as something to be exploited, but emptied himself, taking the form of a slave, being born in human likeness. And being found in human form, he humbled himself and became obedient to the point of death—even death on a cross" (Phil. 2:5–8 ESV). By his teaching and example, Jesus called the world to follow his way of life and participate in the kingdom of God, a community where everyone has enough and no one needs to be afraid. The Spirit is sent into the world to call, guide, and empower the community of Christ's followers in their missional vocation to be the people of God in the particular social, historical, and cultural circumstances in which they are situated. Through the witness of the church to the good news of God's love and mission, the Spirit calls forth a new community from every tribe and nation, centered on Jesus Christ, to be a provisional demonstration of God's will for all creation. And the Spirit then empowers that community to display God's love for the sake of the world.

This missional pattern, manifested in the world through the sending of the Son and the sending of the Spirit out of God's love for the world, is lived out and expressed in the context of the eternal community of love and points to the missional character of God, who seeks to extend the love shared by Father, Son, and Holy Spirit into the created order. The extension of this mission into the created order occurs not only through the sending of the Son and the Spirit but also in the sending of the church. As David Bosch observes, this biblical pattern demonstrates that mission is derived from the very nature of God and must be situated in the context of the doctrine of the Trinity rather than ecclesiology or soteriology. From this perspective, the classical doctrine of *missio Dei* expressed as God the Father sending the Son, and the Father and the Son sending the Spirit, may be expanded to include yet another movement: Father, Son, and Spirit sending the church into the world.[8]

In keeping with the pattern of this sending, the mission of the church is intimately connected with the mission of God in the sending of Jesus and the Spirit. The church is called to be the image of God, the body of Christ, and the dwelling place of the Spirit in the world as it represents and extends the good news of God's love for the world as a sign, instrument, and foretaste of the kingdom of God. However, given the local and particular nature of the church in its various manifestations throughout history, culture, time, and place, the expression of this mission is always contextual and situated in keeping with the commission to bear this witness to the ends of the earth.

Before giving attention to a more detailed summary of the mission of the church, it will be helpful to keep in mind the focal point of the mission of God as it flows from God's life and into the world through Jesus and the Spirit. What specifically is the mission of God in relation to the world? The short answer is, may I suggest, love and salvation. Flowing out of the divine life in Trinity, love is central to the mission of God in the world. When asked which commandment is the greatest, Jesus replied: "You shall love the Lord your God with all your heart, and with all your soul, and with all your mind. This is the greatest and first commandment. And a second is like it: You shall love your neighbor as yourself. On these two commandments hang all the law and the prophets"

---

8. David J. Bosch, *Transforming Mission: Paradigm Shifts in Theology of Mission*, twentieth anniversary edition (Maryknoll, NY: Orbis, 1991), 399.

(Matt. 22:37–40 ESV). In 1 John 4:7–12, the primacy of love is underscored in the relationship of God to the church:

> Beloved, let us love one another, because love is from God; everyone who loves is born of God and knows God. Whoever does not love does not know God, for God is love. God's love was revealed among us in this way: God sent his only Son into the world so that we might live through him. In this is love, not that we loved God but that he loved us and sent his Son to be the atoning sacrifice for our sins. Beloved, since God loved us so much, we also ought to love one another. No one has ever seen God; if we love one another, God lives in us, and his love is perfected in us. (ESV)

Above all things, the church is called to bear witness to the love of God for the world by imitating the life of Christ and living God's love.

The end of the mission of God as it is expressed in the world through the life of Jesus and the witness of the church is salvation. As Paul writes in his letter to the Romans (1:16): "For I am not ashamed of the gospel; it is the power of God for salvation to everyone who has faith, to the Jew first and also to the Greek." As Paul makes clear in the letter, the means of that salvation is the life, death, and resurrection of Jesus Christ who is the Son of God and the Lord of the world. This salvation entails the liberation of the created order—humanity and the entire cosmos—from the powers of sin and death (Rom. 8:2–25). In the same way that the mission of God in Jesus Christ to love the world is passed on to the church, so the mission of salvation and reconciliation is entrusted to the church:

> So if anyone is in Christ, there is a new creation: everything old has passed away; see, everything has become new! All this is from God, who reconciled us to himself through Christ, and has given us the ministry of reconciliation; that is, in Christ God was reconciling the world to himself, not counting their trespasses against them, and entrusting the message of reconciliation to us. So we are ambassadors for Christ, since God is making his appeal through us; we entreat you on behalf of Christ, be reconciled to God (2 Cor. 5:17–20 NRSV).

As many New Testament scholars have pointed out, it is important not to read this idea of salvation from the individualistic perspective of modern Western culture. To do so will be to miss the full scope and grandeur of the divine mission. God's actions are not only on behalf of all of humanity, but of the entire created order as well, such that it "will be set free from its bondage to decay." The fullness and cosmic scope of this mission is captured in the words of Beverly Roberts Gaventa, who writes that, according to Paul in Romans, the mission of God involves the work of rescuing "the world from the powers of Sin and Death so that a newly created humanity—Jew and Gentile—is released for the praise of God in community."[9] Commenting on this conception of the divine mission, Michael Gorman observes: "God is therefore at work creating an international network of multicultural, socio-economically diverse communities ('churches') that participate in this liberating, transformative reality *now*—even if incompletely and imperfectly."[10] He goes on to say that Paul uses numerous words, images, and phrases to articulate a comprehensive vision of God's mission of salvation including liberation, transformation, new creation, peace, reconciliation, and justification.[11]

This salvific mission is rooted in the self-giving, self-sacrificing love of God expressed in the eternal Trinitarian fellowship and made known in the created order through the life, death, and resurrection of Jesus Christ. It is this divine mission that forms the context for an understanding of the mission of the church.

Christendom, the Church, and Mission

Before turning our attention to the mission of the church, it may be helpful to comment briefly on the effects of Christendom as it relates to the church and its sense on mission. The missionary expansion of the church has often been an exercise in the extension of empire through the process of colonization using the Bible as a justification for this activity. While all of the texts that would eventually make up the Christian canon were produced at the margins of empire, the complicity that arose

9. Beverly Roberts Gaventa, "The Mission of God in Paul's Letter to the Romans," in *Paul as Missionary: Identity, Activity, Theology, and Practice*, eds. Trevor J. Burke and Brian S. Rosner, Library of New Testament Studies 420 (London: T&T Clark, 2011), 65–66.

10. Michael J. Gorman, *Becoming the Gospel: Paul, Participation, and Mission*, The Gospel and Our Culture Series (Grand Rapids: Eerdmans, 2015), 24–25.

11. Gorman, *Becoming the Gospel*, 25.

between Christianity and Rome in the advent of Christendom meant that the margins moved to the center and were interpreted accordingly. "Locked in the crushing embrace of the Vulgate, the first official Bible of imperial Christianity, the primary function of the biblical texts became that of legitimizing the imperial status quo, a function that, covertly when not overtly, continued into the modern period."[12]

In reflecting on the missionary expansion of the church over the last two centuries, many missiologists began to be concerned about the particular shape of this missionary enterprise. It has become increasingly clear that Western mission has traditionally been very much an Anglo-European church centered enterprise and that the gospel has been passed on in the cultural shape of the Western church. While this approach contributed to the growth of the church throughout the world, it also presents a challenge in that the formation and structures of the Western church are not missional, but rather have been formed and shaped in the context of a historical and social setting which for centuries considered itself formally and officially Christian.

In this context the church was intimately involved in shaping the religious and cultural life of Western society. This situation led to what is known as Christendom, a system of church-state partnerships and cultural hegemony in which the Christian religion maintains a unique, privileged, and protected place in society and the Christian church is its legally and socially established institutional form. This model of the church, and the outlooks and intuitions that attend to it, are so deeply pervasive that even when the formal and legal structures of Christendom are removed, as in the case of North America, its legacy is perpetuated in the traditions, patterns, structures, and attitudes that are its entailments. The continuance of the intuitions and entailments of Christendom, even in the aftermath of its formal demise, are known as functional Christendom.

From the perspective of Christendom that characterized the established church in the West, "mission became only one of the many programs of the church. Mission boards emerged in Western churches to do the work of foreign mission. Yet even here the Western churches understood themselves as sending churches, and they assumed the

---

12. Stephen D. Moore, "Paul after Empire," in *The Colonized Apostle: Paul through Postcolonial Eyes*, Christopher D. Stanley, ed. (Minneapolis: Fortress, 2011), 22.

destination of their sending to be the pagan reaches of the world."[13] It was assumed that these distant realms would benefit from the influence of Western culture as well as the gospel. In a similar manner many churches developed home mission programs and strategies in order to confront and attempt to hold at bay the emerging secularism of society that threatened to undermine the legacy Christian culture. These programs often involved significant political activism as an important part of preserving the ethos of a Christian society.

This desire to preserve and spread not only the gospel but also the particular ethos and culture of Western Christendom connected Christian mission with colonialism and colonization in the name of the gospel of Jesus Christ.[14] The results of this connection have had disastrous consequences for the practice of mission. Richard Twiss, a member of the Rosebud Lakota Tribe, wrote "Christian mission among the tribes of North America has not been very good news. What worldview influences allowed the Creator's story of creation and redemption to morph into a hegemonic colonial myth justifying the genocide and exploitation of America's First Nations people?"[15] Speaking of his own experience he explains the pressure imposed by white Christians to regard the music, dance, drumming, and ceremony of his Native culture as "unclean" and inappropriate for followers of Jesus. The implicit message was that the old and familiar rituals and experiences had passed away and all things had "become white." "This meant I needed to leave my Indian ways behind me, because I had a new identity in Christ, and it *was not* Indian! The Bible was used to demonize just about everything important to our cultural sense of being one with God and creation."[16]

This social and cultural colonization in the name of Christianity has had devastating consequences and has been all too typical of the interaction between Western mission and the indigenous cultures it has

---

13. Darrell L. Guder, ed., *Missional Church: A Vision for the Sending of the Church in North America*, The Gospel and Our Culture Series (Grand Rapids: Eerdmans, 1998), 6.

14. For example, see Jorge Juan Rodríguez V, "The Colonial Gospel in Puerto Rico," *The Christian Century* blog, January 3, 2017, https://www.christiancentury.org/blog-post/colonial-gospel-puerto-rico.

15. Richard Twiss, "Living in Transition, Embracing Community, and Envisioning God's Mission as Trinitarian Mutuality: Reflections from a Native-American Follower of Jesus," in Amos Yong and Barbara Brown Zikmund, eds., *Remembering Jamestown: Hard Questions About Christian Mission* (Eugene, OR: Pickwick, 2010), 93.

16. Twiss, "Living in Transition," 94.

encountered. A particular set of social and cultural assumptions and presuppositions have stamped the Bible and theology in its image, in this case that of Western culture, and then this is imposed on another group of people in the name of God and truth. When this occurs, the voices of those who do not participate in the assumptions and presuppositions of the majority are marginalized or eclipsed, often under the guise of claims that they are not being faithful to Scripture or the Christian tradition. Christian mission that would bear faithful witness to the gospel of Jesus Christ must resist and repudiate this colonizing trajectory. In light of its history and complicity with the forces of colonization, the mission and witness of the church must be reimagined.[17]

The Mission of the Church

In considering the mission of the church, framed by the concepts of love and salvation, we return to John 20:21–23 (ESV): "Jesus said to them again, 'Peace be with you. As the Father has sent me, so I send you.' When he had said this, he breathed on them and said to them, 'Receive the Holy Spirit. If you forgive the sins of any, they are forgiven them; if you retain the sins of any, they are retained.'" Here the disciples, representing the church, are sent into the world by Jesus after the pattern by which the Father sent the Son. They are called to continue his work. The close and indissoluble link between the mission of the Son and the mission of the church is established here in two ways: first, by the gift of the promised Spirit who had anointed Jesus for his mission at his baptism in the Jordan; now this same Spirit will guide and empower the church as it continues the mission of Jesus. Second, by Jesus's entrusting to the church the authority that was central to his mission—the authority to forgive sins. Lesslie Newbigin points out that what is being communicated in this scene is not simply the general idea that God forgives sin. Rather, it is the specific commission to do something that will otherwise not be done in the world, namely, "to bring the forgiveness of God to actual men and women in their concrete situations in the only way that it can be done so long as we are in the flesh—by the word and act and gesture of another human being."[18]

---

17. For example, Marion Grau, *Rethinking Mission in the Postcolony: Salvation, Society and Subversion* (London: T&T Clark, 2011).

18. Newbigin, *The Open Secret*, 48.

It is the particular and concrete forgiveness of sins that makes possible the gift of God's peace. The restoration of peace or shalom, the all-embracing blessing of the God of Israel and Jesus Christ, may be the most simple, compelling, and comprehensive way of articulating the content of the commission given to the church here. It is the focus of the initial word of Jesus to his disciples: "Peace be with you." This peace that Jesus speaks to his disciples here is one of the most central elements of the presence of God's kingdom in the created order and perhaps its most telling mark. "The church is a movement launched into the life of the world to bear in its own life God's gift of peace for the life of the world. It is sent, therefore, not only to proclaim the kingdom but to bear in its own life the presence of the kingdom."[19] The mission of the church encompasses both the character of its internal communal life as well as its external activities in the world. This comprehensive vision of the mission of the church, the reason for which it was sent into the world, is captured by Michael Gorman in his assertion that "already in the first century the apostle Paul wanted the communities he addressed not merely to *believe* the gospel but to *become* the gospel, and in so doing to participate in the very life and mission of God."[20]

From this perspective the gospel is both a message to be proclaimed—the good news that in Jesus Christ, God is liberating the world from the powers of sin and death and reconciling human beings with God, each other, and the whole of creation in order to establish shalom in the cosmos—and a way of life in the world that provisionally demonstrates this announced reality in the present, even as it anticipates its coming eschatological fullness. The church is therefore the gathered community of the followers of Jesus Christ who believe in this good news and are prepared to live by it. In the words of David Bosch, mission is the participation of the church in the mission of God made known in Jesus Christ, "wagering on a future that verifiable experience seems to belie. It is the good news of God's love, incarnated in the witness of a community, for the sake of the world."[21] This community is sent into the world by the triune God for the purpose of bearing witness to the gospel as a sign, instrument, and foretaste of the kingdom of God.

---

19. Newbigin, *The Open Secret*, 48–49.
20. Gorman, *Becoming the Gospel*, 2.
21. Bosch, *Transforming Mission*, 532.

The church is sent into the world to be the image of God as a sign of the kingdom. The assertion that human beings are created in the image of God is both an ontological status and a vocational calling, a destiny toward which human beings are moving. This eschatological destination is also a future reality that is present now proleptically. As Daniel Migliore states, "Being created in the image of God is not a state or condition but a movement with a goal: human beings are restless for a fulfillment of life not yet realized."[22] Genesis 1:26 connects the human task with the concept of dominion: "Then God said, 'Let us make humankind in our image, according to our likeness; and let them have dominion over the fish of the sea, and over the birds of the air, and over the cattle, and over all the wild animals of the earth, and over every creeping thing that creeps upon the earth'" (ESV).

Rather than reading dominion against the background of the ideology of modern industrial society, however, we must place the concept within the context of the royal theology of the Hebrew Bible. The kings of the ancient Near East often left images of themselves in cities or territories where they could not be present in person. Just as earthly kings erected images of themselves to indicate their dominion over territory where they were not physically present, so human beings are placed upon earth in God's image as God's sovereign emblem or image to represent God's dominion on the earth.[23] Human beings are called to reflect the loving care of God to creation.

Viewing the image of God as connected to our divinely given calling to represent God means that all persons are made in God's image and that all share in the one human *telos.* However, the New Testament writers apply the concept of the divine image particularly to Jesus Christ (2 Cor. 4:4–6; Col. 1:15) who is the clear representation of the character of God. By extension, those who are united to Christ share in his role as the image of God. All who are "in Christ" are being transformed into the image of Christ so that their lives may reflect his glory: "And all of us, with unveiled faces, seeing the glory of the Lord as though reflected in a mirror, are being transformed into the same image from

---

22. Daniel L. Migliore, *Faith Seeking Understanding: An Introduction to Christian Theology* (Grand Rapids: Eerdmans, 1991), 128.

23. Gerhard von Rad, *Genesis*, trans. John H. Marks, Old Testament Library (Philadelphia: Westminster, 1972), 58.

one degree of glory to another; for this comes from the Lord, the Spirit" (2 Cor. 3:18 ESV). In fact, it is this conformity to Christ as the likeness of God for which God has destined humanity (Rom. 8:29; 1 John 3:2). For this reason, Paul proclaims the hope that we will bear the image of God in Christ through our participation in Christ's resurrection (1 Cor. 15:49–53). In short, the entire biblical panorama may be read as presenting the purpose of God as bringing into being a people who reflect the divine character and thus fulfill the vocational calling to be the image of God.[24]

In Matthew's gospel we read that, after the arrest of John, Jesus withdrew to Galilee to fulfill what had been spoken by Isaiah. Then Matthew tells us: "From that time Jesus began to proclaim, 'Repent, for the kingdom of heaven has come near'" (Matt. 4:17 ESV). Similarly, Mark says that the beginning of the gospel coincides with the preaching of Jesus in Galilee: "The time has come," he said. 'The kingdom of God has come near. Repent and believe the good news!'" (Mark 1:15). With this announcement, the gospel writers are declaring that, after long and often difficult years of anticipating the reign of God in the world, in Jesus of Nazareth God's kingdom has come near in a new and decisive way that calls for action among those who have eyes to see and ears to hear. Newbigin poses that, "If the New Testament spoke only of the proclamation of the kingdom there could be nothing to justify the adjective 'new.' The prophets and John the Baptist also proclaimed the kingdom. What is new is that in Jesus the kingdom is present."[25] For those whose thought was shaped by the Hebrew Bible, the inference is clear: the coming of the kingdom of God is no longer a distant, far-off hope but a present reality in the person of Jesus.

The proclamation and presence of the kingdom of God in the person of Jesus calls forth the action of repentance, a turning from the ways of sin and death, from the selfish exploitation and oppression of others. It is a call to a new way of life that is expressed as discipleship. The church is sent into the world after the pattern by which the Father sent the Son to be a sign of the kingdom of God through its proclamation

24. For a more detailed discussion of the church as the image of God, see Stanley J. Grenz and John R. Franke, *Beyond Foundationalism: Shaping Theology in a Postmodern Context* (Louisville: Westminster John Knox, 2001), 192–202.

25. Newbigin, *The Open Secret*, 40.

of the gospel in word and deed and as a community of persons committed both to practicing discipleship in the way of Jesus and to making disciples in keeping with the last instructions of Jesus to his followers, who in Matthew 28:19–20 are to "Go therefore and make disciples of all nations, baptizing them in the name of the Father and of the Son and of the Holy Spirit, and teaching them to obey everything that I have commanded you. And remember, I am with you always, to the end of the age" (ESV).

As the church, following the pattern of Jesus, proclaims the gospel of the kingdom and God's love for all people, and calls on those who hear this good news to repent and become disciples of Jesus, a new way of life in the world is envisioned leading to the formation of a new community—a welcoming and inclusive community that lives the love of God for the world and transcends the divisions so often used to exclude people from the blessing and peace of God's kingdom. As the church pursues and embodies this inclusive vision of new community through gospel proclamation and discipleship in the way of Jesus, it bears the image of God as a sign of God's kingdom.

The church is sent into the world to be the body of Christ as an instrument of the kingdom. As the body of Christ, the church is sent into the world and called to continue the mission of Jesus in the power of the Spirit. While it is certainly true that God is at work outside of the church through, for example, the work of the Spirit convicting the world of sin, the New Testament characterization of the church as the body of Christ leads to the conclusion that it is intended to be a focal point of the mission of God in the world. The mission of the church is shaped by the mission and ministry of Jesus. Two biblical texts from the gospel of Luke, among many that could be cited, point to the mission of Jesus and should characterize the life and witness of the church sent by God into the world after the manner in which Jesus was sent.

The first is found in Luke's account of the inaugural events of the public ministry of Jesus and his reading of the words of the prophet Isaiah as a summary of the work he had been sent to accomplish:

> When he came to Nazareth, where he had been brought up, he went to the synagogue on the Sabbath day, as was his custom. He stood up to read, and the scroll of the prophet Isaiah was

given to him. He unrolled the scroll and found the place where it was written: "The Spirit of the Lord is upon me, because he has anointed me to bring good news to the poor. He has sent me to proclaim release to the captives and recovery of sight to the blind, to let the oppressed go free, to proclaim the year of the Lord's favor." And he rolled up the scroll, gave it back to the attendant, and sat down. The eyes of all in the synagogue were fixed on him. Then he began to say to them, "Today this scripture has been fulfilled in your hearing." (Luke 4:16–21 ESV)

This emphasis on the liberating ministry of Jesus points to an understanding of the church as the community of Christ's followers who join with Jesus in his struggle for the liberation of humanity from the forces of oppression and enslavement. The mission of the church, in keeping with the mission of Jesus, is to proclaim and live out the meaning of God's liberating activity so that those who live under the oppressive powers of this world will see that their liberation from these powers constitutes the mission of God in the world. The church, as the body of Christ, is the instrument of God in this liberating activity of social justice for all.

This concern for the poor and marginalized is powerfully expressed in Matthew 25:31–40 (NRSV):

When the Son of Man comes in his glory, and all the angels with him, then he will sit on the throne of his glory. All the nations will be gathered before him, and he will separate people one from another as a shepherd separates the sheep from the goats, and he will put the sheep at his right hand and the goats at the left. Then the king will say to those at his right hand, "Come, you that are blessed by my Father, inherit the kingdom prepared for you from the foundation of the world; for I was hungry and you gave me food, I was thirsty and you gave me something to drink, I was a stranger and you welcomed me, I was naked and you gave me clothing, I was sick and you took care of me, I was in prison and you visited me." Then the righteous will answer him, "Lord, when was it that we saw you hungry and gave you food, or thirsty and gave you something to drink? And when was it that we saw you a stranger and welcomed you, or naked and gave you clothing? And when was it that we saw you sick or in prison and visited you?" And the king will answer them, "Truly I tell you, just as you did it to one of the least of these who are members of my family, you did it to me."

Likewise, in James 1:27: "Religion that is pure and undefiled before God, the Father, is this: to care for orphans and widows in their distress, and to keep oneself unstained by the world" (NRSV).

These texts point to the calling of the church to participate in the temporal, here-and-now activity of liberation. The concreteness of these texts points beyond common interpretations that imagine the activity of liberation in primarily, or only, a spiritual sense. Embedded in the Hebrew tradition, the call to liberation is to be enacted in the present in such a way that the existing social order is actually changed. Liberation theologian Gustavo Gutierrez speaks of liberation in the three senses—political, cultural, and spiritual—all of which are part of the mission of the church. While these are interrelated, they are not the same—none is present without the others even while they remain distinct. Together they are part of a single, all-encompassing salvific process that takes root in temporal political history but is not exhausted by it. As Gutierrez writes, "we can say that the historical, political liberating event *is* the growth of the Kingdom and *is* a salvific event; but it is not *the* coming of the Kingdom, not *all* of salvation."[26] As the body of Christ in the world, the church participates in this historical process as an instrument of the kingdom of God in accordance with the mission of God and the good news of the gospel.

A second text is found in the story of Jesus and Zacchaeus the tax collector, which concludes with Jesus saying to Zacchaeus: "Today salvation has come to this house, because he too is a son of Abraham. For the Son of Man came to seek out and to save the lost" (Luke 19:9–10 NRSV). The church has been sent into the world after the pattern of Jesus to seek the lost and to proclaim the good news of salvation in Christ. Evangelism is a central aspect of the reconciling mission of God to a lost and broken world.

---

26. Gustavo Gutierrez, *Theology of Liberation* (Maryknoll, NY: Orbis, 1973), 176–77.

In response to those who have separated evangelism from the pursuit of social justice and liberation, note the comment of Zacchaeus in the preceding verse (v. 8): "Look, half of my possessions, Lord, I will give to the poor; and if I have defrauded anyone of anything, I will pay back four times as much." The response of Zacchaeus to Jesus, which includes repentance, reformation, and restoration, leads to the kind of individual transformation that has a direct effect on the social order. Evangelism and social justice are inseparable elements of the proclamation of the good news in Jesus Christ, declaring that God is reconciling all things.

The church is sent into the world to be the dwelling place of the Spirit as a foretaste of the kingdom. The Spirit is given to the church to empower it for participation in God's mission to establish a new community that transcends divisions that so easily divide and cause hostility and suspicion among human beings made in God's image. In the New Testament this vision of inclusive community is focused on the inclusion of the Gentiles in the family of God. Ephesians asserts that the establishment of this inclusive community is part of the eternal purpose of God in order to establish peace in the world.[27] According to Ephesians 1:9–10, God "has made known to us the mystery of his will, according to his good pleasure that he set forth in Christ, as a plan for the fullness of time, to gather up all things in him, things in heaven and things on earth" (NRSV). Michael Gorman observes that in Ephesians 2, we see that the mystery referred to here is made known in the gospel and is "best characterized with respect to humanity as a divine peace mission."[28]

This divine plan is intended to bring unity to that which is currently scattered and fragmented in order to restore harmony to creation. This is the power of God working through Christ and the church, which is Christ's body on earth: "God put this power to work in Christ when he raised him from the dead and seated him at his right hand in the heavenly places, far above all rule and authority and power and dominion, and above every name that is named, not only in this age but also in the age to come. And he has put all things under his feet and has made him the head over all things for the church, which is his body, the fullness of him who fills all in all" (Eph. 1:20–23 NRSV). Commenting on this in

---

27. For a detailed interpretation of Ephesians as a call to participate in the peace of God, see Gorman, *Becoming the Gospel*, 181–211.

28. Gorman, *Becoming the Gospel*, 188.

the context of a detailed exegesis of Ephesians, Gorman writes: "Thus the church, as described briefly here and in more detail in the rest of the letter, is intended by God to be a foretaste of the future cosmic peace and harmony that has been the eternal divine plan."[29] This is summarized in Ephesians 3:8–11 (NRSV):

> Although I am the very least of all the saints, this grace was given to me to bring to the Gentiles the news of the boundless riches of Christ, and to make everyone see what is the plan of the mystery hidden for ages in God who created all things; so that through the church the wisdom of God in its rich variety might now be made known to the rulers and authorities in the heavenly places. This was in accordance with the eternal purpose that he has carried out in Christ Jesus our Lord.

In light of the foregoing, unity in the church is clearly of paramount importance, displaying the church as the foretaste of God's intention to bring peace and harmony to the division of creation that is the result of patterns of sin and death:

> I therefore, the prisoner in the Lord, beg you to lead a life worthy of the calling to which you have been called, with all humility and gentleness, with patience, bearing with one another in love, making every effort to maintain the unity of the Spirit in the bond of peace. There is one body and one Spirit, just as you were called to the one hope of your calling, one Lord, one faith, one baptism, one God and Father of all, who is above all and through all and in all. (Eph. 4:1–6 NRSV)

A central feature of this new community gathered together in the name of Jesus is corporate worship. In the worship of God, the community comes together as one body and declares its adoration of God and thankfulness for the gifts of faith, hope, and love as well as its dependence on God for its witness in the world. Worship is a central element of the witness of the church to the reign of God in the world. As the church

---

29. Gorman, *Becoming the Gospel*, 189.

gathers together in worship, we celebrate God's presence, share concerns, pray, and seek the strength to continue on in faithful witness. As such, worship is a fundamental expression of the mission of the church and not an activity separate from that mission. It is a part of the comprehensive calling for which the church has been sent into the world to bear witness in thought, word, and deed to the love of God for the world. In this way the church is a foretaste of the vision from Revelation 7:9–10 in which "a great multitude that no one could count, from every nation, from all tribes and peoples and languages" stands before God and gives thanks in worship and praise for the salvation of God in Jesus Christ.

Through a new life together of interdependent relationality and corporate worship, the church bears witness to a new world that finds its coherence in the love of God revealed in Jesus Christ and attested by the power of the Spirit. The life is a foretaste of the world as it is willed to be by God. However, the world as God wills it to be is not a present reality, but rather lies in the eschatological future. Hence, Jesus taught his disciples to pray: "Our Father in heaven, hallowed be your name. Your kingdom come. Your will be done, on earth as it is in heaven" (Matt. 6:9–10 NRSV). This is a prayer to bring into being a new reality when God will put everything right and order the cosmos in accordance with the intentions of creation. Because this future reality is God's determined will for creation, as that which cannot be shaken (Heb. 12:26–28) it is far more real, objective, and actual than the present world, which is even now passing away (1 Cor. 7:31). The church in the present is a foretaste of the manifestation of this future eschatological reality for which we live, work, hope, and pray, and in which all of creation finds its connectedness in Jesus Christ (Col. 1:17).

While the elements of the mission of the church to be a sign, instrument, and foretaste of the kingdom of God can be distinguished, they cannot be separated. They are bound together in overlapping and interrelated ways. One particularly helpful example that brings the three together, though without using the same terminology, is the work of Raymond Fung, former secretary for evangelism in the World Council of Churches' Commission on World Mission and Evangelism.[30] Fung offers a strategy for evangelism that includes each of the elements we

---

30. Raymond Fung, *The Isaiah Vision: An Ecumenical Strategy for Congregational Evangelism* (Geneva: WCC Publications, 1992).

have discussed, and suggests that local Christian congregations, in partnership with other people, pursue the Isaiah vision outlined in Isaiah 65:20–23 (NRSV):

> No more shall there be in it an infant that lives but a few days, or an old person who does not live out a lifetime; for one who dies at a hundred years will be considered a youth, and one who falls short of a hundred will be considered accursed. They shall build houses and inhabit them; they shall plant vineyards and eat their fruit. They shall not build and another inhabit; they shall not plant and another eat; for like the days of a tree shall the days of my people be, and my chosen shall long enjoy the work of their hands. They shall not labor in vain, or bear children for calamity; for they shall be offspring blessed by the LORD—and their descendants as well.

In pursuing this vision in partnership with others, we declare to our neighbors that the "God we believe in is one who protects the children, empowers the elderly, and walks with working men and women. As Christians, we wish to act accordingly. We believe you share in similar concerns. Let us join hands."[31] As the church works at this vision, we invite our partners to worship God with us. We say: Doing this work is hard. There are many needs and problems. Occasionally, we need to pause, share concerns, pray, and seek the strength to continue through worshiping our God. "Would you join us? You would be most welcome."[32] In the process of working towards the Isaiah vision, the partners will grow to know and understand each other as trust and friendship develops and we become comfortable with each other. In this context, occasions will emerge when it is appropriate to invite partners to become disciples of Jesus. "Whether you are somebody or nobody, rich or poor, powerful or powerless, you are invited to enter into friendship with Jesus and fellowship with the church. You are called to turn around. Take up your cross and follow Jesus, together with us. We are ordinary people called to do extraordinary things with God."[33] In

---

31. Fung, *Isaiah Vision*, 2.
32. Fung, *Isaiah Vision*, 2.
33. Fung, *Isaiah Vision*, 3.

this model the church is a sign of the kingdom in making disciples, an instrument of the kingdom in working for a better world for those who are vulnerable and those who labor, and a foretaste of the kingdom in worship and life together.

Mission in Context

In summarizing the mission of the church, Kavin Rowe puts it succinctly: the life of the Christian community is the "cultural explication of God's identity."[34] In keeping with the calling of the Christian community to bear witness to the ends of the earth, the church in the aftermath of Pentecost emerged as a multifaceted and multidirectional movement. Its development was not, as it has often been pictured or implied, from Palestine to Europe to the rest of the world. Rather, it moved from Palestine to Asia, Palestine to Africa, and Palestine to Europe and was immersed in the cultural diversities present in these places.[35] It is a story that must be understood not simply as "the expansion of an institution but as the emergence of a movement, not as simply the propagation of ready-made doctrine but as the constant discovery of the gospel's 'infinite translatability' and missionary intention."[36]

This translatability continually results in fresh adaptations of the Christian faith as the message of the gospel spreads throughout the world across national, tribal, linguistic, and ethnic boundaries engaging culture after culture, social setting after social setting, and situation after situation. In this missionary engagement of bearing witness, the church continually reinvents itself to meet the challenges of relating the gospel to new peoples and new cultures. In this activity, the experience and understanding of what it means to be the church arises from the ongoing engagement of the gospel with culture.[37] "There seems to

---

34. C. Kavin Rowe, *World Upside Down: Reading Acts in the Graeco-Roman Age* (New York: Oxford University Press, 2009), 8.

35. The recovery of a theology of place is a vital component for the future development of missional theologies. See, for example, John Inge, *A Christian Theology of Place*, Explorations in Practical, Pastoral, and Empirical Theology (London: Ashgate, 2003); and Craig G. Bartholomew, *Where Mortals Dwell: A Christian View of Place for Today* (Grand Rapids: Baker Academic, 2011).

36. Stephen B. Bevans and Roger P. Schroeder, *Constants in Context: A Theology of Mission for Today* (Maryknoll, NY: Orbis, 2004), 3.

37. For a more detailed discussion on the relationship between theology and culture from this perspective, see John R. Franke, *The Character of Theology: An Introduction to Its Nature, Task, and Purpose* (Grand Rapids: Baker Academic, 2005).

be an inevitable connection, therefore, between the need for Christian mission, on the one hand, and the need for that mission always to be radically contextual. The urgency of mission is linked to the urgency of change, adaptation and translation—in other words, to context."[38] The ongoing engagement of the gospel with cultures of the world results in an irreducible plurality that is reflective of the missional nature of the Christian community. The very nature of the call to take the good news of the love of God to the ends of the earth and embody it among all peoples and situations for the good of the world leads inevitably to diversity.

From this perspective, plurality (not uniformity) characterizes the story of Christianity. The pervasiveness of this missional plurality in the history of the church leads Andrew Walls to conclude that Christian communities through the centuries "are cloaked with such heavy veils belonging to their environment that Christians of different times and places must often be unrecognizable to others, or indeed even to themselves, as manifestations of a single phenomenon."[39] The upshot of this history is that all churches everywhere are culture churches. All bear the marks of the particular cultural settings in which they participate. All are shaped, in ways both conscious and unconscious, by the assumptions and intuitions that are part of their social and historical contexts, even where they express dissent from or explicit resistance to aspects of their cultural surroundings. The cultural embeddedness of all articulations of the gospel and all forms of Christian faith leads Walls to conclude that no particular group of Christians "has therefore any right to impose in the name of Christ upon another group of Christians a set of assumptions about life determined by another time and place."[40]

This poses a challenge to many of the assumptions about mission that have emerged from the Anglo-European Christian tradition. In the words of the authors of *Missional Church*, "The subtle assumption of much Western mission was that the church's missionary mandate lay not only in forming the church of Jesus Christ, but in shaping the Christian communities that it birthed in the image of the church of Western

---

38. Bevans and Schroeder, *Constants in Context*, 31.

39. Andrew F. Walls, *The Missionary Movement in Christian History: Studies in the Transmission of Faith* (Maryknoll, NY: Orbis Books, 1996), 6–7.

40. Walls, *Missionary Movement*, 8.

European culture."[41] This awareness has led to greater recognition of the ways in which the Western church has tended to construe and articulate the gospel in ways that are more reflective of its particular cultural contexts. In addition, this approach to mission had the effect of making the extension and survival of the institutional church its priority. In contrast, understanding the mission of the church as a participation in the mission of God more readily leads to the conclusion that the church is a witness to the gospel and an instrument of the gospel, but not the goal and end of the gospel. The extension of God's mission is in calling and sending the church to be a sign, instrument, and foretaste of the kingdom of God in all the cultures and societies in which it participates. This activity is deeply and radically contextual.

I have suggested elsewhere that the irreducible plurality that results from the infinite translatability and radical contextuality of the gospel is not a problem to be overcome but is actually the intention and blessing of God for the church and the world.[42] Scripture reflects this plurality in multiple ways through the inclusion of a diversity of literary forms such as narrative, law, prophecy, wisdom, parable, and epistle as well as numerous perspectives on the presence and actions of God within each of these forms. The presence of four different gospel accounts offers perhaps the most straightforward example of plurality in the biblical canon. The inclusion of Matthew, Mark, Luke, and John, each with a distinctive perspective on the life and ministry of Jesus, alerts us to the pluriform character of the gospel. This means that true catholic or universal faith is pluralistic. In the words of Justo González, "It is 'according to the whole,' not in the sense that it encompasses the whole in a single, systematic, entirely coherent unit, but rather in the sense that it allows for the openness, for the testimony of plural perspectives and experiences, which is implied in the fourfold canonical witness to the gospel."[43]

The multiplicity of the canonical witness to the gospel is not incidental to the shape of the community from which it emerged and which

---

41. Darrell L. Guder, ed., *Missional Church: A Vision for the Sending of the Church in North America*, The Gospel and Our Culture Series (Grand Rapids: Eerdmans, 1998), 4.

42. John R. Franke, *Manifest Witness: The Plurality of Truth* (Nashville: Abingdon, 2009).

43. Justo L. González, *Out of Every Tribe and Nation: Christian Theology at the Ethnic Roundtable* (Nashville: Abingdon, 1992), 22.

it envisions for the future. As the normative witness to the mission of God, Scripture reflects the plurality of the ancient community. As paradigmatic witness to the mission of God, Scripture also invites greater plurality than that contained in its pages in order that the witness of the church might be continually expanded to the ends of the earth. Embracing and extending this plurality is part of the mission of the church. In the words of Lamin Sanneh: "For most of us it is difficult enough to respect those with whom we might disagree, to say nothing of those who might be different from us in culture, language, and tradition. For all of us pluralism can be a rock of stumbling, but for God it is the cornerstone of the universal design."[44] Attempts to suppress this plurality by means of an overarching, single, universalistic account has led to serious distortions of both the gospel and the community that is called to bear witness to it.[45]

As Lesslie Newbigin reminds us, there is no such thing as a pure gospel. All forms and understandings of the gospel are contextual and culturally situated:

> The gospel always comes as the testimony of a community which, if it is faithful, is trying to live out the meaning of the gospel in a certain style of life, certain ways of holding property, of maintaining law and order, of carrying on production and consumption, and so on. Every interpretation of the gospel is embodied in some cultural form.[46]

Likewise, our knowledge of God, our understanding of the Christian faith, our sense of the calling of God on our lives, and our notions about the mission and witness of the church are deeply contextual. Because of this, Stephen Bevans asserts: "The time is past when we can speak of one right, unchanging theology, a *theologia perennis*. We can only speak about a theology that makes sense at a certain place and in a certain

---

44. Sanneh, *Translating the Message*, 27.

45. For two recent examinations of these distortions, see Willie James Jennings, *The Christian Imagination: Theology and the Origins of Race* (New Haven, CT: Yale University Press, 2011); and Richard Twiss, *Rescuing the Gospel from the Cowboys: A Native American Expression of the Jesus Way* (Downers Grove, IL: InterVarsity Press, 2015).

46. Lesslie Newbigin, *The Gospel in a Pluralist Society* (Grand Rapids, MI: Eerdmans, 1989), 144.

time. We can certainly learn from others (synchronically from other cultures and diachronically from history), but the theology of others can never be our own."[47]

This leads to the conclusion that the mission of the church has been and continues to be shared by diverse theological/ecclesial and ethnic Christian traditions. In relating the many communities of the Christian tradition to the one body of Christ, we turn to the metaphor of the church as a body. In 1 Corinthians 12 we read that the Spirit is at work forming one body, one church out of many parts in which a diversity of gifts is given for the edification of the whole church: "Now there are varieties of gifts, but the same Spirit; and there are varieties of services, but the same Lord; and there are varieties of activities, but it is the same God who activates all of them in everyone. To each is given the manifestation of the Spirit for the common good" (1 Cor. 12:4–7 NRSV). The diversity of the church is the work of the Spirit, with each part providing particular gifts and understandings of the gospel of Jesus Christ on behalf of the whole body for the edification of the whole body in service to one common Lord.

In addition, the various parts of the church are interdependent. They need each other. They cannot fulfill the mission to which they are called apart from their relation to the whole body, for no single part can do all that needs to be done or comprehend all that needs to be said: "If the whole body were an eye, where would the hearing be? If the whole body were hearing, where would the sense of smell be? But as it is, God arranged the members in the body, each one of them, as he chose. If all were a single member, where would the body be? As it is, there are many members, yet one body" (1 Cor. 12:17–20 NRSV). Hence, no part of the church is independent of the rest. The gifts, theological insights, and particular ecclesial practices provided by the Spirit to one segment of the body of Christ are intended for the benefit and edification of the whole church, but none of these are adequate for all times and places.

The Spirit-intended plurality of the body serves as a warning against the temptation of constructing universal forms of church and theology. The many parts of the church are called to participate together in interdependent unity as a part, and only a part, of the embodied witness to

---

47. Stephen Bevans, *Models of Contextual Theology*, rev. ed. (Maryknoll, NY: Orbis, 2002), 4–5.

the truth of the gospel made known in Jesus Christ. All are called to do their part in the mission of God in accordance with the particular social and historical circumstances in which they are situated and the gifting of the Spirit. All have gifts to give and to receive in the edification and building up of the one church. As previously stated, plurality in the Christian community is not a problem to be overcome but is instead the very intention and blessing of God, who invites all people to participate in the liberating and reconciling ministry of the gospel of Jesus Christ.

The participation of the church in the mission of God to reconcile the world through Jesus Christ means that our primary commitment is not to any particular forms of Christian community, but rather to the interaction and relationship between the gospel and the particular cultural contexts in which we are situated. Indeed, we might say that we have no experience of church or its mission apart from the interaction between gospel and culture. Forms of Christian life and mission may be varied and fluid in keeping with new and ever-changing circumstances. In other words, there is no one way to be the church in the world, and appropriate forms of communal life are the product of particular social and historical circumstances. One size does not fit all, and we should expect a plurality of forms of church in keeping with the cultural diversity we see in the world. This serves as a reminder that no one of us, no one of our churches, traditions, or theologies can bear the witness and mission of God alone.

JONATHAN LEEMAN

Yes, but. That's my basic response to John Franke's interesting and elusive chapter.

For instance: Yes, all our doctrinal statements and church practices are culturally embedded. Sure. But the devil's in the details when you make a claim like that. Is Franke talking about musical styles? Or the foundational ingredients of the gospel itself, such as the role of law, guilt, shame, or substitution?

This "yes, but" reaction applies to my other overarching observation. Franke talks about just one side of at least three different coins: love but not holiness; inclusion but not exclusion; salvation but not judgment. In the Bible, these pairs are mutually-defining realities. Attempting to explain one without reference to the other often yields a misunderstanding of both. So, yes, I like what Franke says, but what he doesn't say concerns me.

So let me turn each one of these coins into a question, along with a fourth question about the two-sided coin of unity and plurality.

What Does God's Holiness Have to Do with Mission?

Franke starts with the love of God, which he calls the central character of God's mission. And what a glorious place to begin! The Father loves the Son, the Son loves the Father, both love the Spirit. God's love, says Franke, is "the compelling basis for the extension of the divine mission to the world."

Never once, however, does Franke mention God's holiness. I don't think we can understand God's love (or mission) apart from God's holiness.

Three times the seraphim affirm the holiness of God before making the missional claim that the whole earth is fully of his glory (Isa. 6:3). God then "sends" Isaiah on a mission, yet he sends him—interestingly—with a word of judgment (vv. 9–13). Franke affirms the church's word of salvation. Would he affirm its word of judgment? He never says.

What is God's holiness? As the seraphim's chant implies, God's holiness is his perfect consecration to his own glory (see also Ps. 29:2; Ezek. 28:22). To put it another way, God's holiness *is* the love shared between the three persons. That's how Jonathan Edwards describes it: "the holiness of God consist[s] in his love, especially in the perfect and intimate union and love there is between the Father and Son."[1]

What is love? Theologians from Martin Luther to Karl Barth emphasized the *gift* nature of God's love—that he loves as an unconditional gift (e.g., Deut. 7:8; Jer. 31:3). Yet an older tradition of theologians combined gift with *desire*. Love includes the affections of the Spirit, said Augustine. Love is intoxicated by the beloved and wants to be united to her, said Bernard of Clairvaux drawing from the Song of Songs. Love burns with the heat of a furnace, said Aquinas. When the divine Father beholds the divine Son, there is gift and desire. The Father gives all he is to the Son, and he delights utterly in what he beholds in the Son. "You are my beloved Son. With you I am well pleased" (Mark 1:11; see also, Heb. 1:9).

God's love is always holy, both in what it gives and why it gives. Which is a crucial point when we move from God's intra-Trinitarian love to God's love for humanity. The Father doesn't give us his love indiscriminately or because he is attracted to something lovely in us. Everything we have is from him (1 Cor. 4:7). He loves us for the sake of his Son. He wants the world to delight in the Son as he does, to say, "One thing I ask from the LORD, this only do I seek: that I may dwell in the house of the LORD all the days of my life, to gaze upon the beauty of the LORD" (Ps. 27:4). God's holy love is like a boomerang, swirling outward and drawing us into the arch of its path. "For from him, and through him, and to him are all things. To him be the glory" (Rom. 11:36).

What then does holiness have to do with mission? First, it provides a purpose for mission: worship. Mission exists not "just because" God loves. Mission exists to call people to worship. Franke captures this when he argues that "worship is a fundamental expression of the mission

---

1. Jonathan Edwards, *Treatise on Grace*, in *The Works of Jonathan Edwards*, vol. 21, ed. Sang Hyun Lee (Newhaven, CT: Yale University Press, 2002), 186.

of the church." In corporate worship, he says, "the church bears witness to a new world that finds its coherence in the love of God."

Unholy, idolatrous love opposes the worship of God. Therefore, it's opposed to mission. No holiness, no worship or mission.

Second, relatedly, holiness impels evangelism. God is so utterly consecrated to his own glory that he wants you, me, and everyone else to be consecrated to his glory too. Franke again: "Evangelism is a central aspect of the reconciling mission of God to a lost and broken world."

Unholy, idolatrous love will not share the gospel because, again, it does not value the worship of God. No holiness, no evangelism.

Third, holiness is crucial to mission because it requires repentance, which issues in discipleship, two more matters Franke argues are crucial to the church's mission.

Unholy, idolatrous love does not require repentance or discipleship. No holiness, no Christian discipleship.

So is the love which Franke describes in his chapter a holy love? He never uses the word "holy," but his affirmations of worship, evangelism and service, repentance, and discipleship suggest he at least implicitly affirms the holiness of love. It's the next two questions, however, that leave me uncertain.

Does the Church's Mission Involve Exclusion?

Franke emphasizes the inclusive nature of churches. It's an important note to sound when we consider the exploitations and discriminations of past and present. I think, for instance, of what African Americans have endured for centuries from white Christian America, and I'm not sure whites like me have adequately grasped or mourned our sin. If Paul counted Peter's separation from the Gentiles in Galatians 2 as anti-gospel, so we should count any exclusion of minorities as anti-gospel.

To be clear, however, holy love does exclude. It excludes the unholy and unrepentant. It excluded Adam and Eve from Eden, people from Noah's ark, the Egyptians from Goshen, unclean Israelites from the camp, and Canaanites from the Promised Land. Like a boomerang, holy love gladly embraces all who repent, even the most unlikely, such as the brother-betraying Judah, the foreign-born Ruth, the woman at the well. But holy love finally draws a line between those who love God and those who love idols—like the idol of white supremacy.

Today, holy love draws membership boundaries around the church. It practices church discipline. It baptizes and "fences" the Lord's Table (see 1 Cor. 11:27–32). Churches often blur the line between church and world, thinking that that is loving. They theorize about "centered set" churches, or "belonging before believing." They refuse to confront sin. At worst this evinces a reductionist, human-centered view of love; at best it overlooks the evangelistic power of exclusion, to say nothing of the biblical pattern (e.g., Matt. 18:15–17; 1 Cor. 5). Paul, on the other hand, sees no conflict between characterizing the Corinthians as "ambassadors of reconciliation" and simultaneously calling them to separate themselves as a people (see 2 Cor. 5:20; 6:17).

The idea that love might exclude is counterintuitive to our culture, which has defined love as a process of self-discovery and self-expression at least since the days of novels like *The Scarlet Letter* and *Pride and Prejudice*.[2] But make no mistake, both the God-centered love of the Bible and the human-centered love of the world draw lines, make demands, include some things, and excludes others. The love of God and the love of self both create holy spaces from which the unholy is excluded.

Would Franke agree with all of this? I don't know, because he says nothing about the boundaries and ordinances of the local church. A boundaryless church will last for a few years, even a generation. Typically, however, it will soon abandon the gospel, because it's unprotected from both heresies and hypocrisies.

Why Is a Doctrine of Hell Crucial to Mission?

By the same token, Franke never mentions God's judgment generally or hell specifically. And salvation, he says, is from sin and death. Does that mean salvation from God's wrath (e.g., Rom. 5:9)?

The omission of judgment and hell is curious. In all our thinking about God, sin, salvation, and the church, hell is like the foundation beneath a skyscraper. Pour shallow foundations and your building won't reach very high.

Is God weighty? His presence imposing? His glory beyond reckoning? The unimaginable horror of hell provides an inverse measurement of all this, like the cement and steel piles sunk deep beneath the Burj

---

2. Anthony Giddens, *Transforming Intimacy: Sexuality, Love & Eroticism in Modern Societies* (Stanford: Stanford University Press, 1992).

Khalifa, the world's tallest building built upon the sands of Dubai. Anselm's talk of a transgression against an infinite God requiring an infinite punishment might sound a little too mathematical to some, but the instincts were right. If God is something glorious, then an offense against him is something voluminous, and the magnitude of punishment shows it. Shed blood requires shed blood, says the proportionally precise author of Genesis (9:6). Why? It affirms the *worth* of the victim.

Wrath reveals worth. My siblings and I discovered at a young age, for instance, that lying to our parents yielded a stronger penalty than squabbling over a toy. Why? The truth is worth more than toys. The more precious the reality, the more terrible the consequences. Every jewelry store owner will tell you the same.

To judge is to measure. Take away judgment and you effectively consign life to worthlessness. John Lennon imagined a world with no heaven or hell. He should have read Ecclesiastes. Set "under the sun," it describes this world. What the inspired poet discovered, however, is that removing the eternal measuring tape of God's judgment turns life into a nihilistic garbage ball of "meaninglessness!" because none of the judgments we encounter under the sun make sense. The wise dies like the fool. Evil emerges from the place of justice. And an honest day's work kills you.

Salvation in Ecclesiastes, ironically, is the judgment of God, as the book's final two verses indicate. Only God's judgment will right this world's inverted and senseless measurements. Judgment Day, then, is that glorious day when all of history will suddenly make sense and we will discover the true measure of everything as it's held up to the standard of God's glory.

Why does Scripture offer such sobering images of hell—undying worms and unquenchable fire? Because sin dulls our senses, shrinks our horizons, and anesthetizes us to the poignancy of reality. The doctrine of hell wakes us up to a much bigger, grander universe, like moving from a stick-figure world on paper to the real world. Life is more precious, the stakes higher, God's glory greater than you ever imagined.

Franke affirms worship and evangelism. But his judgment-less and hell-less chapter, ironically, undermines the answer to "Why worship? Why evangelize?" He has removed the disincentives of hell, yes, but in doing that he has also cut off how high the glory and wonder of God can reach.

Are There Any Doctrines or Practices around Which Churches Unite?

Finally, Franke pushes so hard in the open and pluralistic direction for his missiology, one wonders which doctrines and practices unite churches? Can we abandon Nicene Christology? Is it okay to synchronize Christianity with African traditional religion or Zionistic chicken sacrifices? What about "America first" forms of Christian nationalism? Franke objects to "suppressing the plurality." Would he suppress the health-and-wealth charlatans who fleece the poor? If so, on what grounds?

Yes, praise God for the diversity of gifts and experiences enjoyed by the body of Christ through time and space. God is rich and manifold, and his glory is displayed through our very diversity. Franke was exactly right to say that our plurality is not a problem to be overcome but is good for its own sake.

But "pluralism" in these postmodern times is also a euphemism for tribalism and the gods of the group, or autonomy and the gods of the self.

I strenuously disagree with Andrew Walls's claim (quoted by Franke) that Christians from different times and places "must often be unrecognizable" to one another. How quickly have I enjoyed an immediate sense of kinship and fellowship with saints in Brazil, South Africa, Uzbekistan, or Malaysia. The Holy Spirit is more powerful than culture. He's creating a new culture and a new humanity, after all. That's why my church can sing Prudentius's fifth-century "Of the Father's Love Begotten" or Theodulph's ninth-century "All Glory, Laud, and Honor" or read Augustine's *Confessions*.

Different cultures have different idols, but all created cultures after the fall are idolatrous. Different people struggle with different fears, whether their deceased ancestors or the stability of the stock market, but all people struggle to fear God by faith. People are not as different as today's university classrooms insist. We're all sons and daughters of Adam.

Yes, but. Yes, we all read Scripture and write doctrine through our cultural experiences, but Scripture remains the foundation of the church's unity. So we must constantly measure our doctrines and practices against it. I want to think Franke would agree?

CHRISTOPHER J. H. WRIGHT

W hat on earth (or in heaven) might that mean?" I found myself asking (and wrote in the margin), as I read the rich paragraphs in which John Franke outlines his Trinitarian, love-centered understanding of the *missio Dei*—which I welcome and agree with. The point that raised a questioning eyebrow was when, in the midst of that discourse, he states,

> Mission is essential to God's very nature and is expressed in the being and actions of God throughout eternity. . . . Mission is an attribute of God and thus descriptive of God's very nature. One of the consequences of affirming that mission is an attribute of God and inherent in the divine nature is that the mission of God does not have an end point. It does not cease at the consummation of the age but instead continues into eternity as an essential aspect of the divine nature.

It is not that I instinctively disagreed—quite the opposite. But rather that I could sense how such a view of the mission of God extends our understanding of that term beyond the purpose of God for the *redemption* of creation and humanity from their present, respectively, cursed and fallen condition, to encompass the original and eternal purpose of God for creation and humanity *per se*—a purpose that will govern the unimaginable vistas of our life with God in the sin-free eternity of the new creation. In other words, it proposes an understanding of the mission of God (and of humanity) that goes back before Genesis 3 and will continue after Revelation 22.

Traditionally for most missiologists (certainly most evangelical ones), the *missio Dei* has been understood to refer to the action of God the Father in sending the Son, and both in sending the Spirit, for the great work of salvation in history. God's mission means God's purpose and plan for the redemption of the world, promised in the Old Testament, accomplished by Christ in his death and resurrection, and to be consummated at his return. And it is this redemptive mission of God in which the church is called and commissioned to participate. Accordingly, Craig Bartholomew writes,

> Mission in the sense of *missio Dei* begins in the biblical story after the fall, in Genesis 3:15 at the earliest. It is thus unhelpful to speak of creation as missional. Mission flows out of God's great work of *redemption*, and there will thus come a time when the *missio Dei* will cease. Thus, I do not think that God is "eternally missional."[1]

Franke clearly disagrees and argues that God *is* "eternally missional," in the sense that God has a purpose for his creation and for humanity within it, a purpose that will become fully "operational," as it were, when both are redeemed from sin and evil and restored to fulfill all that God desires for it and us. Franke is convinced that the inner Trinitarian love of God that reaches out towards, and flows into, the life of creation is an eternal part of God's being and will therefore continue even after the work of redemption is complete—i.e., beyond the *parousia*, resurrection of the dead, final judgment, and the establishment of the new heaven and new earth where God will dwell with his people forever. Life in that new eternal reality will be *purposeful*. I believe the glimpse we are given of that new creation in Revelation 21–22 supports that assertion. "His servants will serve him . . . And they will reign for ever and ever" (Rev. 22:3, 5). Our dual role of kingly rule and priestly service in the earth (Gen. 1:26–28; 2:15), will be affirmed and eternal—and we can scarcely imagine what that will involve, except that it will bring all our human created potentiality, purged and sin-free, into God-imaging alignment at last with the character, will, and glory of God (cf. the mysterious picture of Rev. 21:24–27).

How might we picture the dual nature of the *missio Dei* as, on the one hand, God's eternal purpose for creation and humanity that reflects God's own being as Trinity-in-love and, on the other hand, God's

---

1. Craig G. Bartholomew, "Theological Interpretation and a Missional Hermeneutic," in Michael W. Goheen, ed., *Reading the Bible Missionally* (Grand Rapids: Eerdmans, 2016), 79.

historical mission of bringing redemption and restoration to a world gone
awry in sin and rebellion? Or, to put it biblically, how can we helpfully
hold together the picture of God's desire for creation and humanity that
we see in the outer frame of the Bible—creation and new creation (Gen.
1–2 and Rev. 21–22), with the great story of God's mission of redemption, centered on the gospel of the Lord Jesus Christ, that fills the canon
of Scripture from the fall (Gen. 3) to the final judgment (Rev. 20)?

Jesus's parable of the vineyard and the tenants (Matt. 21:33–44)
ends with the vineyard owner, once he has dealt with the wicked tenants, handing over the vineyard to those who will properly "produce its
fruit." The vineyard will be restored to its proper owner and its proper
purpose—*after* the sequence of events involving his servants and his Son
and judgment on the abusive and murderous tenants.

Imagine a comparable allegory. A wealthy patron plans and builds a
wonderful estate for resident artists to enjoy and develop—replete with
homes, gardens, and expanses of wild countryside. But it gets taken over
by malevolent usurpers who damage the homes, trash the gardens, pol-
lute the wild areas as waste dumps, fight among themselves, and abuse
the artists who seek to do what the patron intended. The patron embarks
on a lengthy process to reclaim his property—at great personal cost,
including vicious abuse from the usurpers. He cannot proceed with his
original plans until this great and time-consuming task of recovery and
purging is complete. Eventually, however, with the usurpers arrested,
evicted, and imprisoned, he redeems what was his own and restores it to
its original purpose, to be occupied, enjoyed, developed, and enhanced
by artists who understand and reflect his own desires. The owner-patron
is one and the same person, but in the outworking of the narrative his
"mission" has taken two forms: first, his *original* plan in creating the
estate, which could only be fulfilled when, second, his *recovery* plan
had achieved its victory. The "redemptive" part of the story takes up
the bulk of the narrative from our perspective. But the whole point of
the redemption thus achieved was to enable the original purpose of the
owner-patron to be realized and to move forward into a glorious future
of unlimited artistic potential.

Might this be a way of *both* seeing the central place of the *redemptive*
mission of God in Scripture *and* recognizing its crucial goal of enabling
the fulfillment of the *creational* mission of God—namely for God and

redeemed humanity to dwell together in the reconciled and restored creation, fulfilling God's loving purpose eternally?

If there is biblical warrant for such a configuration of the *missio Dei* in its broadest sense, then we need a comparable discernment of the mission of God's people. For after all, as redeemed humans who are being restored in Christ to the unspoiled image of God, we participate in God's creational mission as well as God's redemptive mission. Or, in Franke's terms, the church is not only the *instrument* of the extension of God's kingdom (participating in God's redemptive mission) but also the *foretaste* of it in all the ways we bear witness, in word and deed, to the Trinitarian redeeming love of God in Christ and his glorious purpose for the new creation. So, returning to our allegory, our mission includes *both* calling the usurpers to repentance and alignment with the owner-patron's intention (and to avoid his judgment), *and* living now within that usurped estate as the artists he wanted and has redeemed us to be, in anticipation of the day when the estate will be fully restored and we can fulfill the owner-patron's intentions, for his glory and pleasure and our own. By doing both what we were created for and what we have been redeemed for, we participate to the fullest extent possible in the whole mission of God as revealed in the biblical narrative with its creational frame and its redemptive central narrative.

My second response to John Franke's essay is to propose some nuancing of his strong condemnation of previous missionary work of the church as predominantly Western, colonial, and culture-homogenizing. There is undoubtedly some truth in that accusation (though the relationship between colonial powers and Christian missionaries was far from simple collusion—the former often resisted the latter, a very important point), but two points need to be recognized. On the one hand, there have been many forms of mission in past centuries that do not reflect that stereotype, such as Syrian Christianity's mission to China; Celtic missionary wanderings; Moravian missions; the missions of former West Indian slaves to West Africa; and more recent indigenous mission movements in India and Africa. And on the other hand, the tendency to export cultural assumptions and domination are not confined to Western colonialism; the same accusations have been made (and often recognized by themselves) about, for example, Korean and Brazilian missionary movements.

My third response relates to the later thrust of the essay in the direction of contextual plurality. Here I think Franke suffers from the restriction all of us contributors faced—having to condense positions argued at length elsewhere into a single essay. His argument for hermeneutical and missional plurality can be read more fully in "Intercultural Hermeneutics and the Shape of Missional Theology."[2] Let me say immediately that I entirely accept the reality of, the need for, and the essential biblical warrant for the wide diversity of cultural forms in which the gospel is communicated, received, believed, obeyed, and embodied. I resonate with the writings of Andrew Walls and Lamin Sanneh on this essential "translatable" nature of the biblical faith—that it will embrace people of every tribe and people and language. As Walls has put it, we will not know the fullness of the gospel's accomplishment until we see it gloriously and eschatologically revealed in the multifaceted diamond of all the cultures of humanity, redeemed by Christ and displaying his image and glory.

However, are there boundaries to plurality? Or are there criteria by which we could distinguish between a manifestation of cultural diversity that truly expresses the gospel and one that is deficient, distorted, or indeed subversive of the gospel, or a syncretistic admixture of gospel and the unredeemed features of a given culture? And where are such criteria (if they exist) to be found? Franke seems, to me, so committed to a radically postmodern epistemology that it might be hard for him to answer those questions without denying his own presuppositions. In "Intercultural Hermeneutics" he claims that "mission theology is beyond foundations." But in (rightly) rejecting modern foundationalism based on the autonomous rational self as final authority, he seems to sail close to a radical postmodern relativism. He says that "nonfoundationalist theology does not eschew convictions" but subjects them to critical scrutiny, revision, etc. But what then *are* the criteria for that critique? "The ultimate authority in the church," he concludes, "is not a particular source, be it Scripture, tradition, or culture, but only the living God revealed in Jesus Christ."[3] But how does he *know* that? Where, we must

---

2. In Michael W. Goheen, ed., *Reading the Bible Missionally* (Grand Rapids: Eerdmans, 2016), 86–103. See also: John R. Franke, *The Character of Theology* (Grand Rapids: Baker, 2005), and *Manifold Witness: The Plurality of Truth* (Nashville: Abingdon, 2009).

3. Franke, "Intercultural Hermeneutics," 98.

ask, is the authoritative source of our knowledge of the living God and his revelation in Jesus Christ, if not in the Scriptures? What other access do we have to the person of Christ and all he reveals of God the Father and the Holy Spirit, and the grand missional purpose of this triune God in creation and redemption?

Additionally, he speaks authoritatively (and well) about the essence of the divine nature—the Trinity of love in missional relationship with creation and humanity. In the first part of his essay here, this triune dynamic is presented as very much *foundational* to the rest of his argument. But by what authority does Franke *know* this to be the case, if not from the biblical revelation that this is, in "foundational" fact, the ontological reality of God and all that flows from that reality as regards creation, redemption, and mission? Does our mission ever go "beyond" that foundation and the epistemological confidence of faith that it generates?

Of course there was diversity among the New Testament *churches*. But I disagree that the mere fact that we have four accounts of the gospel indicates that the gospel itself is "pluriform." They are not "four Gospels," but, in each case "*the gospel* according to" each writer. The gospel itself is good news about historical events which were publicly witnessed and undeniable. There is a singular "having-happened-ness" about the gospel. The gospel must be received and lived in multiple cultural contexts, but the gospel itself is not determined by those receptor cultures but by its own historical, unique, unrepeatable, and irreplaceable facticity.

So, I want to applaud John Franke's insistence on the rich and necessary diversity of missional engagement with human contexts and cultures, but to ask for a more careful account of the boundaries and criteria (which the apostles were keen enough to outline for us) by which we can recognize and rejoice in the genuine work of the Holy Spirit and the truth of the gospel, and, conversely, recognize and reject that which is counterfeit and contrary to both.

PETER J. LEITHART

John Franke presents a Trinitarian account of "contextual mission." Trinitarian theology is operative at several levels in his paper. As Augustine had it, the processions of the Son and Spirit from the Father are the eternal and uncreated ground for the mission of Son and Spirit. Not only economically but ontologically, God is a God of mission. Though less explicit, triune unity-in-plurality and plurality-in-unity lurks behind Franke's discussion of the diversity of the church. Paul is explicit that the diverse gifts of the church are various expressions of the one Spirit, and given Franke's Trinitarian framework, we may draw the inference that the Spirit's mission is to produce this variety of gifts.

Trinitarian and specifically pneumatological concerns thus underwrite one of Franke's central worries and one of his central claims. The worry is that the mission of the church can be twisted into a mission of cultural imperialism; the claim is that the church's mission must respect cultural difference, express the "infinite translatability" of the gospel, make room for "the testimony of plural perspectives and experiences," and aim to form an inclusive community.

There is much to commend and affirm here. Though I nowhere mention the Trinity in my own essay, I agree that Trinitarian processions are the divine grounding for the church's mission. Trinitarian theology is easy to integrate into my sacramental missiology: One cannot commune with *this* God through Word and sacrament without being caught up into the *missio Dei*.[1] Franke's emphasis on love as motivation and goal of mission is important, and a point inexcusably lacking in my own contribution to this volume. Franke is right that the church is not an agent of colonial civilizing, and that the gospel blossoms in a variety

---

1. For an excellent development of this theme, see Eugene Schlesinger, *Missa Est: A Missional Liturgical Ecclesiology*, Emerging Scholars (Minneapolis: Fortress Press, 2017).

of linguistic and cultural colorations. I strongly affirm his emphasis on the scope of the gospel and the church's mission, aimed at global shalom, and agree that the gospel is a liberating message. He is right to stress that the church's internal life is as integral to her mission as sending, such that the church, the "focal point of the mission of God in the world" is "to *become* the gospel" (the last a quotation from Michael Gorman). His scheme of the church as sign, instrument, and foretaste of the kingdom is excellent, and I could not agree more strongly that "unity in the church is clearly of paramount importance."

But there are significant flaws in Franke's essay, both at a more general theoretical level and in detail. Welcome and true as the Trinitarian framing is, it leaves his proposal feeling ethereal. For all his talk of cultural contextualization, there is little detail about how that actually happens. This is especially evident in Franke's broad dismissal of Christendom, which, he claimed, turned the church into "an exercise in the extension of empire through the process of colonization using the Bible as a justification for this activity." Franke could provide plenty of evidence to back that up, and, given the scope of the paper, I do not blame him for not doing so. But one can also cite evidence on the other side of the ledger. Missionaries often took the side of the colonized against the colonizers, exercising all sorts of forms of resistance to forms of hegemonic and abusive forms of empire. Las Casas fought members of his own order on behalf of natives of South America, and missionaries stood by Native Americans against the American expansion that horrifically crushed them. For all the church's real failures, it is unjust to ignore the genuine heroes and simplistic to summarize a millennium of church history so brusquely.

In a related vein, Franke complains that some Western churches develop home missions to stave off the advance of secularism and devote energy to "political activism as an important part of preserving the ethos of a Christian society." It is not clear what Franke opposes. Does he think that churches should embrace or adapt to secularism? Franke's mission theology seems to endorse efforts to infuse the gospel into diverse cultures, and so it would be odd for him to complain against societies *having* a Christian ethos. And if many American Christians think (with some justice) that American society is (partially, imperfectly) an expression of the gospel, should they not attempt to preserve it? They *think* they are defending the gains of Christian mission.

This specific example points to a two-sided ecclesiological problem with Franke's view. The one side is evident in Franke's quotation of Lesslie Newbigin's claim that "every interpretation of the gospel is embodied in some cultural form." Franke takes this as an endorsement of his argument in favor of cultural plurality in the church, but Newbigin is making a different, almost opposite point. Franke complains that Western missionary work "has traditionally been very much an Anglo-European church centered enterprise" that "has been passed on in the cultural shape of the Western church." Newbigin's point is that this sort of thing is simply unavoidable, that the missionary is *inevitably* proclaiming a gospel-in-cultural-form. Franke does not seriously grapple with Newbigin's point.

And this is because, on the other side, Franke fails to reckon with the fact that the church has features of a culture. It is not quite right to say it *is* a culture, given the variety of languages, local customs, and tonalities that exist and have existed within the church. But it has cultural features. Christians speak many languages, but they proclaim one gospel and strive to speak biblically about the world; the Bible can be translated into any language, but for all its internal complexity, it is one book with a unified, coherent, and universal narrative and view of reality;[2] the liturgy is performed in many languages with many variations of detail, but it is everywhere a liturgy of Word and meal for those who have entered the church through baptism; the lifeways of Christians are various in many respects, yet we are called to follow the same *cruciway* of the same crucified Lord. Franke favorably quotes Andrew Walls's statement that no Christian has "any right to impose in the name of Christ upon another group of Christians a set of assumptions about life determined by another time and place." To which I ask: What about the Bible?

I suspect that what Franke is getting at is something like this: Christian missionaries enter a new field with a gospel that is inevitably shaped by their own cultural setting (language, way of life, ethos). They must strive to the best of their ability to convey the gospel *itself*, holding their own cultural habits as loosely as possible, adapting to local custom as much as they can. This is always a difficult stance, since, for many

---

2. I suspect that Franke and I differ in our understanding of the unity and diversity of Scripture.

missionaries, their cultural habits are expressions of the gospel. To the best of their ability, they plant a seed, but the way the seed grows will depend on the soil into which it is planted. The missionary should not impose his own theological categories, but let the new converts work things out for themselves, developing a set of beliefs and practices that is both rooted in the gospel and expressive of their own cultural mores.

There is something to be said for this. Many of the most dynamic movements in Africa today are postmissionary churches that sprouted after the missionaries left. In practice, such a hands-off posture is all but impossible, even irresponsible. A missionary preaches the gospel and translates the gospel of John. People convert, and the newly founded church determines from its own study that the Son is a created being. Does the missionary avoid imposing orthodoxy? Does it leave the plant to blossom as it may without an effort to prune? The new converts ask about some ancient ritual that has historically been associated with worship of idols: Can we keep doing this? What is the missionary to say? May she seek to persuade, even if it risks imposing her own gospel-informed cultural assumptions on them?

It is a caricature of Franke's position, but it gets to a genuine problem: He tends to treat the gospel as an acultural, invisible, intangible something that slips easily into whatever cultural form it encounters. He denies that the gospel is pure and unacculterated; his argument implies the opposite, that the gospel can exist with no cultural form. It is as if God carries out his mission without the missionary.

Apropos of my own essay in this volume, I add that Franke's error at this point is related to the almost complete absence of sacramental and liturgical theology in his paradigm. As soon as we say that the church performs specific rites of entry and festivity, we are saying it has the character of a culture. We might say that the church is a metaculture, translatable into a variety of cultural forms but providing a new operating system that gets installed into an existing culture so that it begins to run differently.

If the church has culture-like features, the gospel is not *infinitely* translatable; it can be translated into any existing language, but it can only say *this* and *that* in that language. It cannot say, "Cursed be Jesus." By the same token, the church cannot be *merely* inclusive; it must also *ex*clude. New Jerusalem has open gates, but there are angelic guardians at the gates (Rev. 21). The gospel cannot take hold without altering, sometimes radically, the culture to which it comes. Sometimes the gospel sparks a culture war, not because of any missionary malpractice but because the gospel is a word of judgment as well as salvation. As often as not, when the gospel arrives, things fall apart.

Individuals fall apart too. Franke quotes a Native American convert who charges that after conversion, "I had a new identity in Christ, and it *was not* Indian!" This is characterized as a process of "becoming white." Even if we strip off the racial component (difficult in practice, of course), a convert does take on a new identity that is not, or not exactly, Indian. Instead of a member of the old tribe, he becomes a member of the new Christian tribe; he receives a new name. We ought to say that the converted Indian comes into his own, and that all his cultural heritage is perfected in Christ. That is true even if we have enormous difficulty sorting out what it means in practice. Still, there must be a moment when "old things have passed away" because "the new has come." Conversion is a death to an old self and an old community, rebirth to a new self and community. Franke would have benefitted from trying to think through the problem of conversion-and-culture from the perspective of baptism.

As a result of these moves, Franke distorts Paul's portrait of the church as the body of Christ. It is, as he claims, a vision of the church as one and many, but in Paul the diversity is not a diversity of theological or ethnic traditions. Paul envisions a church of one spirit and mind, striving for one purpose (Phil. 1:27; 2:2–3), blessed with a diversity of gifts of the Spirit. Ethnic groups do produce treasures, and John envisions kings bringing them into New Jerusalem (Rev. 21:24). But Paul is not speaking of natural gifts and cultural traditions brought into the church but the varieties of gifts that the Spirit produces within the church. The New Testament is clear that the church consists of people from every tribe, tongue, people, and nation. By reading the gifts of the Spirit as diverse cultures, Franke does not highlight Paul's accent on unity, found even in those passages that speak of diversity (cf. Eph. 4:1–16). Given the Trinitarian framing that Franke uses, these ecclesiological errors raise questions about theology proper. If the Christian community is, as Kavin Rowe says, the "cultural explication of God's identity," then the church must be one as well as many, one *as much as* it is many.

And if the church is the cultural explication of God's identity, then the church is not *merely* a sign, instrument, and foretaste but also an *end*. This Franke explicitly denies: The church is "not the goal and end of the gospel." I disagree. The goal of the gospel is to bring sinful people into the perichoretic communion of the triune Persons. One and many, the church in union with God is the end precisely because it is, forever, the human and cultural "explication of God's identity."

SACRAMENTAL MISSION:
ECUMENICAL AND POLITICAL MISSIOLOGY

PETER J. LEITHART

Evangelicals have written much of late about mission, emphasizing the place of mission within the biblical story; the ecclesial dimensions of mission, with the church reconceived *as* a mission, as missional; the missional significance of the church as "countersociety"; the connections between the church's mission and biblical concerns for justice, peace, poverty relief, and community development. Inevitably, some have risen in defense of older conceptions of mission. While they often acknowledge that evangelism and discipleship bear fruit in social transformation, they emphasize the priority of preaching, evangelism, individual conversion, and personal discipleship. For the sake of convenience, I will refer to the advocates of the broader vision of mission as "revisionists" and the defenders of older evangelical models of mission as "traditionalists."[1]

---

1. Outside the contemporary context, these labels are misleading. Traditionalists defend a view of mission that is only about a century old, and revisionists have been carrying on revision for decades. Indeed, neo-evangelicalism, insofar as it departs from fundamentalism, is defined by its broader conception of mission. In his 1947 *The Uneasy Conscience of Modern Fundamentalism*, Carl Henry condemned the narrowing of the gospel in fundamentalism: "Whereas once the redemptive gospel was a world-changing message, now it was narrowed to a world-resisting message.... Fundamentalism in revolting against the Social Gospel seemed also to revolt against the Christian social imperative.... It does not challenge the injustices of the totalitarianisms, the secularisms of modern education, the evils of racial hatred, the wrongs of current labor-management relations, and inadequate bases of international dealings" (quoted in David J. Bosch, *Transforming Mission: Paradigm Shifts in Theology of Mission* [Maryknoll, NY: Orbis, 1992], 404). John Stott confessed that he had changed his mind about mission by the 1970s. Writing in 1975, Stott said, "I now see more clearly that not only the consequences of the commission but the actual commission itself must be understood to include social as well as evangelistic responsibility, unless we are to be guilty of distorting the words of Jesus" (quoted

Though I have deep sympathies with the revisionists, I believe missional theologians have left critical dimensions of mission badly underdeveloped. Attending to these areas of weakness will, I hope, bolster the revisionist project and perhaps go some way to harmonizing revisionist and traditionalist approaches to mission. Simply put, revisionists often ignore the role of sacraments in the church and mission. That is simply put but potentially misleading, since for some readers "sacramental" will conjure images of dark rites in smoky cathedrals that have little to do with mission, while for others the term will evoke the notion of "re-enchantment" that does not capture my intentions either. It is potentially misleading too because I do not wish to emphasize sacraments to the exclusion of teaching, preaching, pastoral correction, and other ministries of the word. Word and sacrament must work together, but that is just my point: in evangelical missiology, they do *not* work together.

The Forgotten Sacraments

The problem with contemporary missiology can be illustrated by comparing the role of baptism and the Supper in the New Testament with recent treatments of mission. Baptism first: Matthew 28:18–20 is Jesus's great "Go" to the remaining apostles. He commissions his disciples to teach his commandments and discipline peoples, and he makes baptism an integral part of that mission. Grammatically, "make disciples" (*mathēteuō*) is the imperative, with "baptizing" and "teaching" as the participles that describe the instruments by which disciples are made. Grammatically again, the object of disciple-making is *ta ethnē*, people *groups*,[2] and groups are also the objects of the baptizing and the teaching. When the Spirit falls at Pentecost, the eleven-turned-twelve immediately carry out Jesus's commission as they baptize three thousand in a day (Acts 2:38–42). As the word spreads in the book of Acts, so does the water: Philip baptizes the Ethiopian eunuch (Acts 8:36–38), and Peter determines that baptism cannot be withheld from Gentiles who have received the Spirit (Acts 10:47–48; 11:16). Tabitha is baptized

---

in Bosch, 405). Mid-twentieth-century debates among evangelicals themselves recapitulated debates within the ecumenical movement at the beginning of the century (Bosch, *Transforming Mission*, 368–510).

2. See the extended discussion of this point in John Piper, *Let the Nations Be Glad!*, 3d ed. (Grand Rapids: Baker, 2010), 182–204.

(Acts 16:15), and so is the Philippian jailer (Acts 16:33), the Corinthians (Acts 18:8), and the Ephesians (19:3–5).

The Gospels begin with the mission of a baptizer, and Matthew ends with the sending of eleven baptizers. After Pentecost, they preach *and baptize.*

And the meal: John the Baptizer comes with a stern message of repentance, calling for a fast. Jesus comes eating and drinking, and meals are basic to his ministry.[3] He welcomes tax gatherers and prostitutes, arousing the indignation of Pharisees, with whom he also eats. He teaches that table manners are the stuff of discipleship (Luke 14). He spends the hours before his arrest having a meal with the Twelve, and when he rises from the dead he restores the community of the apostles by sharing a meal with them by the Sea of Galilee. As the Spirit impels the apostles into mission, they carry on Jesus's table fellowship, confident that Jesus is with them by his Spirit. The baptized in Jerusalem are devoted to prayer, the apostles' teaching, and the breaking of bread (Acts 2:42). Disciples gather to break bread, and Paul implies in 1 Corinthians 11 that the gatherings of believers are gatherings for meals. After the sea baptism of his shipwreck, Paul gives thanks and breaks bread in a Eucharistic meal (Acts 27:35).

John baptizes; Jesus commissions the apostles to baptism; they baptize. John fasts; Jesus eats and drinks with his disciples; they go out eating and drinking. Carrying on the mission of Jesus, the apostles preach and teach. They *also* baptize and break bread.

Water and bread are essential features of the early church's existence as *ekklesia*. In ancient Greek, *ekklesia* is a political term, describing a citizen assembly of the ancient *polis* (city). By calling Christian communities *ekklesiai*, early Christians were claiming that their assemblies were citizen assemblies of a heavenly *polis*, now planted in the midst of the earthly *poleis* (cities) of the Roman world.[4] Like the ancient *polis*, the Christian *ekklesia* had a rite of entry into membership, water baptism. Like the ancient *polis*, the Christian *ekklesia*'s communal life

---

3. For discussions of how Jesus's meals attack the symbols and praxis of first-century Judaism, see N. T. Wright, *Jesus and the Victory of God*, Christian Origins and the Question of God, vol. 2 (Minneapolis: Fortress Press, 1996); also Marcus Borg, *Conflict, Holiness, and Politics in the Teachings of Jesus* (London: Bloomsbury, 1998).

4. For more on this, see my *Against Christianity* (Moscow, ID: Canon Press, 2003), and the literature cited.

was organized around a feast. Baptism and the Supper ritualized the church's existence as a counter-*polis*.

How do traditionalist and revisionist treatments of mission match up to this ancient expression of the church's existence as a counter-*polis*? The kindest answer is, not altogether well.

Kevin DeYoung and Greg Gilbert offer a traditionalist rejoinder to revisionist missiology in their recent book, *What Is the Mission of the Church?* To formulate a precise and focused definition of mission, they devote a chapter to the sending passages of the Gospels and Acts. On Matthew 28, they write, "'Baptizing' implies repentance and forgiveness as well as inclusion in God's family (Acts 2:38, 41)."[5] No doubt; but before it "implies" anything, the commission to baptize requires the *act* of baptizing. About this, DeYoung and Gilbert have very little to say. They summarize the mission of the church as, "We go, we proclaim, we baptize, and we teach—all to the end of making lifelong, die-hard disciples of Jesus Christ who obey everything he commanded."[6] To distinguish between a church and a "bunch of Christians," DeYoung and Gilbert note that members of a church "covenant together to take on certain responsibilities," including the duty "to make sure the Word is preached regularly among them, to make sure the ordinances—baptism and the Lord's Supper—are regularly practiced, and to make sure that discipline is practiced among them."[7] Those are the only references to the "sacraments" in their book.

From the other army in the mission wars, neither baptism nor the Lord's Supper make it into the index of Christopher Wright's magisterial revisionist text, *The Mission of God*. Wright occasionally refers to the sacraments. Discussing the relation of evangelism and social renewal, he comments suggestively that in Rwanda the "blood of tribalism" proved "thicker than the water of baptism," a depressing reminder that "successful evangelism, flourishing revivalist spirituality and a majority Christian population did not result in a society where God's biblical values of equality, justice, love and nonviolence had taken root and

---

5. Kevin DeYoung and Greg Gilbert, *What Is the Mission of the Church? Making Sense of Social Justice, Shalom, and the Great Commission* (Wheaton, IL: Crossway, 2011), 46.

6. DeYoung and Gilbert, *What Is the Mission of the Church?*, 63. The only other reference to baptism in the book is in a quotation of 1 Corinthians 1:17–18.

7. DeYoung and Gilbert, *What Is the Mission of the Church?*, 232.

flourished likewise."[8] Yet Wright does not develop the point, and he never mentions the Lord's Supper.

The neglect of these "ordinances" is pronounced in the work of John Piper. He argues that "mission is not the ultimate goal of the church. Worship is. Missions exists because worship doesn't. Worship . . . is the fuel and goal of missions. It's the goal of missions because in missions we simply aim to bring the nations into the white-hot enjoyment of God's glory. . . . But worship is also the fuel of missions. Passion for God in worship precedes the offer of God in preaching."[9] From Piper's book, though, one would never suspect that the Supper is a primary focus of worship. He never mentions the Supper. Piper provides a splendid analysis of Jesus's commission to *ta ethnē* but includes no discussion of how baptism is involved in this mission.

This is an unbalanced essay, largely because it does not give much attention to the role of preaching and teaching in mission and discipleship. My unbalanced essay is an effort to correct an existing imbalance. It attempts to bring contemporary evangelical missiology more fully into conformity with biblical standards by emphasizing the role of baptism and the Supper in missions,[10] and by explaining how a sacramental missiology

---

8. Christopher J. H. Wright, *The Mission of God: Unlocking the Bible's Grand Narrative* (Downers Grove: InterVarsity Press, 2006), 321. Remarkably, even in Wright's more practically oriented *The Mission of God's People* (Grand Rapids: Zondervan, 2010), he never refers to the Lord's Supper and discusses baptism only briefly (p. 284). See also Dean Flemming, *Recovering the Full Mission of God: A Biblical Perspective on Being, Doing and Telling* (Downers Grove, IL: InterVarsity Press, 2013), whose observations on the connection of mission with baptism and the Lord's Supper are sound but very brief (e.g., 95–96, 108).

9. John Piper, *Let the Nations Be Glad!*, 35–36.

10. Not all writers on mission neglect the sacraments. Michael Goheen's exegesis of Peter's Pentecost sermon is a succinct summary of points I develop below: "The baptism to which Peter calls his fellow Jews defines this new community: they are gathered around the Messiah to share in the work of the Spirit. Baptism is eschatological: it is entry into the sphere of the age to come, made possible by the death and resurrection of Christ and experienced in the Spirit's work. Baptism is also missional: to enter this community is to become part of a people gathered and restored by the Messiah and equipped with the Spirit to continue the missional calling of Israel, to be a contrast society that continues the end-time gathering of the Messiah in the interim period before the final judgment. Newbigin captures both the eschatological and the missional significance of baptism and the church when he writes 'to be baptized is to be incorporated into the dying of Jesus so as to become a participant in his risen life, and so to share his ongoing mission to the world. It is to be baptized into his mission'" (Michael W. Goheen, *A Light to the Nations: The Missional Church and the Biblical Story* [Grand Rapids: Baker, 2011], 135). Similarly, the Supper is "charged with eschatological and missional significance. It is a meal that is to nourish restored Israel in its kingdom life. It is the means by which God's people are empowered and enabled to embody the life of Christ for the sake of the world as they participate in what was accomplished in the crucifixion." Eucharist is integral to mission because "Christ himself is present in the meal and gives his own life to his people" (142).

will correct and enhance our theology of mission. My understanding of "sacrament" will become clearer in the next two sections. For now, it is necessary only to state that I share the Protestant view that there are only two "sacraments"—baptism and the Lord's Supper—and I hold recognizably Protestant views on traditional questions like the efficacy of baptism, the real presence of Christ in the Supper, and so on. I assume that baptism and the Supper are signs of the eschatological society of the church, *effectual* signs that *make* as well as *mark* that new society.[11]

Here is a skeletal outline, then, of what is to come in this essay:

- Every theology of mission rests on or implies a soteriology, but soteriology is intertwined with anthropological convictions. To know what it means for humans to be saved, we must have some inkling of what humans are. We must start with a doctrine of creation.
- If we are to grasp the nature of mission, we have to understand the nature of the church. To understand the nature of the church, we again need a biblical anthropology. Again, we must start with creation.
- If we are to formulate a balanced missional *theology*, we must highlight the role of baptism and the Supper. If we are to carry out the mission of the church *in practice*, baptism and the Lord's Supper must play a prominent role.
- That previous point holds because sacramental theology and practice hold together what missiology often separates—creation and new creation, evangelism and socio-political engagement, individual and community, personal discipleship and active involvement

---

As Goheen makes clear, baptism and the Lord's Supper are not "mere symbols" but formative rites for the missional church. Some other evangelical writers have emphasized the importance of sacraments as well. See Michael Horton, *The Gospel Commission: Recovering God's Strategy for Making Disciples* (Grand Rapids: Baker, 2011), 171–82; Darrell Guder, ed., *Missional Church: A Vision for the Sending of the Church in North America* (Grand Rapids: Eerdmans, 1998), 159–66.

11. I put "sacrament" in quotation marks because I have reservations about the way baptism and the Lord's Supper are theologically isolated from the rest of the church's life, treated as strange moments and actions that demand explanation, and are treated as two things in the same sacramental genus. It is beyond the scope of this paper to pick apart these questions. One observation will have to suffice: Baptism and the Lord's Supper are no odder than membership rituals, dinner clubs, and other rites that mark the groups to which we belong. For further discussion of "sacraments in general," see my *The Baptized Body* (Moscow, ID: Canon Press, 2007); in summary form, "Signs of the Eschatological *Ekklesia*," in Hans Boersma and Matthew Levering, eds., *The Oxford Handbook to Sacramental Theology* (Oxford: Oxford University Press, 2015), 631–44.

in mission, piety and vocation, soteriology and ecclesiology, grace and human action, church and world. In a word, sacraments hold together nature and the supernatural by refusing to separate them in the first place.

The burden of this essay is to put flesh on these bones, and it does so in three stages. First, I outline a biblical theology of mission-and-sacraments; second, I discuss more systematically what baptism and the Supper contribute to the theology of mission; finally, I return to the political ecclesiology described briefly above to fill out the practical implications for mission.

Biblical Roots of Sacramental Missiology

Sacramental theology has more often been the site of a dualistic separation of nature and supernature than a locus of their integration.[12] Sacraments have been viewed as supernatural, quasi-magical, intrusions into a world that normally runs by other rules. To recognize the importance of sacraments for missiology, we must first rethink sacraments from the ground up, starting with creation.

When God created male and female, his first gift was the gift of food: "Behold, I have given you every plant yielding seed that is on the surface of all the earth, and every tree which has fruit yielding seed; it shall be food for you" (Genesis 1:29 NASB). Adam and Eve began their life in the garden-sanctuary, the most prominent feature of which was trees with their fruit.[13] They were invited to eat from the tree of life, enjoying a feast in the presence of God. The world was a table spread for them, and so was the garden. Their most "spiritual" experience was also their most normal experience—eating. Before sin, Adam and Eve had no need of baptismal entry, since the gate of the garden was wide open. But they did participate in a created sacrament, a meal in the presence of God, the original Lord's Supper.

---

12. See especially Alexander Schmemann, *For the Life of the World: Sacraments and Orthodoxy* (Crestwood, NY: St. Vladimir's Seminary Press, 1973), Appendix 1: "Worship in a Secular Age."

13. On the garden as sanctuary, see James B. Jordan, *Through New Eyes: Developing a Biblical View of the World* (Eugene, OR: Wipf & Stock, 1999); L. Michael Morales, *The Tabernacle Pre-Figured: Cosmic Mountain Ideology in Genesis and Exodus* (Leuven: Peeters, 2012); Gregory Beale, *The Temple and the Church's Mission: A Biblical Theology of the Dwelling of God*, New Studies in Biblical Theology (Downers Grove, IL: InterVarsity Press, 2004).

They were not to remain in the garden forever, but, like the river that arose in Eden and flowed through the garden, they were to spread out, multiplying and filling the four corners of earth as they subdued and ruled it. It was a mandate, also a definition, because human beings made in the image of the world's Creator cannot but be world-creators. God created Adam and Eve as son and daughter, servants of God's garden-sanctuary, a prince and a princess who were to mature to be king and queen of the creation, the source of a race of kings and queens, all advancing creation from glory to glory.

Human life was to be a frictionless cycle of work and worship, a rhythm of labor and liturgy: Each Sabbath, Adam and Eve would have eaten with God in the garden and then ventured into the world to glorify it. On the next Sabbath, they would have returned to the garden to enjoy the products of their labor in the presence of God. Worship would fuel them for a new week of work in the world, work that would again culminate in worship. Over time, humanity would form the world into a civilization, pursuing technological and artistic enhancements of creation. The garden too would have changed. Adam and Eve's descendants would have learned to bake bread and to ferment wine, and so too the fresh fruit of the garden would have given way to the solid food of bread and the mature drink of wine. Human beings would have brought the gold of Havilah to adorn the garden. From the beginning, the trajectory of history was from garden to temple to cosmic temple city. That was the original human mission.

Nothing in the Bible indicates that this original mandate or definition was cancelled after sin and death entered the world. After they ate from the tree of knowledge, Adam and Eve were cast from the garden (Gen. 3:25). That was a gracious exclusion, a necessary discipline. But it had the effect of separating zones of life that had originally been united. Human beings no longer had access to the presence of God, and their efforts to rule the earth were rendered more difficult, but they and their descendants continued to fill, subdue, and rule the earth. Separated from communion with God, human beings filled the world with idols and innocent blood, men (*especially* men!) taking dominion without submitting to the Lord of the sanctuary, the High King. They continued to rule, but they no longer ruled as table companions of their Creator.

The problem that needed fixing after the fall was this division between garden and world, the split between communion with God and dominion. That is the setting in which God set out on his mission to restore humanity, and his goal was to restore humanity to fellowship that would produce *godly* dominion. One day, he promised, he would crush the serpent's head and allow sons of Adam and daughters of Eve to return to the garden. Delivered from Satan, they would again create as table companions of the Creator. God's mission was to reestablish table communion with humanity and to qualify human beings to share meals with him, to harmonize labor and liturgy once again. God's mission was to baptize humanity back into his presence so they could resume the Lord's Supper.

Though this restoration is completed in the cross and resurrection of Jesus, it began earlier. After the baptism of the flood (1 Peter 3:21), Noah built an altar to offer an "ascension" offering (Heb. *'olah*), the first altar and the first ascension in the Bible (Gen. 8:20). In the Bible, altars are tables (Ezek. 41:22; 44:16), where Yahweh eats ("consume" is "eat," Heb. *'akal*) his bread (cf. Lev. 21:6, 8, 17, 21–22; 22:25, all using *lechem*, "bread"). Though Noah did not eat any of the animals he offered, he established the first site for table communion outside of Eden. His "ascension" offering ritually enacted his elevation. Set in a newly made world, Noah was a new and advanced Adam, elevated to rule over the animals and given authority to use the sword against murderous men. Later, Noah planted the first humanly-constructed garden, a vineyard, and enjoyed the wine that gladdens the heart.[14] In all this, we see an early stage in God's mission to restore human beings to their original position as royal table companions of the High King enabled to rule the world with justice.

The call of Abraham has been rightly understood as crucial in the biblical theology of mission,[15] but here as elsewhere the sacramental dimension of the Abrahamic covenant has not been sufficiently stressed. Abram was called from Ur in the aftermath of the scattering of the nations at Babel (Gen. 11:1–8). God promised that he would be the agent to extend God's blessing to all the families of the earth, families

---

14. Commentators commonly condemn Noah for drunkenness, but the imagery of the incident is Sabbatical: After the flood, Noah is a new Adam, enthroned in a refreshed earth, enjoying a rest signified by wine. See Jordan, *Through New Eyes*.

15. Wright, *Mission of God*, 221, observes that the Abrahamic covenant is both "a mission statement by God" as well as a call to faith and obedience.

divided from one another by language and worship. Through Abram and his seed, God would unify the scattered Babelic nations so that every tribe and nation shares in the blessing of the one God. In contemporary terms, the mission that grows from the Abrahamic covenant is both ecumenical and political: It is political *because* it is ecumenical, political because it will unify the nations in the blessing of God.

Abram built altars—more than any other character in the Bible—to mark critical moments and places in his life and to symbolize God's covenant. After the Lord first promised to give him the land, Abram built an altar (Gen. 12:7) to represent Abram's claim to the land and signify that the land is to be the space on which God would erect his table among men, the new Eden where he would replant his garden. Abram moved to the mountain east of Bethel, pitched his tent between Bethel and Ai, and built an altar to call upon the name of Yahweh (12:8). The configuration anticipated the later erection of the tabernacle and temple: Beth-El, the house of God, on the west, a tent pitched on a mountain, complete with an altar for calling the Name.[16] After his sojourn in Egypt (12:10–20), Abram returned to the altar between Bethel and Ai (13:4) and divided the land with Lot (13:5–18) before conquering the land to rescue him (14:1–24). Again the reference to the altar foreshadowed Israel's later exodus and conquest of the land. Abraham's final altar was on Mount Moriah (22:9), where Isaac, the child who came from his dead body, symbolically died and rose, replaced by a substitute ram. Altar-building highlighted the centrality of worship in the Abrahamic covenant. Yahweh's mission was to bless the nations as they came to

---

16. Michael Morales (*Who Shall Ascend the Mountain of the Lord? A Biblical Theology of the Book of Leviticus*, New Studies in Biblical Theology [Downers Grove, IL: InterVarsity Press, 2015]) notes that the east-west orientation runs throughout Genesis. Ararat, where the ark rests after the flood, is a new Eden, and so the movement of the men of Babel "to the east" replicates Cain's eastward movement from Eden, which is movement from the presence of God in his sanctuary. Morales finds hints of this orientation in the Abrahamic narratives, not normally read as cultic texts. Like the men who founded Babel, Lot "journeyed east" (Gen. 13:11), a choice that "took him outside the bounds not merely of the Promised Land but of the Promised Presence of God." Abram meanwhile sets up an altar on a mountain between Bethel (west) and Ai (east). Morales comments, "These untypically precise details are not gratuitous, but serve rather to continue the east-west motif, and the cultic theology of the divine presence" (71). In Genesis, we see a sequence of west-east connections: "Eden—Cain's city at the primordial beginning of the world; Noah's ark–Babylon at the beginning of the new world after the deluge; Abram's altar—Sodom at the beginnings of Israel after the scattering of the nations" (72). All this is linked to the east-west orientation of the garden of Eden (Gen. 3) and the tabernacle.

worship at the altar-table of Abraham. They would be blessed as they were admitted to the new-Edenic tables that were scattered throughout the land.

Circumcision needs to be seen in this context. In the flood, Yahweh set out to destroy flesh, understood not as humanity as such but humanity in sinful rebellion against the Creator.[17] All flesh had become corrupted (Gen. 6:12), so Yahweh determined to destroy all flesh in the flood (Gen. 6:13, 17). Even after the flood, however, human beings continued to display the violence and corruption of flesh, most markedly at Babel. Between Genesis 9 and Genesis 17, there is no mention of flesh. It comes back into focus when Yahweh commanded Abraham to circumcise every male member of his household. By cutting away flesh, Abraham renounced the way of life that filled the earth with violence, the way of life that led to the hubris and rebellion at Babel. God enlisted Abram's household in his mission to overcome flesh. Cutting off the flesh of the foreskin, Yahweh began to form one people that was not dominated by flesh. In marking the children of Abraham with *this* sign, Yahweh began to form a people that will walk according to Spirit. Those who were circumcised form a new-Adamic nation gathered around the altar-table of Yahweh.

The Mosaic order built on Abraham's flesh-cutting and altar-building. Circumcision continued to be the qualifying mark for membership in Israel and entry into the festive community of Israel. In place of Abraham's many altars, Moses erected a single bronze altar at the foot of Sinai, part of a sanctuary set that replicates the original sanctuary of Eden. For the first time since Adam and Eve ate the fruit, human beings passed by the cherubim at the garden gate to minister in the presence of God. Priests were consecrated to enter the house of Yahweh and to eat the bread of his presence. Common Israelites became unclean, but Yahweh instituted purification rites, often involving water baptism, which allowed them to come into his courts. Israel was invited to draw near to eat, drink, and rejoice before the Lord (Deut. 14:26). Circumcision and cleansing rites offered admission; once admitted, Israel feasted before the Lord.

Under Torah, the original rhythm of work and worship, labor and

---

17. This paragraph summarizes the longer argument in my *Delivered from the Elements of the World: Atonement, Justification, Mission* (Downers Grove, IL: InterVarsity Press, 2016).

liturgy was restored, albeit in a limited way. Yahweh commanded Israel to work six days and keep the Sabbath as a holy day, and he commanded them to bring the products of their battles and their handiwork to adorn the Lord's house. Israel was not permitted to enter the inner sanctuary, but they were allowed to draw near to the God who had drawn near to them. At Sinai, Israel began to offer peace offerings (the first reference is in Exodus 20:24), a shared meal between the worshiper and the Lord, the first time that human beings ate with the Creator since the expulsion from Eden. Yahweh's mission to restore humanity was carried forward as he brought one people near to become his priests and table companions. The rhythm of life and liturgy, the traffic between tabernacle and world, was not frictionless, but it was possible because the God of Israel made a way for Israel to return to his presence.

The conquest fulfilled the Mosaic order by establishing the tabernacle system in the land promised to Abraham and Israel. As in the flood, Yahweh judged the wicked; unlike the flood, he employed human beings—men who have cut off the flesh—to carry out his judgment. The goal of the conquest was to establish the Lord's sanctuary, with its altar and throne, in the land. Israel targeted the altars and shrines that had polluted the promised land, and once they controlled the land, they erected the Lord's altar and his tabernacle at Shiloh. Yahweh's mission was to purge the land of the defilements of flesh and to establish his royal table in the midst of it, and he brought Israel into that mission.

Circumcision and Torah marked Israel from the nations, but the goal was always the Abrahamic one of uniting the nations in the blessing of Abraham. Under Torah, that blessing took the concrete form of a shared meal. Once Israel settled in the land (and began its cycle of feasts), strangers, aliens, and other Gentiles were invited to share in the festivities (Deut. 16:11, 14). That international aim of Israel's ministry became more obvious in the writings of Israel's prophets. Zion would be a source for the life-giving instruction of God that flows to the nations (Isa. 2:2–4; Mic. 4:2–3). Nations would stream to Zion to learn his ways (Isa. 2), to feast on meat and wine at his altar-table (Isa. 25), to bring their treasures to adorn the sanctuary (Isa. 61:1–8), and to celebrate the Feast of Booths (Zech. 14:14–19).

The trajectory set by Torah and the prophets comes to a climax in the ministries of John and Jesus. John comes baptizing; Jesus comes eating and drinking. John offers baptism for repentance and cleansing, to prepare a people to receive the coming king. As king, Jesus sets up a table, welcoming Jews and Gentiles, the unclean and sinners, to share a meal with God. As various parables make clear, those meals are the very substance of the kingdom Jesus announces. They are the beginning of the wedding feast that the king throws for his son (Matt. 22:1–14); they are the feast of fatted calf set out by the joyful father for prodigals (Luke 15:11–32); they are the king's banquet.

Jesus describes the mission of Israel and of the disciples by reference to these meals. Servants of the king go into the highways and byways to invite guests to the kingdom's feast. Those who refuse the invitation will be condemned to sit outside, watching as the nations come from the east and west, north and south, to recline with Abraham, Isaac, and Jacob in the Father's kingdom (Matt. 8:11). In Jesus, humanity is restored to God, and so is restored to itself and to its vocation. In Jesus, human beings are remade as priests and kings, new Adams and Eves, servants of the Lord's house and rulers of his world. In the water and at the table, John and Jesus restore the harmony of liturgy and life.

The church *is* that renewed humanity, and its sacraments proclaim this gathering as the fulfillment of Yahweh's mission. Baptism announces that sons of Adam and daughters of Eve can again draw near, and the Lord's Supper is the site of communion, where God gives himself as food to his people, where his people feast in his presence without veils or barriers. Baptism and the Supper *effect* the very restoration they proclaim. As people from every tribe and tongue and nation are baptized, they are united to one another in their union in the body of Jesus. Baptism is not a *picture* of the nations being reunited; baptism *reunites* the nations. The Supper is not a *picture* of nations feasting together in the presence of God; it *is* the feast of the nations in the presence of God. The eucharistic feast is political and ecumenical, or rather, political because ecumenical, since the baptized nations that share the eucharistic feast constitute the *polis* of God. The feast is an "engine" for mission. Those who feast on the body and blood of Jesus are empowered by the Spirit as witnesses. But the meal is not only a means to assist mission. It is the aim and goal of mission, the *now* of the wedding feast still to come, the wedding feast to which the mission of the church and the history of the world are directed, the wedding feast to which the church invites the nations.

Sacramental Missiology

Much more could be said, but perhaps this sketch suffices to show that purification and meal, baptism and the Supper, have been centerpieces of the mission of God and the life of the people of God since the beginning. Perhaps I have made plausible the notion that God's mission is to restore the original harmony of liturgy and life, and that this intention comes to a focus in the Christian sacraments.

How might a sacramental missiology affect traditionalist accounts of mission? What shift is involved when we emphasize not merely preaching, evangelism, and teaching but also baptizing and eating? How does a sacramental missiology enhance or correct revisionist accounts of mission? How does it keep together what missiology separates?

Above all, the sacraments keep the church and her mission Christ-centered. That may seem a preposterous claim in the light of the history of "sacramental" churches, which do not seem to have a strong track record of maintaining a Christocentric life. During the Latin Middle Ages, the Roman Church, centered on the Mass, was distracted by relics, the cult of the saints, Mariology, and other deviations from the gospel. Whatever the intentions of the theologians and bishops, popular piety was not focused on Christ. Christ was the fearsome *Pantocrator* who glared down from the cathedral ceiling. Saints were gentler and more approachable. Mainline churches of the past century, furthermore, were often liturgical and sacramental, but that did not prevent them from collapsing into secular social agencies.

It would take more than this essay to make a case, so I will simply assert it: The perversions of the medieval Catholic church did not arise from an overemphasis on sacraments but from bad sacramental theology. Instead of a table, the Catholic church gathered at a tomb; instead of a meal before the unveiled face of God, the church erected barriers, ordinarily reserving the host and wine to the priests. The meal was not the feast of God's baptized table companions but a spectacle for the baptized to watch from a distance.[18] Likewise, the perversions of

---

18. The Reformers *emphasized* the sacraments just as much as the Catholics. Arguably, Luther attributed *more* efficacy to sacraments than Catholics did. But for Luther baptism marked the baptized as a member of the Christian priesthood, and for him *all* of the people of God were invited to share in the feast of the kingdom.

mainline Christianity do not arise from an emphasis on sacraments *per se* but from perverse sacramental theology, sacraments detached from the Word and discipleship.

Both medieval and modern churches understood and practiced sacraments within a distorted natural-supernatural framework. The Catholic Mass hardly resembled a normal meal; the Host was not daily bread, and lay Christians did not drink the wine. Theologically and liturgically, the Mass reopened the chasm between liturgy and life that the Supper is designed to bridge. It was dissonant at the very point where there was supposed to be harmony. In reaction to overly supernaturalist ecclesiologies, liberal churches introduced dissonance from the other side, dismantling the boundary between church and world, Eucharist and common table, and reducing mission to do-gooding.

When baptism and the Supper are rightly understood and practiced, they keep Christ at the center of Christian living. Baptism is *not* a mark of the believer's decision but rather of *God's* gracious decision, an indicator that the baptized is claimed in and by Christ. Baptism thus inaugurates the Christian life as life in union with Christ, life under the Lord whose name is imposed in baptism. Discipleship grows out of baptism, which continually recalls the baptized to their baptism, as a *continuing* reminder that they are in and under Christ.[19] Uprooted from baptism, discipleship can turn legalistic: Christian living means Doing This and Not Doing That. Or it can turn antinomian: Grace liberates from law; follow the motions of your renewed heart. Baptism is a gift of God in Christ, and, *precisely for that reason*, demands that the baptized work out his or her salvation in fear and trembling. Baptism brings the mission of the church to bear on individuals: By baptism, outsiders are brought into the garden that is the church, into the community that gathers around the communion table. Discipleship grows out of baptism because baptism inaugurates a way through life in union with the Way who is Life.

Shared regularly, at least weekly (Calvin), the Supper too keeps the Christian life focused on Jesus. However we work out the physics and metaphysics of real presence,[20] Christians can unite in affirming Paul's

---

19. Many theologians have said this. For a succinct summary of the points I am making, see Horton, *The Gospel Commission*, 171–77.

20. Calvin's formulation is, to my mind, superior to alternatives. The problem Calvin addresses is how the heavenly Jesus can give himself to us as food, and for Calvin the answer is the Spirit: God the Father feeds us the flesh and blood of his risen and exalted Son by the

statement that the bread we break is *koinonia* in the body of Christ, and the cup of blessing is *koinonia* in his blood (1 Cor. 10:16–17). However it works, eating bread and drinking wine is communion in Christ. When mission focuses on the Eucharist, it takes the form of an invitation to the feast, the feast that *is* participation in Christ's body and blood. As we share bread and wine, we proclaim Christ's death. We participate in the body and blood of the Crucified, and so share in his cross. As Thomas Aquinas said, while natural bread turns into the eater, the bread of the Eucharist turns the eater into itself. As we participate in Christ in bread and wine, we are conformed to his image.[21] Each week, we do what Adam and Eve were created to do—eat in the presence of God. And at the end of each meal we are sent out in the fullness of God's food to labor in his world, to carry out the human mission in the world.

Sacraments overcome the dichotomy of individual and community. The Spirit baptizes *individuals*, but baptizes them into the one *body* that has many members and many gifts (1 Cor. 12:12–13). Baptism unites the baptized to Christ; baptism also unites the baptized to the church that is the body of Christ, being, as the Westminster Confession puts it, the "solemn admission into the visible church." Baptism makes clear that the Christian life is a life in community, that an isolated Christian is an anomaly if not an absolute impossibility. Evangelism culminates in baptism because evangelism aims to form *communities* of disciples and to incorporate more and more into those communions. Baptism is the context for discipleship because the church is the context for growth in Christlikeness. Similarly, the Supper expresses the corporate character of the Christian life: "We are one body because we all partake of the one bread."

Together, baptism and the Supper announce the fulfillment of the Abrahamic promise of the reunion of the human race under the blessing of Abraham's seed. The church is not yet a reunified humanity; it is not the eschatological form of the city of God. But the church *is* God's city, the reunion of nations in the seed of Abraham and under the Abrahamic blessing. Unity is a note of the church: as the body of Christ, she is

---

power of the Spirit. We truly feed on Christ; we truly receive his resurrection life; we are able to do so because the Spirit lifts us to heaven or brings Christ down.

21. It is critical, of course, to resist isolating the Supper from the rest of the life of the church. The bread is given with the Word and in the midst of a community life characterized by pastoral correction and mutual edification.

(potentially) home to every tribe, tongue, people, and nation. The Spirit incorporates Jew and Gentile, slave and free, male and female into the one temple of God. Unity is also the church's *mission*: she is sent to the world to disciple all people groups by baptizing them, teaching them the commandments of Jesus, and welcoming them to the table of the Lord. In this, the church is God's instrument to fulfill his mission to reunite the human race. Baptism and the Supper do not merely announce this fulfillment but, as works of Christ's Spirit, *make it happen*. Tutsi and Hutu are united by dying together in the waters of baptism; all nations come to have a place at the table of the Lord.

That mission of reunifying humanity can go awry. Baptized Christians can betray their baptisms, taking up machetes to slaughter one another in the streets. Christians who share the Supper together can steal from one another during the week. Sacraments have their full effect only in churches devoted to the Word and mutual discipline. Baptized Christians must be taught that they are brothers to all other baptized Christians; all who share the table have to be reminded that they are table companions of one another. Even here, the sacraments have their effect, serving as standards by which the church is judged. Like Israel's priests, the baptized are under stricter standards than others. Murder is always sin; when a baptized person murders a baptized person, he assaults the name as well as the image of God. Sacraments make visible John's warning that we cannot love God if we do not love our brothers.

The church's mission of unity can go awry in other directions as well. In the liberal theologies that dominated the nineteenth and early twentieth centuries, the gospel was a message about the Fatherhood of the God and the brotherhood of man. That contained enough truth to mislead, but the slogan was turned to secular uses in the great Kantian institutions of the UN and the EU.[22] Sacramental missiology erects roadblocks to this secularization. Baptism and the Supper signify and form a reunited humanity, but they do so in a way that keeps Jesus, his

---

22. This has rarely tempted evangelicals, but the ecumenical missions movement engaged in a mighty struggle over the role of the gospel in the church's mission. As Bosch puts it, "Mission became an umbrella term for health and welfare services, youth projects, activities of political interest groups, projects for economic and social development, the constructive application of violence, etc." Some so stressed the *Dei* of *missio Dei* that they excluded the church itself from mission. Mission is whatever is happening in the world outside the church (Bosch, *Transforming Mission*, 383).

cross, and his resurrected at the center. Yes, all nations are to be reunited, and yes, that is a chief goal of the church's mission. But they are united by *baptism*, which means by sharing in the death of Jesus. Humanity can be reunified only by first dying in baptism. Yes, all nations have a place at the table, but the only table copious enough to receive all tribes and nations is the Lord's Table, communion with the Christ who died and has now been raised. Humanity can become one body *if* humanity partakes of one loaf. Baptism and the Supper maintain the Christic foundation of the church's mission of unity. Sacraments provide a canon to test and judge our missiology. They are continuous correctives, disabusing the church of the temptation to seek the kingdom without the King.

Much recent evangelical discussion of mission has focused on the relationship between mission and social justice. Revisionists claim that poverty relief, defense of oppressed minorities, rescue of sex slaves or the unborn are inherent in the mission of the church. Traditionalists claim that these are secondary to the church's main business of evangelism and disciple-making. On the one side, some worry that the church might turn into another NGO; on the other side, some complain about a dualism that reduces the gospel to a message of personal salvation and truncates the mission of the church to "mere evangelism." The worries on both sides are justifiable. The church can and has become a service agency stripped of anything like the good news of judgment and salvation that is the message of the apostles. Bad theology has led some churches to withdraw from wider dimensions of the church's work.

How might this issue look from the perspective of a sacramental missiology? On the one hand, the sacraments indicate that the pursuit of justice and mercy is integral to the church's life and mission. Those who die with Christ in baptism rise to present the members of their bodies as instruments of justice (Rom. 6:1–14; *dikaiosūnē*), participating even now in the resurrection *of the body*. Instead of bowing to idols, indulging in sexual license, or doing the violent and oppressive works of the flesh (cf. Rom. 1:18–32), the baptized are to worship God, maintain purity, and advance justice. Baptized into the Light to share his light, we are to expose the works of darkness. Baptism seals us with the Spirit, who impels us into his warfare against the works of the flesh. Crucially, we are empowered to advance God's justice *only* by dying to Adam and rising to newness of life. Mission begins with death to the world and

God's gracious rescue from death. Baptism indicates that only those who are dead and risen in Jesus are free to devote their bodies to God's justice. Justice is inherent to the life of the baptized, but it is a justice that depends entirely on the gracious death-dealing and life-giving God.[23]

Jesus's social agenda took the form of festivity. He came eating and drinking, and invited sinners to share his Father's joy. He came healing and cleansing, turning outcasts into table companions. Once they were at the table, Jesus instructed his disciples by teaching them the table manners of the kingdom. Jesus warned his disciples not to compete for prominent places at the table but to humble themselves, trusting the Lord to exalt them. He forbade them to use their tables to bargain for benefits and urged them instead to welcome the marginal and rejected who cannot repay them, again trusting their Father to reward them at the resurrection (Luke 14). Rich and poor both have a place at this table. The rich do not have special privileges; they are bread-eaters and wine-drinkers like everyone else. They are not even benefactors of the poor but are joined in a shared meal at the table of the heavenly Benefactor. Every time the church celebrates the Supper, she embodies the just society. As John Milbank remarks somewhere, the meal is the model of Christian charity: not a handout, not a renunciation, but a joyful *sharing* of the good gifts of God.

If the mission of the church leads to baptism, then it makes justice-warriors who deploy their bodies as instruments of God's righteous kingdom. If the mission of the church is to invite the world to share in the Lord's table, then it invites them to share in the yet imperfect city of God, the city already just in Christ and becoming just by the Spirit. A vision of the just society that grows out of the Eucharist will be Christ-centered. A sacramental missiology will insist that the just society can exist only through Jesus, who is the embodiment of God's

---

23. This is not "magic." To "you died in baptism," Paul adds, "therefore, consider yourself dead to sin." We are called to conform our "self-image" and our lives to what baptism does to us. Baptism works because by it the Spirit makes us citizens of Christ's city. Baptism incorporates the baptized into the church, the body of the incarnate Son animated by the Spirit. Within that body, the baptized is supposed to be instructed, trained, and deployed to do God's justice. A faithful church will remind the baptized constantly of this baptism: Remember, you died; therefore, consider yourself dead; therefore, devote your body to justice. If the church into which the baptized is baptized does not pursue God's justice, baptized members are not likely to be trained and deployed to advance God's justice. Baptism performs the "magic" of uniting us to Christ in his body, but its long-term efficacy depends, in general, on the health of the body.

justice, and that the cross and resurrection of Jesus are the source of all genuine social justice.

The Practice of Sacramental Missiology

We can bring these reflections to a practical focus by considering the political import of a sacramental missiology. As noted above, the most common term for the church in the New Testament, *ekklesia*, is a political term. To call the Christian assemblies *ekklesiai* was, at least, to claim that the church was a new city of God founded within the existing cities of humanity. More strongly, it implied that the power center of the world had shifted from the political institutions and gatherings of the Roman world to the modest table fellowships of baptized Christians. Ask a pagan, "Where is the *ekklesia* of Ephesus?" and he would point you toward the agora. Ask a Christian the same question and he would direct you to a house church tucked somewhere in the honeycomb of the city's residences. That is where the future of Ephesus is being decided. That is the real decision-making body of the city.

That is no fantasy. The future of Ephesus really did lie with the church rather than the city's political institutions. It is always so, if the church does not forget herself. As the city of God, formed by baptism and gathered around Word and table, she is God's urban renewal movement, God's city sent to transform the world's cities to make them over into images of the perfect city yet to come.

What does this mean? How does a sacramentally formed church with a sacramentally formed mission challenge and renew the polities of the world? How are sacramentally formed churches instruments of God's justice? How does a sacramentally formed church determine the future of the surrounding culture?

At the most basic level, the church has a political impact by virtue of her sheer existence. In a world where rulers were often considered at least demi-divine, the early church vigorously, often courageously, refused to worship any but the living God or to acknowledge any but Jesus as universal king. Since the whole of her communal life was organized as a response to the Lordship of Jesus, her communal existence was necessarily distinct from the surrounding social and political order. The church strives to be a "contrast society" because she essentially and unavoidably *is* one.

The church's political setting today is not as different from that of the early church as we may suppose. Totalitarian regimes dispensed with the theological apparatus; they have no room for transcendence. But their rulers play essentially the same role as the divine kings of ancient Mesopotamia and Egypt. They are objects of cultic devotion, their visages are ubiquitous, their word is law. A faithful church is a standing challenge to totalitarianism simply by being a faithful church. Liberal democracies have even more stripped-down theological foundations, but they can be functionally totalitarian. Liberal polities sacralize liberalism and so become intolerant of anything deemed illiberal. Liberal polities engage in self-sacralization. A church that preaches an exclusive gospel or denounces certain actions as sin can fall afoul of liberalism's totalitarian demands for tolerance. By speaking and living in accord with God's Word, the church poses a political challenge to totalitarian and liberal regimes.

The sacramental life of the church is fundamental to this political role. The sacraments are visible, active rituals. They may be performed in private, but they cannot be performed invisibly. If the Word of God makes the church audible, the sacraments are the core of the church's visibility. Since they are irreducibly essential to the church—that is, there is no church where baptism and the Supper are not practiced—the church is irreducibly visible. And as long as she is irreducibly visible, she stands as an empirical society in the midst of the world.

The church may fail. She *has* failed. And that failure betrays the truth declared and effected by baptism and the Supper. It is no accident that modern churches have both neglected sacraments and accommodated to liberal (and sometimes to totalitarian) regimes. Neglecting sacraments, the church denies her own visibility as a society in the world and thus easily adjusts her mission and life to what liberal (or totalitarian) regimes permit. A non-sacramental church is an invisible church and can slip quietly into her assigned role. A church that remembers what her rites are for, a sacramental church, being visible, will not leave public space unmolested. She *must* intrude, and intrudes with the claim that she is the *ekklesia*, the ruling body of the city, the community that will determine the city's future.

The previous paragraphs offer a formal description of the church's political role, but the public form of the church has specific contours and content. The sacraments are rites performed with particular created things under particular circumstances typically accompanied by particular words. And in their *specific* content, the sacraments manifest visibly the counterworldly character of the church. In a world addicted to autonomy, baptism declares that we belong to another. Even our bodies do not belong to us (1 Cor. 6:12–20). A church that baptizes, and shapes its loves and life to baptism, will resist the allures of false freedoms. In a world that believes in inherent human goodness, baptism declares that we must die and be buried to live just lives. In a world of scapegoating, baptism calls the baptized to a life of continuous confession and repentance. In a world of tribalism and nationalism, baptism joins men and women from all nations into one body. In a world of greedy consumerism, the Supper embodies a community of goods shared in joy and thanksgiving. In a world that pursues self-fulfillment, God's table companions are conformed to the self-giving of Jesus. In a world founded on materialism, the bread of the Eucharist confirms that we do not live by bread alone. In a world that separates religion and life, the Supper demonstrates that the mundane world of eating and drinking is caught up in the life of communion with God.

A church shaped and inspired by the sacraments will pursue a mission of global scope. Nothing is in principle outside the scope of the church's concern and mission.[24] In baptism, all are clothed in Christ, and a baptized people cannot be unconcerned with the abuse and exploitation of women, with the indifference of the rich or the degradation of the poor, with racial hatreds and genocide. A church that baptizes will call the nations to peace, but a church that baptizes will also know that peace is a gift of the Spirit that comes from the open tomb of Jesus. In the Supper, all share in the body and blood, and a Eucharistic people cannot be unconcerned with world hunger, with the short-sighted abuse

---

24. As the Mercersburg theologian John Williamson Nevin put it, the catholicity of the church has an "extensive" and "intensive" dimension. Extensively catholic, no territory of the world can claim independence from Christ and his mission. Intensively catholic, no area of human existence is impervious to the transforming influence of the gospel. Nevin wrote, "It is full as needful for the complete and final triumph of the gospel among men, that it should subdue the arts, music, painting, sculpture, poetry, etc., to its sceptre, and fill them with its spirit as that it should conquer in similar style the tribes of Africa or the islands of the South Sea. Every region of science, as it belongs to man's nature, belongs also to the empire of Christ; and this can never be complete, as long as any such region may remain unoccupied by its power" ("Catholicism," *Mercersburg Review* [1851]: 12–13).

of the land that produces grain and grapes, with loneliness and depression. A Eucharistic church will call the nations to communion, but a Eucharistic church will also know that communion among the peoples of the earth is possible only when they share the blessing of Abraham.

As emphasized throughout this essay, both sacraments highlight the unity of the body of Christ. By one Spirit we are baptized into one body; baptism is the ritual mark of the unity of the people of God who have one Lord, one faith, and worship one God and Father of all. We persist in being one body because we regularly partake of one loaf. Through the water, bread, and wine, the body is made one and persists in being one. As noted above, this has been central to the mission of God at least since the nations were divided at Babel. Baptism and the Supper declare that this long mission is coming to a culmination in the body of Christ; and they not only declare but also bring into reality that fulfilled, unified people of God. Unity is a goal of the mission of the church. We proclaim the gospel to gather people from every tribe and nation into the one new humanity that is the church. But pursuit of unity is also a dimension of the political activity of mission. By maintaining unity or reestablishing broken fellowship, the church comes to visibility as the contrast society, as a unified humanity in a world of fragmentation and coerced unity.

Here as everywhere, the sacraments provide mirrors for self-examination, canons by which we may judge ourselves. Baptism says we are the new Adamic humanity, the post-Babelic race; in reality, we are not. And so our continuing divisions belie our baptism. The Lord's feast is spread for every nation and tribe and tongue, but Christians do not even allow other *Christians* to share the meal with them! Our Eucharistic practice thus belies the Eucharist we celebrate. As the apostle Paul said, when believers come together, it is *not* for the Lord's Supper; their divisions vitiate the Supper. The church can nevertheless fulfill its political mission only by repenting and conforming our corporate life to the truth of baptism and the Supper.

We can bring this down to the individual level as well. A baptized person called to political office is obligated to pursue that vocation *as a baptized person.* He is identified with Jesus, and that identification and name transcend any party affiliation or national identity. A church that teaches its members to live out of their baptism will warn such a politician to remember that he wears the name of Jesus. He will regard other believers as brothers and table fellows regardless of their political party, race, or nationality. That does not necessarily imply agreement on every policy issue, but it does mean he will recognize a unity that transcends differences of policy. He will have enemies, as every principled leader does. Baptized in the name of Jesus, he will strive to love his brothers and sisters, his neighbors, and even his enemies. He will do good to all people, speak truth without fear, and pursue the interests of Jesus's kingdom above all things, even the advantages of his own country. Living out his baptism in his public office, he will pursue justice, love mercy, and walk humbly with God. He will use his political power not to buttress the strong, wealthy, and well-connected, not to repay his donors, but to ensure justice for all. He will be an advocate especially for those who have no resources of their own. As he shares bread and wine at the Lord's table, he will be conformed to the death of Jesus, made a faithful witness, taught to take the lowest seat. Though a political leader, he remains under the discipline and oversight of the church. His pastor will be ready to teach, correct, and rebuke him if he adopts policies that conflict with the Scriptures or if he uses political tactics that are at odds with his baptism and his participation in the Lord's Supper. Discipling a Christian who is a political leader means discipling him *as a political leader*.

We can follow through similar thought experiments with other vocations. A baptized businessman is obligated to live a life of justice and love toward his employees, his customers, and his competitors. Since he wears the name of Truth, he will not allow his marketing department to mislead the public about his products and services. Baptized into the Word, his word will be yes, yes and no, no. He will recognize that his baptism places him in the body of Christ, under the oversight of the shepherds who serve the Good Shepherd. If he strays from the way of his baptism, his pastor will call him back, teaching and rebuking and, if necessary, barring him from the Lord's Table if he persists in sin. Baptized as a table companion of God and God's companions, he will learn, perhaps slowly and painfully, the table manners of the kingdom. He will learn how to live with his brothers by learning what it means to eat and drink with them.

In all these ways, the mission of the church opens up into a cultural mission. The church need not be sponsor of cultural activities, though in some circumstances she may well be. Churches have opened hospitals, founded colleges, sponsored artists and craftsmen, incubated social and economic initiatives of various kinds. The church not only promotes the development of civil society but in some settings *is* civil society, giving talented leaders their first taste of leadership, nurturing an alternative to oppressive political regimes, teaching the truth about human dignity and freedom in a world of lies.[25] Much of the church's cultural mission, though, is indirect, as the church forms believers by Word, sacrament, and discipline to fulfill their callings in the world Christianly. By the power of the Spirit, the church that baptizes and feasts becomes a place where the broken harmony of liturgy and life is restored. It becomes a place where disciples learn to live together by learning to eat together.

Discipleship *must* open into this cultural mission. The baptized do not cease to be baptized when they enter their workplace, the board room, the factory floor, the Senate chambers, the classroom. They do not cease to be table companions at the Lamb's feast when they leave church. They must study to know how they are to conduct themselves as the baptized in those settings, and their pastors must study to guide them in that effort. In this sense, on virtually any definition, social justice is inherent in the mission of the church, since any discipleship worthy of its name must train the baptized to follow Jesus wherever they are and wherever he leads.

Conclusion

Here is the mission of the church, then: Set up God's table. Invite folks to dinner. Make sure they wash up. Teach them how to eat together.

---

25. See the fascinating account of "China's Christian Future," *First Things* (August 2016).

RESPONSE TO PETER J. LEITHART

JONATHAN LEEMAN

If this is the first piece of Peter Leithart you've ever read, I expect you are both stimulated and slightly confused. Consider a passage like this:

> Baptism and the Supper *effect* the very restoration they proclaim. . . . Baptism is not a *picture* of the nations being reunited; baptism *reunites* the nations. The Supper is not a *picture* of nations feasting together in the presence of God; it *is* the feast of the nations in the presence of God. [italics in original]

Is he saying that baptism *effects* salvation *ex opere operato*—meaning, the sacraments are actually *doing* the saving and uniting—like a Roman Catholic might say? Or is Leithart just talking about the visible church? That baptism and the Supper are what transform an otherwise unaffiliated group of Christians—presto!—into a local church?

Leithart doesn't say. And I don't think he means to.

Here's another claim you might have found both stimulating and ambiguous:

> [The house church in Ephesus] is where the future of Ephesus is being decided. That is the real decision-making body of the city. . . . As the city of God, formed by baptism and gathered around Word and table, she is God's urban renewal movement, God's city sent to transform the world's cities to make them over into images of the perfect city yet to come.

Once again, what does Leithart mean? Does he mean that healthy churches will impact the city around them? Or does he mean something more grandiose, like, the church (in some non-institutionally specified

177

sense of that word) gradually overtakes a society's institutions, including its government, until its magistrates submit to the direction and discipline of ministers and re-orient the society to serve the church? Again, Leithart doesn't clarify, though I understand him to mean something closer to the latter.

With both of these matters, my agreement with Leithart's chapter depends on which way I tilt my head.

Metaphysics

What's crucial to realize is that quietly humming in the background of Leithart's chapter is his own theory of metaphysics, sort of like the computer code behind the words and images on your computer screen. I think it will serve us to take a moment to look at his metaphysical "code."

A couple of times Leithart disparagingly refers to a nature/supernature dualism. Often we think of things as having a fixed nature, and that whatever that nature is makes a thing what it is. Leithart, building on Paul's discussion of the "elements of the cosmos" in Galatians and Colossians, conceives of the universe in more relational categories. Things are what they are in relation to other things, and most determinately in relation to God. Nature, we might say, is entirely history and sociology. You *are* your history, your relationships and roles with respect to other people, the various things you believe, the practices you maintain, the institutions you build and occupy, the liturgies you follow. Nature is not separate from cultural, ritual, and institutional patterns, but includes them. As Leithart puts it elsewhere,

> For Paul, *physis* and *nomos*, physics and law, nature and culture are not finally separable. Human beings can be "naturally" Jews, not simply by birth but by conformity to the nomic [law] regulations and patterns of life of Torah. One can be "naturally" circumcised. What we would separate into "ritual" and "natural" Paul joins together. And this expresses an anthropology: Human beings are defined by the social and cultural setting in which they live, move, and have their being. Jews are not simply generic human beings who happen to practice and live Jewishly.

Conformity to Jewish norms, performance of Jewish rites, and adherence to Jewish institutions give them Jewish *nature*.[1]

You might think of Leithart as the standard sociologist who says that all reality is "socially constructed," except he's a theologian saying that all reality (down to the quarks) is socially constructed by God and maintained (or not) by humans.[2]

The Sacraments

This metaphysical backdrop then impacts the two points of ambiguity cited above. I'll spend most of my discussion on the sacraments.

If nature depends in part on the customs, institutions, and rituals of a people, then a "change in the cultural, ritual and institutional patterns that define those natures is a change of human nature," says Leithart.[3]

What that means is that baptism and the Lord's Supper are not just natural *signs* of something supernatural; they effect what they signify.[4] They deliver you into a new reality. Yes, it's a new *social* reality, but remember, all reality is social. Now, a Protestant might demand, "There is also a deeper spiritual reality that baptism *doesn't* effect, right?" Yet here Leithart digs in his heels and refuses to answer the way a Protestant might want.[5] Don't be "distracted seeking a deeper, more secretive and hidden grace," he says elsewhere.[6]

My guess is that, if pushed into a corner, Leithart would concede a distinction between the visible and the invisible church. I assume he would say the thief on the cross belongs to Christ's eschatological humanity. But where Christopher Wright's chapter leans too far toward the universal church, leaving the local church basically unmentioned, Leithart's chapter seems solely interested in the visible church, as if

---

1. Peter J. Leithart, *Delivered from the Elements of the World: Atonement, Justification, Mission* (Downers Grove, IL: InterVarsity Press, 2016), 29.

2. Ibid., 40.

3. Ibid., 41.

4. See ibid., 221–23.

5. E.g. Peter J. Leithart, "Signs of the Eschatological Ekklesia: The Sacraments, the Church, and Eschatology," in Hans Boersma and Matthew Levering, eds., *The Oxford Handbook of Sacramental Theology* (New York: Oxford University Press, 2015), 640–41.

6. Ibid., 641.

that's all that matters: "Membership in that body is the eschatological gift."[7] And that gift is real, the firstfruits of eternity.

So is baptism effectual with regard to the visible or to the invisible church for Leithart? I think his answer is "yes"—not quite like a Roman Catholic would say "yes," but giving grounds to the growing critique he is trending in a Roman direction, whether on justification or otherwise.[8]

What do we make of all this? I like his metaphysical emphasis on the relational and historical nature of reality. Yet in the final analysis I think it's reductionistic. Created things have a basic substance created by God and are therefore dependent on him (see Acts 17:28). God might relate positively with both a fish and a person, but the fish and the person are still different things.

For my part, I'd recommend affirming the distinctions between Creator and creation, and then construing matters of identity and relationship through the Bible's covenantal storyline. With the advent of the new covenant, we are served by a doctrine of two ages, which affirms the present simultaneity of the age of creation and the age of new creation.[9] Creation is *real*. New creation is also *real*. Unbelievers abide in one age. Believers abide in both. The thing is, we don't have Holy Spirit eyes. We cannot see what God sees. And the overlap of the ages requires us to doctrinally affirm both a visible and an invisible church, just as God and the new covenant work of the Spirit remain invisible to us.

The new covenant, recall, is granted through a word of forgiveness and the regeneration of the heart (Jer. 31:31–34; Ezek. 36:24–27). This is the first constitutive moment for ecclesiology: people coming to faith through the preached word. But a second constitutive moment is required, which is what the ordinances offer.[10] They make the church visible or public. Oliver O'Donovan writes,

---

7. Ibid., 641.

8. E.g., Thomas Schreiner, *Faith Alone: The Doctrine of Justification* (Grand Rapids: Zondervan, 2015). 176–77.

9. See my *Political Church: The Local Assembly as Embassy of Christ's Rule* (Downers Grove, IL: InterVarsity Press, 2016), 274–78.

10. See John Webster, "The 'Self-Organizing' Power of the Gospel: Episcopacy and Community Formation," in Richard N. Longnecker, ed., *Community Formation: In the Early Church and in the Church Today* (Peabody, MA: Hendrickson, 2002), 183; also, Bobby Jamieson, *Going Public: Why Baptism Is Required for Church Membership* (Nashville, TN: B&H Academic, 2001), 141–44.

The sacraments provide the primary way in which the church is "knit together," that is, given institutional form and order. Without them the church could be a "visible" society, without doubt, but only a rather intangible one, melting indeterminately like a delicate mist as we stretched out our arms to embrace it. In these forms we know where the church is and can attach ourselves to it. They are at once "signs" of the mystery of redemption wrought in Christ, and "effective signs" which give it a palpable presence in a participating church.[11]

O'Donovan goes on to affirm that the Supper should not be viewed as "'a sacramental grace which affects the believer in a different way from other kinds of grace'; rather its work has to do with the formation of the body."[12]

So, yes, baptism "effectually" binds the one to the many, and the Supper "effectually" binds the many into one.[13] But let's not muddle our metaphysics. The word "effectually" should be used sociologically and politically. It is not *ex opere operato*. The church on earth requires two constitutive moments, and we must not elide or blur those two moments together.

Government

Another crucial piece of the Leithart's theology of the church and mission—an almost hidden plank throughout his chapter—is his objective view of the sacraments. "Baptism is *not* a mark of the believer's decision but rather of *God's* gracious decision," he observes. Hence, he can be a paedobaptist and paedocommunionist. (A credobaptist like me would say the ordinances are both objective and subjective. The *subject* needs to confess.)

This plank impinges on our previous discussion about the effectual nature of the ordinances, but it also impacts his approach to the state. Building on his metaphysic, Leithart can envision the transforming of cities, the Christianizing of society, and the theoretical success of

---

11. Oliver O'Donovan, *Desire of the Nations: Rediscovering the Roots of Political Theology* (New York: Cambridge University Press, 1999), 172.

12. Ibid., 180.

13. Bobby Jamieson's excellent *Going Public* uses this language throughout.

something like the Constantinian settlement for at least two reasons. One, he possesses a postmillennial eschatology, which is implicit throughout his chapter. Two, the practice of paedobaptism does not *require* but does *allow for* the "Christianizing" of a nation in a way that believer's baptism does not. If you baptize almost every new citizen of a nation into membership in the state-established church, you can have a "Christian" nation, where church membership and citizenship broadly overlap. Hence, to be English is to be Anglican, and to be Spanish is to be Roman Catholic. It wasn't only Constantine's conversion that made Christendom what it was. As much as anything, it was paedobaptism.

So Leithart concludes his chapter affirming that a baptized senator doesn't leave his or her baptism when entering the Senate. I agree. Not only so, but the senator should be instructed and discipled by the church's pastors. Yes, yes.

But let's keep several things in mind. The church-as-an-organized-collective holds the keys of the kingdom for declaring the *what* and the *who* of the gospel, not the senator. No senator should be fiddling with the doctrine of the Trinity like Constantine did, at least in his or her capacity as a senator. Second, church officers don't have competence or authority in matters of public policy any more than they have competence or authority in law or medicine. So a pastor should teach on taxes from Romans 13, but I'd caution him against taking a pastoral stand on, say, a flat tax versus a progressive tax rate. The Bible doesn't say, and we need to leave such matters in the realm of Christian liberty, lest we undermine the gospel or play law-declaring Lord.

In short, Leithart's "practice of sacramental missiology" could use clearer institutional lines in addition to the need for clearer metaphysical lines. The church-as-an-organized-collective has one kind of authority, the state another. And so in every other domain of life. Pastors should teach the Bible. Church members then go into the workplace to work for good, whether in politics, law, medicine, or otherwise. But they remain finite and fallen, occupants of the age of creation. They don't have a God's-eye view on the best tax rates, legal tactics, or medical procedures. Non-Christians, in fact, will often out-competence them. To think otherwise reveals an over-inflated belief in our ability to bring heaven to earth now.

CHRISTOPHER J. H. WRIGHT

I enjoyed Peter Leithart's essay just as much for its deserved "rebuke" of a significant gap in my own writing as for its robust advocacy for a stronger, more biblical focus on the sacraments in our evangelical ecclesiology and missiology.

I begin, however, with a quibble over his use of the terms "traditional-ists" and "revisionists"—a labelling that he acknowledges in footnote 1 is "misleading." It is indeed. I would not regard "as revisionist" the wide spec-trum of evangelical theologians and practitioners of mission who believe that, viewed in the light of the whole Bible, the mission of God's people integrates many forms of practical service and engagement in the world around the centrality of the gospel and its proclamation. If anything, we might claim to be "restorationist"—recovering that comprehensive under-standing of mission from the narrowing that occurred in the first half of the twentieth century in understandable but unfortunate reaction to the liberalism of the social gospel. That was certainly how John Stott saw his decision to "express himself differently" in 1975 from how he had in 1966—he believed he was *returning* to a more faithfully biblical understanding (of the Great Commission, in context), not "revising" the traditional one. And since the Lausanne Congress of 1974 (and well before that, of course, in the strong challenge of Carl Henry in 1947, as Leithart points out), this has been a major emphasis in the classic documents of the Lausanne Movement, and the World Evangelical Alliance, and many of the most renowned and experienced theologians of mission in the evangelical family.[1]

Then, I must immediately hold up my hand and agree that I did not pay enough attention to the sacraments in either of my two main books on mission. I can at least point out that I have emphasized their

---

1. See the extensive survey of documents and authors I cite in John Stott and Christopher J. H. Wright, *Christian Mission in the Modern World* (Downers Grove, IL: InterVarsity Press, 2015), 41–54.

importance in another book, *Salvation Belongs to Our God,*[2] though admittedly without observing their importance in relation to the mission of the church. However, Leithart is right. It is an omission of a vital dimension of biblical faith and Christian worship, and I am grateful to him for pointing it out and for explaining how and why it matters in our thinking and practice of mission. We live and learn, and I shall endeavor to correct this in future teaching and writing on mission.

I immediately warmed to the initial reason Leithart advances his argument, namely that the sacraments bind together creation and redemption, reminding us of our created humanity (in all dimensions of our physical, spiritual, and social integrity) and pointing out the union and rhythm of life, work, food, worship, and communion with God that we find in the opening (and closing) chapters of the Bible. He is right to say that some theologies of mission have a very inadequate doctrine of creation, and therefore also of the new creation. As a result of that, they have tended to inject a dichotomy between the material and the spiritual. The sacraments, to the contrary, hold them together "by refusing to separate them in the first place."

Reading on, I find myself sometimes agreeing and sometimes asking for greater explication. Leithart's description of "the problem that needed fixing after the fall" is a helpful corrective to the one-sided view that I critique in my own essay (represented by DeYoung and Gilbert), that the primary (if not the only) issue at stake is how sinful humans can come into the presence of the holy God. The whole narrative of Scripture is then read searching for answers to that problem. Now, I do not for a moment deny that that *is* a fundamental problem—our alienation from fellowship with God because of our sin and rebellion. But focusing on that alone can tend to produce a one-directional mission concern: since Genesis 3 all human beings are destined for hell; how then can they ever be saved and go to heaven to dwell with God? The answer, prefigured in Old Testament sacrifices, is the atoning sacrifice of Christ for our sin, through which we can know we will be among the righteous on the day of judgment described in Revelation 20. Again, let me insist, I do not deny that glorious truth. But from the earliest chapters of Genesis we see that there is a wider problem than sinners getting back into the presence of God. The first expression of

---

2. *Salvation Belongs to Our God: Celebrating the Bible's Central Narrative* (Downers Grove, IL: InterVarsity Press, 2008), 130–135.

human longing after the escalating story of sin in Genesis 3 and 4 and the tolling bell of death in Genesis 5 is Lamech's naming of his son "Noah," in the hope that "he will comfort us in the labor and painful toil of our hands caused by the ground the LORD has cursed" (Gen. 5:28). Something needs to be fixed with the earth as well as humanity (and it will be, says Rev. 22:3). In the flood narrative, "the earth" is mentioned multiple times, both in judgment and in deliverance; animals are saved along with Noah's family; and God's covenant is emphatically made with "all life on earth." Again, God's purposes clearly include creation as well as the human beings.

So, Leithart rightly sees the mission of God as not merely *saving* humanity from sin but also *restoring* humanity to its rightful and *godly* (= image of God) dominion within God's creation. I would like, however, a little more textual support before expressing it in quite the way he does, as "God's mission was to reestablish table communion with humanity and to qualify human beings to share meals with him. . . . God's mission was to baptize humanity back into his presence so they could resume the Lord's Supper." Perhaps this language is justified in the overall context of biblical theology, but it is hard to read straight out of Genesis itself.

Leithart's emphasis on the place of food, eating, feasting, and drinking in the Bible is welcome. Along with others, I have neglected it but have been encouraged to enjoy it (both the concept and the practice!) by books such as Tim Chester's *A Meal with Jesus*[3] and the fascinating missional reading of the feasts of Deuteronomy by Mark Glanville.[4] It is also explored in challenging detail by Michael Rhodes[5] (and modelled in his own community among lower-income residents in Memphis). There is certainly something strongly sacramental here, which is focused in the Lord's Supper but extends beyond it to the missional power of shared food and communal meals that dissolve the boundaries of wealth, and race.

While it is right that altars in the Old Testament were symbolic tables and therefore spoke of the table fellowship between God and his people, several thoughts occurred to me in relation to Leithart's emphasis on this. First, we should note that the Israelites were warned to understand the

---

3. Tim Chester, *A Meal with Jesus: Discovering Grace, Community and Mission around the Table* (Nottingham, UK: Inter-Varsity Press, 2011).

4. Mark Glanville, "A Missional Reading of Deuteronomy," in Michael W. Goheen, ed., *Reading the Bible Missionally* (Grand Rapids: Eerdmans, 2016).

5. Michael Rhodes, *Practicing the King Jesus Economy* (Grand Rapids: Baker, forthcoming).

limitations of the idea of the sacrifices as "food for God." God did not reject their sacrifices, but not because he was hungry and needed them (Ps. 50). The idea of sharing food with God was there in metaphor but given some careful theological qualification. Second, while Abraham's altar-building worship in response to God's call and promise are notable elements of Genesis, I'd like more textual evidence that the blessing of the nations (so intrinsic to the Abrahamic covenant) would be, in Leithart's terms, "as they came to worship at the altar-tables of Abraham." And again, that they "would be blessed as they were admitted to the new-Edenic tables that were scattered throughout the land." Third, however, and possibly even supportive of the point I'm questioning, there are other texts that Leithart might have cited, where the nations are envisaged as coming to, or praying in, the temple—which implies some kind of access to the altar-table (whether literally or symbolically). For example, Isaiah 2:3; 56:6–7; 55:1–2; 60:7, and Solomon's remarkable prayer in 1 Kings 8:41–43.

Fourth, it is not quite true that the fellowship offerings prescribed in Exodus 20:24 were the "first time that human beings ate with the Creator since the expulsion from Eden." The meal that Abraham had Sarah prepare for the three "men"—one of whom turned out to be the LORD (in Genesis 18)—could surely qualify (though, to be fair, it is God eating in the presence of humans rather than the other way around, but that in itself is astonishing). And that was an occasion filled with intense missional significance (see verses 18–19).

Fifth, I'm surprised that Leithart does not mention that mysterious note at the climax of the making of the covenant at Mount Sinai, when Moses and Aaron, Nadab and Abihu, and the seventy elders of Israel went up and "saw the God of Israel . . .; they saw God *and they ate and drank*" (Ex. 24:10–11, my emphasis). This must surely mean more than that, even though they saw God, they stayed alive enough to eat their picnic. It is a profoundly sacramental conclusion to the ceremony of blood that had sealed the covenant in words to be quoted by Jesus himself at the Lord's Supper (Ex. 24:8). Tragically, of course, the next time we hear of the Israelites eating and drinking, it is in the presence of other gods in the great apostasy of the golden calf (Ex. 32:6)—which makes it all the more a sign of God's forgiving grace that the second half of the book is so taken up with the building of the tabernacle, precisely so that God could continue to dwell in the midst of his people and they could come to his table with their offerings (Ex. 25:8; 29:45–46).

Sixth, while the significance of the altar as a place of table fellowship is undoubtedly true, Leithart omits what is surely also another point of primary significance: the altar was the place of atonement. This is not the place to survey the range and differentials of the sacrifices in Leviticus 1–7, but the *need* for atonement because of the reality of sin and uncleanness, and the *making* of atonement by the priests for those who bring their sacrifices, are very clear. Those who come into table fellowship with God must come via the provision God made for atonement. When it comes to his discussion of the Lord's Supper, Leithart stresses that our feasting in that sacramental meal is on the body and blood of the Lord, and therefore focuses us on the cross, just as baptism takes us through death, death with Christ and rising to new life. But, as in the references to the Old Testament sacrifices, I sense a gap here in not including that primary element of what we do in the Supper—in "remembering the Lord's death" and its atoning power, as in the words of the Anglican Book of Common Prayer, 1662: "a full, perfect, and sufficient sacrifice, oblation, and satisfaction, for the sins of the whole world."

While I agree that the failures of both the medieval Roman Catholic Church and the mainline and often liberal Protestant churches have stemmed from *bad* sacramental theology (separating the sacraments from the realities of life as lived by ordinary Christian people in the created order), I would like more clarity on Leithart's claim that baptism and the Lord's Supper actually *effect* the restoration they proclaim. Perhaps it's my own Protestant heritage, but are they not *signs* (in the fully biblical sense) of the reality to which they point? And is Leithart's claim of *effecting* not rather contradicted later when he points out that, in fact, in our fallen humanity, even as baptized participants in the Lord's Supper, we fail to *be* what we *are*, we fail to live in the ways those sacraments point to? That does not invalidate them at all. On the contrary, it elevates their importance in the constant walk of discipleship and mission.

In conclusion, I love the way Leithart uses his biblical understanding of sacramental theology to *hold together* what is so frustratingly often separated in this whole mission debate. His work provides another biblical motivation and focus for integrating all that we do in mission around the centrality of the gospel of God's grace, which both sacraments proclaim and impart to those who participate in them in repentance, faith, and obedience.

JOHN R. FRANKE

Peter Leithart's essay on sacramental mission is both an important contribution to a frequently underdeveloped aspect of the mission of the church, particularly in evangelical circles, as well as a truncated one that "does not give much attention to the role of preaching and teaching in mission and discipleship." Leithart states that the reason for this "unbalanced essay" is an effort to correct an "existing imbalance" among evangelical communities to bring their missiology "more fully into conformity with biblical standards."

On the need to correct the existing imbalance, I appreciate Leithart's approach and share his concerns. The marginalization of the sacraments in the life and thought of evangelical (and other) churches is at odds with both Scripture and the tradition of the church. It is often suggestive of a disdain for the past history of Christian communities and individualist notions of salvation and ecclesiology that move in a sectarian direction and work against the concerns for unity to which the sacraments point and for which our Lord prayed. As Leithart makes clear in his essay, the significance of unity in the church for mission cannot be overstated.

As our nation, and much of the world, faces an increasingly fragmented and hostile environment, the significance of the unity for the mission of the church, as Leithart makes clear, can hardly be overstated. Yet Christians are so often at the forefront of fostering division and discord in society and the church. Leithart reminds us of the ongoing calamity that while the table of the Lord "is spread out for every nation and tribe and tongue," many Christian communities "do not even allow other *Christians* to share the meal with them!" Surely it is one of the great ironies and tragedies in Christian history that disputes about the meaning and practice of the sacraments have been the very source of so much of the disunity and hostility amongst would-be followers of

Christ, contradicting the unity that they are intended to convey. In the midst of the current cultural moment and in the face of the history of the church, it seems like a particularly important time to remember the witness of the New Testament concerning the unity of the church. Perhaps the most significant text on this theme, one that neither Leithart or I have mentioned in our respective essays, is found in John 17. After praying that his disciples would be sanctified in truth and that he had sent them into the world as he had been sent, he turns his attention not only to their unity but also for the unity of all who would believe through their word—the church.

In John 17:20–23 we read:

> I ask not only on behalf of these, but also on behalf of those who will believe in me through their word, that they may all be one. As you, Father, are in me and I am in you, may they also be in us, so that the world may believe that you have sent me. The glory that you have given me I have given them, so that they may be one, as we are one, I in them and you in me, that they may become completely one, so that the world may know that you have sent me and have loved them even as you have loved me. (NRSV)

It is worth noting here the close connection being made between truth, the sending of the church, and the unity of the church. The sending of Jesus into the world is to proclaim the truth, to be the light of the world, in order that the world might believe. The church is entrusted by Jesus with the continuance of that mission as those sent by Jesus into the world to proclaim the reality that Jesus had been sent by the Father to reconcile the world to God. The unity for which Jesus prays is to be a prime indicator of this truth. Hence it is to be a visible unity and not simply an invisible one. It can be seen by the world and is a visible testimony to the reconciling love of God in Jesus Christ. This indicates that the unity of the church is vitally connected with its life and witness and as such is a central aspect of its mission in the world.

This concern for unity is prominent in other parts of the New Testament as well. For instance, in the letter to the Ephesians, the church is called upon to adopt attitudes and practices that will promote peace in the church and is urged to maintain the unity of the Spirit. "Be completely humble and gentle; be patient, bearing with one another in love. Make every effort to keep the unity of the Spirit through the bond of peace. There is one body and one Spirit, just as you were called to one hope when you were called; one Lord, one faith, one baptism; one God and Father of all, who is over all and through all and in all" (Eph. 4:2–6). Unity is not simply an invisible reality but also a calling that is to be manifested in visible ways through the cultivation of the disciplines of humility, gentleness, patience, and forbearance with others.

The letter to the Philippians connects these qualities to the life of Jesus, who did not consider equality with God something to be grasped, but instead humbled himself, taking the form of a servant. and urges that the church follow this example (Phil. 2:1–11). The letter to the Galatians speaks of the qualities of love, joy, peace, patience, kindness, goodness, faithfulness, gentleness, and self-control as the fruit of the Spirit (Gal. 5:22–26). This way of the Spirit is essential for the unity of the church.

These texts point to the importance of the visible unity of the church as a testimony to our neighbors of the truth of the gospel. The mission of the church is vitally connected with an appropriate and visible manifestation of its unity in the midst of its diversity, and the failure to maintain this unity will significantly compromise its witness to the world. In the midst of the deep divisions currently shaping our culture, the followers of Jesus would do well to remember his prayer that we might all be one. This doesn't mean we will all come to agreement on the social and political issues of the day. It does mean that the unity we share in Christ transcends our differences and calls on us to love each other in spite of them. This is a way of life that our world needs to see. As Leithart points out, it is exactly in the oneness of the community that the church is established as a contrast society; and it is in the sacramental life of the church that this unity is liturgically visible.

On these basic concerns I heartily agree. However, I also believe that the preaching, teaching, evangelistic, and disciple-making aspects of the church's mission need to fully support the sacramental vision of complete unity in the midst of diversity. This unity is not found in ideological or theological sameness and uniformity. It is precisely at this point that a biblical theology of plurality such as I have briefly described in my essay and more fully elaborated elsewhere is a necessary component to the sacramental mission developed by Leithart.[1]

Since Leithart has not developed the fullness of the church's mission with respect to preaching and teaching, I am not sure what he would make of this claim. But I do think it is precisely at this point that many evangelicals as well as other Christians will find Leithart's (and my) assertions of the importance of unity problematic. They simply don't think it comports with their particular understandings of theology. The goal of theology is to develop one right system of doctrine and teaching that is faithful to the Scriptures. And where Roman Catholic, Orthodox, Reformed, Lutheran, Arminian/Wesleyan, Baptist, evangelical, mainline, conservative, liberal, etc. don't agree, then of course they can't be united together since they don't share the same views. This becomes all the more problematic from the perspective of these modes of thought when the views that are held are mutually exclusive regarding matters such as God, Jesus, the nature of the Bible, the proper forms of biblical interpretation, salvation, the mission of the church, and the like. They ask: How can we possibly be one if we don't agree on such fundamental issues related to the Christian faith? How indeed? From my perspective, the unity of the church is not to be found in shared theological and ecclesial position but in the work of the Holy Spirit and living presence of Christ.

In 1 Corinthians 12 we read that the Holy Spirit is at work forming one body, one church out of many parts in which a diversity of gifts are given for the edification of the whole church: different gifts but the same Spirit; different kinds of service but the same Lord; different kinds of working but the same God at work; to each the manifestation of the Spirit for the good of all. The diversity of the church is nothing less than the work of the Spirit in enabling the church to bear witness to contextual plurality with each part providing particular gifts and understandings of the revelation of God in Jesus Christ and for the edification of the whole body in service to one common Lord.

The focal point of the Spirit's work is the living presence of Christ, wherein the unity of the church is ultimately found. My late teacher Tom Oden put it like this:

---

1. See John R. Franke, *Manifold Witness: The Plurality of Truth* (Nashville: Abingdon, 2009).

The circle of the Christian tradition has an unusually wide circumference without ceasing to have a single, unifying center. It is Christ's living presence that unites a diverse tradition, yet that single presence is experienced in richly different ways. Christ's presence is experienced sacramentally by the liturgical traditions, spiritually by the charismatic traditions, as morally inspiring by the liberal traditions, as ground of social experiment by the pietistic traditions, as doctrinal teacher by the scholastic traditions, as sanctifying power of persons and society by the Greek Orthodox tradition, as grace perfecting nature by the Roman Catholic tradition, and as word of Scripture by the evangelical tradition. All of these traditions and the periods of their hegemony have experienced the living and risen Christ in spectacularly varied ways. But nothing else than the living Christ forms the center of this wide circumference.[2]

The affirmation of the unity of the church in the midst of its massive diversity seems to me to cry out for a corresponding theology of plurality in order to provide an account of the church's mission that does justice to both the unity and diversity of the church. I agree entirely with Leithart on the sacramental unity of the church but would add that this necessitates the development and communication of a pluralist Christian theology. This is a matter of utmost importance for the mission of the church and its witness to the gospel. The plurality of the church is not simply a historical reality but also the very intention of God. The visible unity of the church in the midst of this plurality is not simply wishful thinking but is God's very desire and intention. Faithfulness to the divine vision of unity and oneness in the midst of diversity and difference is a demonstration of the truth of the gospel and an invitation to a new way of life. When we practice this way of life, our salvation, and that of the world, draws near.

---

2. Thomas C. Oden, *After Modernity . . . What? Agenda for Theology* (Grand Rapids: Zondervan, 1990), 176–77.

RECALIBRATING A CHURCH FOR MISSION

JASON S. SEXTON

The Church: Being and Acting

The essays and responses in this volume reflect a conversation that has reached into the particularities of the church's mission and how to effectively be church in the contemporary world. The conversation brings with it a fundamental underlying question: Indeed, what *is* the church? Moreover, what is the church *doing*? What *ought* it to be doing? And how do these questions relate to one another? Evangelicals in particular, known as people of emphasis, have an additional question: Are they (and their churches) carrying out their mission to the full extent they could be? And are churches actually carrying out the mission they *claim* to be? Under a helpful fourfold rubric, Helen Cameron provides a method of nuancing the various voices at play in any given theology, and she identifies these as theology (or in our case, *mission*) that is "operant," or what they actually do; "espoused," or what they *say* they do; "normative," having to do with sources of authority; and "formal," which is the professional kind done by, well, professionals.[1] Such a way of nuancing the church's mission might also be helpful for readers of this book as they consider how they and their churches might approach their ongoing mission today.

This leads to another pressing question: Are churches today carrying out the mission they would like to be, and in the ways they wish to? And are these things the very things God would have his people do in this present moment? During the assemblage of this volume, we highlighted a number

---

1. Helen Cameron, et al., *Talking about God in Practice: Theological Action Research and Practical Theology* (London: SCM Press, 2010), 49–56.

of strong forces active within the US (and, by extension in some respects, the global) context which require more intense and ongoing conversations than the rich ones already conducted in this book. These views are a reflection of conversations already happening within households, congregations, and missions organizations as well as academic, civic, even corporate and nonprofit organizations that are working to serve the church in some manner, helping it to advance in what God has called it to be and do.

We recognize that the voices in this volume are not reflective of everything with which the church in its missionary action may be tasked to do in particular settings. The writers of this volume have real limitations, are each Anglophile males, and possess British PhDs. Yet each in one way or another is connected to the church around the globe. Nevertheless, with these limitations, we struggle to reckon with challenges of, for example, the Black church in the United States, or the Brown church, the Native Indian, or the Asian ecclesial experience, and how these particular dynamics shape various ways that our evangelical sisters and brothers carry out the task of the church's mission, which one can see from this book looks very different across the evangelical spectrum. We also have major limitations when it comes to understanding those outside our own ecclesial traditions, which echo in the backdrop of this volume's essays and responses. Yet with this, we have tried to articulate ideas that are biblical and transferrable among a range of contexts, and offer for your analysis and engagement the explorations within.

The Ecclesial Backdrop of the Views

While each of the positions in this volume has been clearly and substantially articulated by its particular representative—"Soteriological Mission" by Jonathan Leeman; "Participatory Mission" by Christopher Wright; "Contextual Mission" by John Franke; and "Sacramental Mission" by Peter Leithart—I'm not sure that any of them fully captures the dynamic public and political witness of the church,[2] nor has the significance of church qua church been established. It's been more or less assumed throughout: a church exists, it has a mission, and we focused most of the time looking at what that mission is or how to carry it out most meaningfully. But

---

2. Aside from the authors' particular and significant single-volume contributions, which have been discussed throughout, on the church's public role, see Jennifer McBride, *The Church for the World: A Theology of Public Witness* (New York: Oxford University Press, 2012); for the political, see Amy E. Black, ed., *Five Views on the Church and Politics* (Grand Rapids: Zondervan, 2015).

certainly the church's activities—things like prayer, preaching, and actual presence (and the fact that the church *is* at all)—bears witness to the church's reality as an alien phenomenon in the world. Its constitution is strange inasmuch as it is supernatural, far beyond Robert Bellah's notion of the lifestyle enclave, and displays a gathering together of people from all walks of life—wealthy and poor, educated and uneducated, skilled and unskilled, black and white and brown and Asian, and everything else—the "new humanity" (Eph. 2:15), bound together in love.

None of the contributors in this volume drew in explicit ways from their ecclesial traditions, or at least it wasn't particularly noticeable. One might of course recognize that Peter Leithart and John Franke are Presbyterians, that Chris Wright is Anglican, and that Jonathan Leeman is a Baptist of a very conservative kind in some ways. But none of these are identifiably and exclusively *Presbyterian*, nor exclusively *Anglican*, nor exclusively *Baptist*. The visions presented could be shared by nearly any tradition that wishes to think through Scripture and what it refers to, and are in this sense ecumenical in their own ways. Yet on the other hand, each author's understanding of the church and its mission is more than theoretical and academic—each view is part of a deeply personal journey and is wrapped up in each contributor's identity as a participant in the life of a real church and its mission. Each contributor has personally followed his understanding of the church's mission into a vocational calling and lifestyle that have not been without their own demands, and in some cases have meant great personal and professional cost for the contributors. Yet each of their efforts has also yielded demonstrable results and genuine fruit as they have discharged their work in service to the Lord and to the mission of the church.

But again, what is *church*?

The English word "church" derives from the German *Kirche* and Dutch *kerk*, coming into English through the Scottish *kirk*, deriving ultimately from the Greek notion, κυριακόν, which means something like "belonging to the Lord," originally applying to a church building. In Latin, the word *ecclesia* and its derivatives, also referring to a building, comes from the Greek, ἐκκλησία, meaning an assembly, and coming later to refer to the gathered Christians.[3] When given special theological import by the apostle Paul, who refers to both the local congregation and the universal church as more

---

3. F. L. Cross and Elizabeth A. Livingstone, eds., *The Oxford Dictionary of the Christian Church* (New York: Oxford University Press, 2005), 346.

specifically ἐκ τοῦ θεοῦ or ἐκ τοῦ Χριστοῦ, the idea gave the term its more specifically Christian coloring: the church *of God* or the church *of Christ*.

Taken an additional step, the late John Webster notes that in the case of 2 Corinthians 5:18, "an operative notion of ἐκ τοῦ θεοῦ will require us to invest a great deal of theological energy in the depiction of the person and work of the reconciling God."[4] This sets up what Webster refers to as "the dominating feature of Christian ethical geography, of a theological depiction of the space for the church's endeavor which is established by the action of the triune God, and which it is the chief task of Christian moral theology to map."[5] Furthermore, from this new creative (2 Cor. 5:17), divine activity—ἐκ τοῦ θεοῦ—is displayed in a fundamental sense "the determinative divine action which generates the community of reconciliation."[6] Consequently, this action by God enables the community of reconciliation (or church), by its very existence, to be the community embodying the message of reconciliation (2 Cor. 5:19).

As such the church is now *creatura verbi divini* (creature of the divine Word), grounded in God's unique revelation of Jesus Christ by the power of the Spirit, which then becomes the ground of the church's *catholicity* or universality. There is *one* church, rooted in the universal truth of God's revelation in Christ and by true faith, which constitutes the *communio sanctorum*, the communion of saints. This *holy* communion has its holiness not by its own intrinsic status but because of the sanctifying action of the Holy Spirit, wherein the church also finds its *apostolic* function by which it witnesses the identity and universality of God's revelation in Christ.[7] Therefore the church exists in its constitution *as* church, by grace being one, holy, catholic, and apostolic, the marks also found listed in the Creed.

The Dynamic, Living Church

While the church's existence finds its life grounded in the divine Word by the power of the Holy Spirit and thus constituted as a witnessing community, Jesus informed his followers in Acts 1:8 that they would also receive

---

4. John Webster, *Word and Church: Essays in Christian Dogmatics* (Edinburgh: T&T Clark, 2001), 215.

5. Ibid., 216.

6. Ibid., 220.

7. Christoph Schwöbel, "The Creature of the Word: Recovering the Ecclesiology of the Reformers," in Colin E. Gunton and Daniel W. Hardy, eds., *On Being the Church: Essays on the Christian Community* (Edinburgh: T&T Clark, 1989), 126–29.

power and, as a community, will be his witnesses. The future tense verb here for "will be" is in the indicative mood (not imperative; i.e., there is no command to *go be witnesses*) and as such indicates that by their very constitution as church, they already are witnesses, and a witnessing community, with marks remaining as real and vital as ever. This dynamic highlights the witnessing nature of the church, but also its ongoing dynamic life.[8] The dynamic power operates in centrifugal fashion, maintaining the marks— one, holy, catholic, apostolic—and yet turning them outward actively in such a way that it becomes even more fitting to describe the church as a unifying, sanctifying, reconciling, and proclaiming community, as Charles Van Engen and Darrell Guder have suggested. As such, the church is these things by virtue of its constitution by the Holy Spirit, by virtue of its union with Christ, and by virtue of its dynamic life as this witnessing community. Being sent, then, the church in a sense shares, testifies of, and in this way holds out in extended fashion the salvific action of God the Father, who reconciles sinners, bringing people into a safe harbor, granting shelter from the storm, bringing lost sons and daughters home from their sojourn in troubled waters. In that sense, the church is a ship, constantly moving on the ever-changing sea of ebb and flow, storm and calm, living as a beacon of hope on a special journey of rescue and redemption.

Called, Gathered, and Sent

On its special mission of redemption, the church never loses its quality of being the church, over which the gates of hell will never prevail. While some of the contributors had critique of others' use of Scripture, how normative (or not) it might be, this certainly makes up one of the fundamental features of the church. It is not only divinely called as a *creatura verbi* (creature of the Word) but it is also a creature gathered around Scripture. In a sense, the church is gathered by the sacraments, a point acknowledged by all contributors after being made forcefully as the essence of Peter Leithart's argument. Yet Leithart also concedes to Franke at one point that his proposal lacks space for the *missio Dei*. The church's constitution is also focused on conversion, proclamation, action, and service. The reality of the theological description here, of course, is that all three of these dynamics of the church's constituted life—called, gathered, sent—occur simultaneously and ongoingly.

---

8. For a robust account of this ecclesial life, see Pete Ward, *Liquid Ecclesiology: The Gospel and The Church* (Leiden: Brill, 2017).

Issues throughout this book at times conflated the ideas of church, which by its constitution as a creature of the Word is a community of worship and of mission. At least one contributor has suggested that sanctification must take place *before* mission. But again, this betrays the notion of the character of the church: called, gathered, sent . . . simultaneously. To suggest degrees of holiness before worship or mission may indeed invoke a tacit Pelagianism, especially if the logic might be applied to salvation, and especially if testifying to and proclaiming this salvation is one of the church's primary privileges (which I believe it is). At best, this tendency might create second-class citizens within the church, if folks can ever find their way there. But the most dynamic churches, more contextually aware, indigenously rooted, majority-world, ethnic, etc., seem to be carrying on with their life and mission in radical ways, with various forms of increased holiness looking markedly different than what, say, some of our churches in North America would ever recognize; where newly-celibate polygamists care for the wives they still cohabitate with and provide for, to list just one real-world example in some emerging evangelical situations, which has far-reaching implications that we have been far less quick to explore in our context, whatever our view on the mission of the church might be.

Throughout the spread of the church's mission of proclamation, sanctification, unification, and reconciliation exists a divinely wrought experience of justice, which brings us back to the gospel, the good news about God: that God was in Christ reconciling the world. And how does this message remain front and center of the church's life so that it may most effectively carry out its mission of seeing this hope develop in the world? It is our prayer that this book will assist some of that effort, helping churches within the evangelical movement take a serious moment of pause, critical self-reflection, and then carry on with the mission we've been brought into as the Spirit-and-Word-constituted church—as the world's most significant public actor, and as the vessel privileged to bear witness to the most important message of reality there ever was, is, and ever will be: again, God was in Christ reconciling *the world*. And God has given us this ministry, this ongoing mission, of reconciliation. God will one day bring this about ultimately, irrefutably, and in the highest sense, healing through Christ everything that is now broken. God himself will accomplish this mission, for God's own glory, through Christ our Lord. Amen.

SUBJECT INDEX

A

Abraham
  blessing of, 174
  obedience of, 70
  plan for, 24, 27, 65
  promise to, 67, 69–70, 186
Abrahamic covenant, 70–71, 78, 160–67, 186
Adam
  commission of, 93, 105
  creation and, 20, 23–28, 68, 158–59
  descendants of, 139, 167
  exclusion of, 136, 159
  plan for, 24
  sins of, 61, 66, 93, 162
"Age of Creation," 29, 33, 180, 182. See
    also creation
"Age of New Creation," 29, 33, 58, 180
altar-tables, 160–63, 185–87
annihilationism, 56–57
anthropological view, 157, 178
apostles
  baptism and, 153–54, 169
  keys of kingdom for, 35–36
  message from, 107, 118, 145
  role of, 20, 78
Aquinas, 135, 167
ascension, 61, 66, 77, 160
atonement, 22, 27, 30, 187
Augustine, 31, 135, 139, 146

B

Bailey, Sarah Pulliam, 9
baptism
  absence of, 103–4
  apostles and, 153–54, 169
  as church ordinance, 38–39, 45, 155–56
  disciple-making and, 28–29
  ecumenical-political mission and, 14–15
  Lord's Supper and, 14–15, 28–29, 34,
    38–39, 153–60, 164–81, 185–87
  mission and, 105
  of political leader, 174–75
  role of, 148, 150, 153–57, 166
  unity and, 163–70, 174–77

Barth, Karl, 12, 135
Bartholomew, Craig G., 65, 66, 128, 141
Beale, Greg, 26, 93, 158
Bell, Colin, 90
Bellah, Robert, 195
Bernard of Clairvaux, 135
Bevans, Stephen B., 128, 131
biblical story, 66–102, 141, 152
"binding and loosing," 36–37
Black, Amy E., 194
Boersma, Hans, 157, 179
Böhmer, Karl E., 99
Bosch, David, 112, 118, 152, 153
Burke, Trevor J., 114

C

Calvary Chapel, 10
Calvin, John, 62, 166
Cameron, Helen, 193
Campus Crusade for Christ, 9
Camus, 32
Cape Town Commitment, The, 65, 81, 83,
    84, 89, 102
catholicity, 173, 196–97
Chester, Tim, 185
Christ. *See* Jesus Christ
Christendom, 114–17, 147, 182
Christian witness, 14, 100, 107–8
church
  as-its-members, 21, 34–37, 40–47, 53,
    58–59
  as-organized-collective, 20–21, 33–35,
    39–49, 53, 58–59, 97, 182
  authority of, 14, 19–21, 35–40
  being, 104, 193, 196–98
  budget for, 10–11, 17
  cultivating, 80–85, 97, 103
  defining, 63–64, 193, 195–96
  diversity of, 132–33, 139, 144–48
  doctrine of, 7, 12
  dynamic church, 197–98
  faithful church, 170–72
  gathered-for-worship, 48–49, 59–60

199

as image of God, 119–21
living church, 197–98
meaning of, 7
megachurches, 10–11
mission of, 7–15, 17–60, 63–105,
    107–50, 152–98
mission statement for, 8, 11
nature of, 157
ordinances in, 28–29, 33, 37–40, 45, 62,
    96–97, 137, 155–56, 180–82
political presence of, 14–15
primary tasks of, 14
prophetic role of, 49–50
recalibrating for mission, 193–98
scattered-in-world, 48–49
suburban megachurches, 10–11
theology of, 8, 55–56
unity of, 134, 139, 164–70, 174–77, 190–93
vision of, 118, 150
witness of, 111–13, 117, 121, 125–26,
    131, 194–95
worship in, 48–49, 59–60
church work, 17–19, 32–33, 38–45,
    113–14, 127
circumcision, 39, 162–63, 178
colonization, 101, 114–17, 143, 147
"community blessing," 70–74
compassion, 80–82, 85–88, 98, 102
Confessions, 139
"consequences of sin," 22, 30, 54–55,
    58–62, 66–67
consumerism, 35, 89, 173, 175
contextual mission view, 14, 107–51, 194
corruption, 11, 32, 50, 67, 76, 162
creation. See also new creation
    age of, 23–35, 58, 180, 182
    caring for, 42, 80–82, 88–90, 93, 98, 103
    doctrine of, 157, 184
    redemption and, 80–81, 88, 116, 145,
        152, 184
    sin and, 66–68
creational disorder, 49, 68, 83
creational mission, 142–43
cross, 65–69, 74–76, 81–82, 94–95, 103,
    160, 171
crucifixion, 75–76, 79, 148, 156, 167
cultural diversity, 14–15, 98–102, 107–17,
    128–34, 144–48

cultural mission, 14–15, 91, 175–76
curse
    of death, 28, 77
    on earth, 66–67
    sin and, 30, 58, 67, 89, 140–41, 184–85

D

David, King, 60, 71
DeYoung, Kevin, 13, 46, 50, 68, 70–72, 76,
    93–94, 103, 155
diakonia, 48
disciples
    being, 14–21
    discipleship, 44, 79–80, 101–3, 120–21,
        136, 152–57, 166–67, 176, 187–89
    making, 14–21, 26–31, 38–40, 44–47,
        97, 153, 191
"drama of Scripture," 65–66, 79
Duncan, Ligon, 45

E

earth, curse on, 66–67
earth, heaven and, 77, 88, 95–96, 124–26,
    140–41, 182
ecumenical missiology, 152–53, 161, 164,
    168, 195
ecumenical movement, 9, 108, 153
ecumenical-political mission, 14–15
Edwards, David L., 56, 135
Edwards, Jonathan, 31
ekklesia, 154–55, 171–72
"elevator work," 33–35
enslavement, 9, 122
Ephesus, 84, 171, 177
eschatological wrinkle, 26, 29–35, 53–54, 58
"eternally missional," 141. See also mission
Eucharist, 156, 166–67, 170, 173–74
evangelicalism, 7–16, 152
evangelism, 18, 80–83, 98, 124
Eve
    creation and, 23–24, 26–28, 158–59
    descendants of, 139
    exclusion of, 136
    sins of, 61, 66, 93, 162
ex opere operato, 37, 177, 181
exclusion, power of, 136–37
exodus, 22, 27, 50, 64, 71–74, 161
expansionism, 8, 13, 62

F

faithful church, 170–72
faithful witness, 14, 117, 126, 175
fall
  creation and, 23
  fixing problem after, 159, 184
  Israel and, 93–94
  sacramental mission and, 14
  sin and, 66, 140–41
  wrath of God and, 27
Fiddes, Paul S., 109
"Five Marks of Mission," 80–91, 103
Flemming, Dean, 156
Flett, John G., 12, 108, 109
foundationalism, 100, 134, 144–45
Franciscan era, 9
Franke, John R., 14, 53, 93, 98–102, 105,
    107–51, 189–93, 194–95, 197
Fudge, Edward W., 56
fundamentalists, 13–14, 19, 53, 95, 152
Fung, Raymond, 126–27

G

Gaventa, Beverly Roberts, 114
genocide, 9, 102, 116, 173
Giddens, Anthony, 137
Gilbert, Greg, 13, 46, 50, 68, 70–72, 76,
    93–94, 103, 155
Glanville, Mark, 185
global missions, 11
God. See also mission
  accomplishment of, 73–77, 197–98
  as "eternally missional," 141
  glory of, 28–29, 77, 91, 106, 141
  healing from, 14
  holiness of, 134–36
  image of, 25, 66, 93, 111–12, 119–21,
    143, 168, 185
  judgment of, 26–29, 33–35, 41, 137–38
  kingdom of, 31–32, 50–51, 57–60, 86,
    91, 108–12, 118–26, 130, 143, 170
  love of, 111–14, 121, 126, 129, 134–37,
    141–43, 190
  obeying, 24–25, 42–44, 70–79, 84–88, 111
  participatory acts of, 14
  reign of, 14
  rule of, 23–24
  Word of, 24, 36–37, 45, 172

  wrath of, 27, 30, 51, 92, 137
Goheen, Michael W., 65, 66, 99, 141, 144,
    156–57, 185
González, Justo L., 130
Gorman, Michael, 114, 118, 124, 147
government, 9, 21, 37, 178, 181–82
Graham, Billy, 10
Grau, Marion, 117
Great Commission
  Adam and, 66, 91–93
  elements of, 78–88
  importance of, 70, 77
  purpose of, 18, 46–51, 71, 78–88
  understanding of, 183
  work of, 38
Grenz, Stanley J., 7, 120
Guder, Darrell L., 12, 116, 130, 157, 197
Gutierrez, Gustavo, 123

H

Hades, 77. See also hell
harmony, restoring, 15, 124–25, 164–66,
    176
heaven
  authority in, 38, 88
  earth and, 77, 88, 95–96, 124–26, 140–41,
    182
  eternal possibilities of, 31–32, 43, 82, 184
  Lord of, 88
  preaching about, 45
  views on, 22–23, 30–31, 34–36, 138
hell
  consequences of, 56–57
  doctrine of, 137–38
  eternal possibilities of, 43, 56–57, 184
  Hades, 77
  images of, 137–38
  preaching about, 45
  purgatory, 95
  views on, 30–31, 56–57, 92, 95, 137–38
Henry, Carl, 152, 183
Hesselgrave, David J., 18
holistic gospel, 19, 22–23, 75–76, 95
holistic mess, 76, 95
holistic mission, 19, 22–23, 50, 75–77,
    80–82, 95, 98, 103
Holmes, Stephen R., 109, 110
holy communion, 196

Holy Spirit
   message of, 107, 146
   power of, 14, 121–26, 167, 176, 196–97
   presence of, 68, 184
   work of, 32–33, 84, 121, 132, 145–46,
      156, 180, 192
Horton, Michael, 157
Hughes, Philip E., 56
humanity, saving, 21–23, 26–29

I

idolatry, 70, 89, 100, 136, 139, 149
image-recovery work, 26, 49
immortality, 56–57, 75
imperialism, 56, 115, 146
Indian Removal, 9
individualism, 35, 114, 189
Inge, John, 128
instrumental intention, 69, 106
interdependence, 14, 126, 132–33
Israel, 24–27, 50–52, 63–79, 85–94, 103–6, 110

J

Jamieson, Bobby, 39, 180, 181
Jennings, Willie James, 131
Jesus Christ
   ascension of, 61, 66, 77, 160
   body of, 11, 37, 112–14, 121–24,
      132–33, 139, 150, 164, 167, 174–75
   coming of, 29–30, 33, 57, 60–61, 65
   disciples of, 14–21
   as image of God, 119–21
   as king, 22–23, 29–30, 45, 60–61, 80,
      159–60
   kingly work of, 20–21, 23–29, 33–35,
      39–41, 49–54, 58–62, 66
   leadership of, 80–81
   Lordship of, 22, 66, 79–82, 88–90, 171
   obeying God, 24–25
   priestly work of, 20–21, 26–30, 33–35,
      40–41, 49–54, 58–62, 66
   resurrection of, 24–25, 51, 61–69,
      74–82, 94–95, 103, 141, 160, 171
   as savior, 28
John the Baptist, 79, 120, 154, 163–64
Jordan, James B., 158, 160
judgment, mediating, 26–29, 33–35, 41,
   137–38

Judgment Day, 138
justice, 80–88, 98, 102–5, 124, 169–76

K

Kahn, Genghis, 43
Keillor, Garrison, 34
kingdom
   of God, 31–32, 50–51, 57–60, 86, 91,
      108–12, 118–26, 130, 143, 170
   keys of, 28, 35–36, 182
   of priests, 27–28
   sons of, 25–26, 41–43, 52
kingdom people, 11
"kingly rule," 61, 66, 93, 141
"kingly story," 23–29
"kingly work," 20–21, 23–29, 33–35, 39–41,
   49–54, 58–62, 66
koinonia, 167
Kuyper, Abraham, 40

L

Lausanne Movement, 12, 183
law, giving of, 72–73
law, interpreting, 36–37, 94
Leeman, Jonathan, 13–14, 17–62, 92–97,
   134–39, 177–82, 194–95
Leithart, Peter J., 14–15, 26, 47, 58, 103–6,
   146–50, 152–96, 197
Lennon, John, 138
Levering, Matthew, 157, 179
liberation, 31, 35, 113–14, 122–24
liturgical theology, 59, 103–5, 149, 165–66,
   191–93
liturgy and life, 15, 164–66, 176
Longnecker, Richard N., 180
Lord's Supper
   baptism and, 14–15, 28–29, 34, 38–39,
      153–60, 164–81, 185–87
   as church ordinance, 38–39, 155–56
   disciple-making and, 28–29
Luther, Martin, 135

M

Madley, Benjamin, 9
Manifest Destiny, 9, 10
Marks, John H., 119
McBride, Jennifer, 194
McCall, Thomas H., 109

Meal with Jesus, A, 185
megachurches, 10–11. *See also* church
Melchizedek, King, 60
metaphysics, 166, 178–82
Migliore, Daniel, 119
ministries
    church work and, 17–19, 32–33, 38–45, 127
    flexibility of, 11
    mission statement for, 8, 11
    works of, 48–49
mission
    accomplishment of, 73–77
    adapting, 14
    bearing witness, 107–50
    broad mission, 14, 18–26, 29–34,
        41–47, 50–59, 76
    budget for, 10–11
    Christendom and, 114–17
    of church, 7–15, 17–60, 63–105,
        107–50, 152–98
    church work and, 17–19, 32–33, 38–45,
        113–14, 127
    colonialized missions, 8–9
    consummation of, 76–77, 95–96
    contextual mission view, 14, 107–51, 194
    corporatized missions, 8–9
    cultural mission, 14–15, 91, 175–76
    defining, 17–21, 63–65, 78–80
    dividing, 20–22, 32–35, 44, 53–54,
        60–61, 95, 124–26
    ecumenical-political mission, 14–15
    "eternally missional," 141
    five marks of, 80–91, 103
    fundamentalist perspectives, 13–14, 152
    global missions, 11
    holistic mission, 19, 22–23, 50, 75–77,
        80–82, 95, 98, 103
    of Israel, 68–79, 164
    mandating of, 77–82
    meaning of, 8–12
    model of, 9
    narrow mission, 14, 18–26, 29–35, 40–47,
        50–59, 76
    nature of, 90, 157
    need for, 45
    participatory mission view, 14, 63–106, 194
    practice of, 90, 116, 184
    prioritizing, 10

    recalibrating church for, 193–98
    of redemption, 14, 17–62, 79, 83, 140–42,
        197–98
    sacramental mission view, 14–15, 152–94
    soteriological mission view, 13–14,
        17–62, 157, 194
    theology of, 8, 55–56, 66, 75, 85, 157–60
    views on, 13–16
    vision of, 8–15, 114–28, 170–71, 191–93
Mission of God, The, 155
mission statement, 8, 11, 79–80, 160
Missional Church, 12, 129
missional dimension, 48, 73, 90–91
missional intention, 69, 90–91, 106
missional pattern, 112, 117–25, 137
missional theology, 49, 99–100, 105, 128,
    153, 157–58
missionaries
    church members as, 11
    need for, 45, 143–49
    work of, 32, 50, 68, 91
"Missionary Roots of Liberal Democracy," 32
Montoya, Inigo, 7
Moore, Stephen D., 115
Morales, L. Michael, 158, 161
Moses, 36, 71–72, 79, 94, 162, 186
Mount Moriah, 161
Mount Sinai, 73, 186

N

nations, scattering of, 67–68, 104, 160–61
Native Americans, 9, 116, 147, 150, 194
neo-evangelicalism, 152
Nevin, John Williamson, 173
new creation. *See also* creation
    church work and, 33, 45, 113–14
    citizens of, 65–66
    distinctions of, 180
    doctrine of, 157, 184
    eschatological wrinkle and, 29, 58
    eternity of, 140
    glimpse of, 141–42
    purpose for, 143
    resurrection and, 24–25, 50–51
    salvation and, 113–14
new humanity, 47–49, 139, 174, 195
Newbigin, Lesslie, 9, 15, 50, 57, 90–91,
    98–101, 108, 117–18, 120, 131, 148, 156

Niebuhr, Gustav, 9
Noah, 24, 27, 61, 67–68, 136, 160–61, 185
nominalism, 42, 44
Nugent, John C., 43

O

obedience, 24–25, 42–44, 70–79, 84–88, 111
Oden, Tom, 192, 193
O'Donovan, Oliver, 180, 181
Olthuis, James, 101
oppression, 59, 76–77, 96, 100–101,
    120–22, 169
Ott, Craig, 12, 109
"Ozymandias," 32

P

parousia, 66, 76–77, 141
participatory acts, 14
participatory mission view, 14, 63–106, 194
persecution, 59, 77, 96
Pinnock, Clark H., 56
Piper, John, 30, 31, 153, 156
Plantinga, Cornelius, 22
polis, 154–55
political activism, 116, 147, 174
political missiology, 152–57, 161–64,
    171–81, 191, 194
postmodern discourse, 101–2, 139, 144
pragmatism, 10, 44
"priestly service," 51, 60, 66, 93, 141
"priestly story," 26–30, 33
"priestly work," 20–21, 26–30, 33–35,
    40–41, 49–54, 58–62, 66
"prophetic" role, 49–50
Protestant evangelical discourse, 15
purgatory, 95. See also hell

R

reconciliation
    ambassadors of, 137
    community of, 197
    message of, 27, 39, 113–14, 196–98
    mission of, 198
    redemption and, 68, 110, 197
    salvation and, 113–14
redemption
    creation and, 80–81, 88, 116, 145, 152, 184
    mission of, 14, 17–62, 79, 83, 140–42,
        197–98

participatory mission view and, 63–106
reconciliation and, 68, 110, 197
resurrection and, 110, 141
soteriological mission view and, 17–62
reductionism, 13, 137, 180
restorationist, 183
resurrection
    ascension and, 61, 66
    cross and, 65–69, 74–76, 81–82, 94–95,
        103, 160, 171
    new creation and, 24–25, 50–51
    participation in, 120
    redemption and, 110, 141
revisionists, 152–55, 165, 169, 183
Rhodes, Michael, 185
Rodríguez, Jorge Juan, 116
Rosner, Brian S., 114
Ross, Cathy, 80
Rowe, Kavin, 128, 150

S

sacramental mission view, 14–15, 152–95
sacramental theology, 62, 157–58, 165–66,
    187–88
sacraments, forgotten, 153–58
salvation
    declaration of, 29–30
    mission for, 34–35, 197
    nature of, 19
    new creation and, 113–14
Salvation Belongs to Our God, 184
Sanneh, Lamin, 108, 131, 144
Satan, 24–25, 75–77, 95, 160
scattering of nations, 67–68, 104, 160–61
Schlesinger, Eugene, 146
Schmemann, Alexander, 158
Schreiner, Thomas, 180
Schroeder, Roger P., 128
Scripture
    canon of, 55, 102, 142, 184
    diversity of, 102, 107–14, 128–30, 148–51
    drama of, 65–66, 79
    study of, 102
Sexton, Jason S., 7, 12, 109, 193–95
Shelley, Percy Bysshe, 32
sin
    of Adam and Eve, 61, 66, 93, 162
    consequences of, 22, 30, 54–55, 58–62,
        66–67

creation and, 66–68
curse and, 30, 58, 67, 89, 140–41, 184–85
forgiveness of, 76, 118
powers of, 113–14, 118–20, 125
as "root cause," 68, 93–94
world of, 65, 83, 102, 121
social justice, 124, 169, 171, 176
social life, 70, 104
society, engaging, 80–81, 85–88, 93, 103
socio-political missiology, 152
"sons of the kingdom," 25–26, 41–43, 52
soteriological mission view, 13–14, 17–62, 157, 194
Spirit. *See* Holy Spirit
Stetzer, Ed, 13
Stott, John, 18, 42, 46, 47, 56, 152, 183
Stranger, The, 32

T

Ten Commandments, 66
Thatcher, Margaret, 43
Themelios, 13
theology
of church, 8, 55–56
liturgical theology, 59, 103, 105, 149, 165–66, 191–93
of mission, 8, 55–56, 66, 75, 85, 157–60
missional theology, 49, 99–100, 105, 128, 153, 157–58
sacramental theology, 62, 157–58, 165–66, 187–88
timeline wrinkle, 26, 29–35, 53–54, 58
Torah, 70, 104, 162–63, 178
traditionalists, 152–55, 165, 169, 183
Trail of Tears, 9
transformationism, 43, 68, 95, 114, 124, 152
Tree of Life, 61, 158–59
Trinitarian life, 14, 105, 110, 114
Trinitarian theology, 109–14, 135, 140–47, 150, 196
Trinity, 63, 109–14, 140–47, 182
Trump, Donald, 43
Twiss, Richard, 116, 131

U

unity, 134, 139, 146, 163–77, 189–93
universality, 71, 196
Uzziah, King, 60

V

Van Engen, Charles, 197
views
contextual mission view, 14, 107–51, 194
on mission, 13–16
participatory mission view, 14, 63–106, 194
sacramental mission view, 14–15, 152–95
soteriological mission view, 13–14, 17–62, 157, 194
violence, 67, 77, 96, 162, 168
Von Rad, Gerhard, 119

W

Walls, Andrew F., 80, 129, 139, 144, 148
Ward, Pete, 197
Warfield, B. B., 22
Webster, John, 180, 196
Weston, Paul, 12
What Is the Mission of the Church?, 13, 103, 155
wheel metaphor, 82–83, 96–97
White, Robert S., 90
witness
bearing witness, 49, 77, 91, 107–50, 197
of church, 111–13, 117, 121, 125–26, 131, 194–95
faithful witness, 14, 117, 126, 175
witnessing communities, 14, 108, 197–98
Woodberry, Robert, 32
worship
in church, 48–49, 59–60
corporate worship, 125–26, 136
gathered for, 48–49, 59–60, 125
as political act, 60
social life and, 70, 104
Wright, Christopher J. H., 12–14, 18, 42, 46–47, 63–106, 140–45, 155–56, 160, 179, 183–88, 194–95
Wrogemann, Henning, 99

Y

Young, Amos, 116

Z

Zacchaeus, 123–24
Zikmund, Barbara Brown, 116

SCRIPTURE INDEX

Genesis
1 77
1–2 . . . . 90, 142
1:1 88
1:26 119
1:26–28 . . . . 89, 93, 141
1:28 . . . . 23, 66
1:29 158
2:15 . . . . 26, 66, 89, 141
3 . . . . . . 30, 58, 89, 142,
          161, 184, 185
3:15 . . . . 67, 141
3:25 159
4 . . . . 67, 185
5 185
5:1 23
5:28 185
5:29 67
6 67
6:12 162
6:13 162
6:17 162
8:20 160
9 162
9:5–6 36
9:6 138
11:1–8 160
11:1–9 67
12 67
12:1–3 . . . . . . 69, 70, 71
12:7 161
12:8 161
12:10–20 161
13:4 161
13:5–18 161
14:1–24 161
17 162
17:1 70
18 186
18:18–19 69
18:19 . . . . 24, 70
19 70
22:9 161
26:4–6 70
34 104

Exodus
4:22–23 24
19:4–6 . . . . 50, 73
19:6 27
20:24 . . . . . . .163, 186
24:8 186
24:10–11 186
25:8 187
29:45–46 187
32:6 186

Leviticus
1–7 187
18:1–4 64
19:2 64
21:6 160
21:8 160
21:17 160
21:21–22 160
22:25 160

Numbers
3:7–8 26
8:26 26
18:5–6 26

Deuteronomy
4:6–8 . . . .64, 70, 73, 93
4:35 79
4:39 79
7:8 135
14:26 162
15:4 87
16:11 163
16:14 163
17:18–20 24
28:9–10 73
29–32 74

1 Kings
5:1–12 104
8:41–43 . . . . . 104, 186
8:60–61 73
9:3 104

2 Chronicles
26:6–10 60

Psalm
1 72
2 60
8:5 23
19 72
27:4 135
29:2 135
50 186
51:4 94
96 68
96:1–3 64
110 60
119 72
148 68

Proverbs
29:7 88

Isaiah
2:2–4 163
2:3 186
6:3 134
6:9–13 135
43:1–2 79
43:7–21 69
43:8–13 69
43:10–12 77
43:21 64
45:20–25 69
53:6 75
55:1–2 186
56:6–7 186
58:6–8 86
58:10 86
60:1–3 86
60:7 186
61:1–8 163
65:20–23 126
66:19 79

Jeremiah
23 60

31:3 135
31:31–34 . . . . . .28, 180

Ezekiel
28:22 135
34. 60
36:24–27 180
41:22 160
44:16 160

Hosea
1:9 64
2:23 64

Micah
4:2–3 163
6:8 86

Zechariah
7:9 86
14:14–19 163

Matthew
3:2 79
3:9 25
4:17 120
5:3–10 25
5:6 85
5:14–16 86
5:16 64
6:9–10 126
6:33 85
8:11 164
8:12 . . . . .25, 52
13:38 25
16. . . . . .20, 35, 36
16:13–20 36
16:18 40
16:19 . . . . .38, 40
17:26 25
18. . . . . .20, 35, 36
18:15–17 137
18:15–18 40
18:16 36
18:17–18 36
18:18–20 38
18:19–20 . . . .36, 38, 39
21:33–44 142
22:1–14 164
22:37–40 113

23:23 86
25:31–40 122
28. . . . . .20, 35, 155
28:16–20 . . . . . .66, 70
28:18–19 25
28:18–20 . . . . .38, 153
28:19–20 121
28:20 . . . . .38, 47

Mark
1:11 135
1:15 . . . . .79, 120
10:37 30
10:42 30
10:45 30

Luke
3:38 23
4:16–21 122
14. . . . . .154, 170
15:11–32 164
19:9–10 123
24:44–47 94
24:45–48 78
24:48 77

John
3:16–17 111
13:34–35 45
17:20–23 190
20:21 109
20:21–23 117
20:23 40

Acts
1. . . . . .66, 68, 93
1–4. 77
1:8 . . . . . . .77, 107, 196
2. . . . . .66, 93
2–6 68
2:1–4 107
2:5–12 107
2:38 . . . . .79, 155
2:38–42 153
2:41 . . . . .38, 155
2:42 154
2:42–46 45
2:44–45 87
3. . . . . . . .68, 71, 90, 93
4. . . . . .73, 94

4:32–38 87
5. . . . . .77, 90, 96
6. . . . . .76, 77, 95
7–8. 104
8:36–38 153
10:47–48 153
11:16 153
11:27–30 87
13. 87
16:15 154
16:33 154
17:28 180
18. 85
18:8 154
18:24–28 84
20:20 84
20:27 84
27:35 154

Romans
1:5 . . . . .71, 78
1:16 113
1:18–32 169
5:9 137
5:20 94
6:1–14 . . . . . .105, 169
8:2–25 113
8:21 69
8:22–23 23
8:29 . . . . .25, 120
9:24–26 64
11:36 135
12:1 29
13. 182
13:1–7 36
15:18 78
16:19 78
16:26 . . . . .71, 78

1 Corinthians
1:17–18 155
3:5–9 84
3:10–15 105
3:16 28
4:7 135
5. 137
5:2 35
5:4 36
5:5 35
5:12 36

6:12–20 173
7:31 126
10:16–17 . . . . . .62, 167
10:17 38
11. 154
11:27–32 137
11:29 39
11:33 39
12. 192
12:4–7 132
12:12–13 167
12:17–20 132
15:23–28 25
15:49 25
15:49–53 120
15:58 51

2 Corinthians
3:18 120
4:4–6 . . . . .86, 119
5:17 196
5:17–20 113
5:18 196
5:19 196
5:20 137
6:16–17 39
6:17 . . . . .28, 137
8–9 87
10:5 85

Galatians
1:6–9 35
2. 136
2:10 87
3:13 28
3:19 94
3:23 94
4:1–7 26
4:4–5 28
4:6 25
5:22–26 191

Ephesians
1:9–10 . . . . .69, 84, 124
1:12 65
1:20–21 51

1:20–23 124
2. 124
2:1–10 29
2:8–10 78
2:11–20 29
2:14–16 75
2:15 195
2:19 25
2:20 105
3:8–11 125
3:10 49
4:1–6 125
4:1–16 150
4:2–6 191
4:11–13 48
19:3–5 154

Philippians
1:27 150
2:1–11 191
2:2–3 150
2:5–8 111
2:10–11 29
3:20 25

Colossians
1:9–10 48
1:15 . . . . .25, 119
1:15–20 . . . . . . .88, 89
1:17 126
1:20 . . . . .69, 75
2:13–14 28
2:15 75
3:15–17 48

1 Thessalonians
1:3 78

2 Thessalonians
1:8 78
1:8–9 51

1 Timothy
6:17–19 87

2 Timothy
2:12 . . . . .25, 29
3:15–17 72

Hebrews
1:2–3 89
1:9 135
2:14 75
11:8 78
12:26–28 126
13:15 29

James
1:27 123
2:14–17 87

1 Peter
1:1–2 64
2:5 28
2:9 28
2:9–12 . . . . . .50, 63, 73
2:13–3:7 50
2:24 75
3:21 160

1 John
3:2 . . . . .25, 120
3:17–18 87
4:7–12 113
4:8 109

Revelation
1:5 51
4. 60
4–7. 51
5. 68
7:9–10 . . . . .69, 126
20. . . . . . . .89, 142, 184
20:6 25
21. 150
21:24 . . . . .43, 150
21:24–27 141
21–22. .88, 90, 141, 142
22. 140
22:3 . . . . . .67, 141, 185
22:5 141